Volume One

Favorites, Friendships, Food, and Fantasy

Literature-Based Thematic Units for Early Primary

Ann Lukasevich
University of British Columbia
Language Department, Language Arts/Early Childhood

Florence Pieronek
University of British Columbia
Language Department, Reading Education

Contributors:

Anna Maria Bilotta ■ Anne Coulombe ■ Susan R. Radford

Addison-Wesley Publishing Company

Menlo Park, California · Reading, Massachusetts · New York
Don Mills, Ontario · Wokingham, England · Amsterdam · Bonn
Paris · Milan · Madrid · Sydney · Singapore · Tokyo
Seoul · Taipei · Mexico City · San Juan

Acknowledgments

We recognize that the manuscript would not have reached its reality without the expertise of Oliva Dela Cruz, who spent endless hours typing and formatting the manuscript. In addition, special thanks to Lois Fowkes at Addison-Wesley for her encouragement and assistance from the beginning to the completion of the project.

Senior Editor: Lois Fowkes

Production Manager: Janet Yearian

Production Coordinator: Claire Flaherty

Design Manager: Jeff Kelly

Text and Cover Design: Paula Shuhert

Illustrations: Rachel Gage

This book is published by Innovative Learning™, an imprint of Addison-Wesley's Alternative Publishing Group.

ISBN 0-201-81844-2

1 2 3 4 5 6 7 8 9 10-ML-97 96 95 94 93

This Book is Printed
on Recycled Paper

Preface

This handbook was written to help teachers enhance emergent literacy growth through the use of integrated, literature-based, thematic units in a supportive, print-rich environment that enables young children to explore and learn effectively. Specifically, these units have been designed for teachers who are interested in learning how to use literature to promote the growth of the communicative process (listening, speaking, reading, writing).

This is a practical resource in two volumes that focuses on how to implement well-planned integrated, literature-based, thematic units that stress the development of effective strategies required of independent, self-directed competent readers and writers. The unit content is developmentally appropriate and is based on recent theory and research in the field of emergent reading and writing. In addition, the units have been extensively field-tested for several years in schools in a large urban area with an enrollment that includes diverse abilities and cultures.

The first section of the handbook discusses research related to sound current theory and practice in the area of emergent literacy.

The second section discusses salient aspects of implementing the units. It introduces teachers to the Transactive Teaching/Learning Model which provides the daily framework for each unit. Since effective questioning is crucial to good teaching, this section also details strategies (Barrett's Taxonomy) that can be used to ensure that young children develop many levels of thinking. In addition, other key elements used in the units are explored, including integration, the print-rich learning environment, and grouping patterns. A comprehensive overview of the units is also provided.

The third section describes the daily teaching and learning activities for two of the four literature/language thematic units (Old Favorites, Friendships) that are of high interest to young primary learners (K–1). Each plan includes numerous suggestions for teacher-directed activities in large- or small-group settings as well as ideas for independent activities. Suggestions are also given for integrating the units with other subject areas such as art, music, drama, science, social studies, and mathematics.

The appendix, Section Four, discusses appropriate assessment for this age level and contains assessment instruments.

Contents

Emergent Literacy: From Theory into Practice

Introduction

Literacy, the ability to read and write, is a basic life skill. It begins early, long before a child enters school, and is an ongoing, natural, developmental process. What happens once the child enters the school system is crucial; "research reveals that the returns are the highest from the early years of schooling when children are first learning" (Anderson et al, 1985). A child's success in school is dependent on literacy skills that will significantly influence his or her chances of leading a productive life and enjoying the benefits of our literate society.

This book focuses on an integrated reading-writing literature program for the early primary school years. Before describing the program, three major questions will be addressed:

- What is meant by the term *emergent literacy?* What are the implications for teaching?

- How can teachers effectively promote emergent literacy through quality teaching?

- How can teachers effectively structure classroom environments to support quality teaching for emergent literacy?

What Is Meant by the Term *Emergent Literacy?* What Are the Implications for Teaching?

Over the years, there has been a noticeable increase in research in the area of literacy and literacy acquisition, spearheaded by the work of researchers such as Clay (1966, 1975), Durkin (1966, 1989), Ferreiro (1978, 1986), Bissex (1980), Wells (1981), Ferreiro and Teberosky (1982), Holdaway (1982), and Graves (1983). As a result, a wealth of literature has been published on the literacy development of young learners, and extensive research has been focused on this area. Much of this research has been longitudinal in nature and has recorded growth in literacy development, changing how literacy is viewed and defined. Many definitions of literacy, depending on the writer's point of view and research focus, have emerged.

Traditionally, literacy has been defined as the ability to read and write. Contributions from developmental learning have led to new definitions and new ways of looking at literacy and literacy development. For example, Hillerich provides the following definition: "Literacy is that demonstrated competence in communication skills which enables the individual to function, appropriate to his age, independently of his society and with a potential for movement in society." (1976, p. 29) Another global definition is provided by Cambourne, who describes literacy as "a word which describes a whole collection of behaviors, skills, knowledge, processes and attitudes. It has something to do with our ability to use language in our negotiations with the world. Often these negotiations are motivated by our desires to manipulate the world for our own benefit. Reading and writing are two linguistic ways of conducting these negotiations." (1988, p. 3)

Cambourne's definition reinforces what was stated earlier by Holdaway (1982), who also felt that both reading and writing were necessary for full literacy. He believed that power resided in the ability to write, while reading was essential to participate in one's particular culture.

Clay found that literacy was an emerging set of knowledge and skills that begins to develop very early in the lives of young children, who accumulate a little here and a little there as they move about their preschool settings (1989, p. v).

The term or concept now appearing in literature focusing on the young learner—*emergent literacy*—was first used by Marie Clay in 1966. It has since been used extensively by educators interested in the development of early reading and writing. Much research has supported Clay's emergent literacy perspective (Calkins, 1983; Clark, 1976; Snow, 1983; and Teale, 1978, 1982). As with so many terms in education, one finds a variety of definitions and conceptualizations of what emergent literacy is believed to be. It is a term that is not easily defined. Hillerich suggests that it is "a continuously developing ability to function in all aspects of language, from oral to printed form. Its inception occurs long before schooling begins and its fruition continues long after kindergarten ends." (1988, p. 24)

Salinger also noted that the term acknowledges the importance of children's attention to the varied uses of print in the environment (1988, p. 202). It emphasizes the continuum of language growth from oral language through mastery of reading and writing and focuses on what children themselves do to become literate.

Furthermore, Temple and Gillet point out that it "names a learning process that occurs over a lengthy period, gaining strength as it goes. The term makes no distinction between reading and writing, since . . . children learn about the uses and forms of written language, reading and writing, at the same time" (1989, p. 111).

However, Pikulski suggests that "emergent literacy is not so much an approach as it is a way of looking at and thinking about how young children acquire functional, reliable reading and writing skills. *Emergent* suggests something that is dynamic and becoming, not a specific point or period in time, and *literacy* stresses the interrelatedness of the language arts." (1988, p. 76)

In order to promote this type of growth effectively in emergent readers and writers during the early primary years, teachers need to be aware of the following:

- Listening, speaking, writing, and reading should be viewed as one total representational process rather than as isolated, separate subjects to be learned. This means that they must be integrated within the total language arts program and curriculum generally (Butler and Turbill, 1984; and Goodman, 1986).

- Parents play a very important role in the growth of their child's literacy (Clay, 1975; Holdaway, 1980; Snow, 1983; and Teale 1978, 1982). It has been established that all children entering school are well on the road to literacy. Teachers must be aware of this fact and provide appropriate experiences that will foster continued growth in literacy development. In addition, they must strive for continued parental involvement.

- The presence of good books and other printed materials are crucial to the development of emergent literacy, not only in the school but also in the home. Research conducted by Durkin showed that children who read early without any formal instruction had many experiences of stories being read to them (1961, 1966). Much later, Wells conducted an important longitudinal study of the language development of children aged from one to five years and found that the most significant predictor of achievement at age seven was the child's knowledge about the conventions of reading at school entry (Bristol Study of Language Development, 1985). The greatest factor in providing this knowledge was the extent to which the child's parents encouraged an interest in books and in reading and writing, and in particular how often they read to their child. In addition, two key findings reported in *What Works, Research About Teaching and Learning* were that parents were their children's first and most influential teachers and that the best way for parents to help their children become better readers was to read to them (1987).

- Teaching as well as instructional programs must be developmentally appropriate and geared to individual needs, allowing for the individual differences found in all classrooms. The focus in curriculum planning must be from an emergent literacy perspective that emphasizes the children's ongoing natural development of skills in reading and writing rather than the accumulation of prerequisite subskills (Strickland and Morrow, 1988).

- Meaning and understanding are crucial to the literacy process. Children need to view writing and reading as a means of communicating information.

- Children for whom English is a second language (ESL) are a special challenge for teachers. Many of these children live where they hear little English spoken and have had limited access to books written in English. As a result, concepts such as letters, sounds, words, and sentences may be new to them. Teachers need to provide many varied experiences to introduce these children to the language of books and structure of stories while expanding the oral language they already have. In addition, teachers should ensure the maintenance of their first language as well as an appreciation of their cultural heritage. This means that the teacher's job is not to change the children's language, but rather to build on their strengths and expand on the language they bring to school. As Jagger points out, "children can think logically, learn effectively, and talk intelligently in any dialect" (1980, p. 28).

How Can Teachers Effectively Promote Emergent Literacy Through Quality Teaching?

Teachers wishing to promote growth in emergent literacy in the classroom must adapt their teaching roles so that they can work effectively with large groups (shared language period), small groups (interest groups, ability groups, friendship groups, cooperative groups, partners, and special-needs groups), and individuals. Teachers function as facilitators, consultants, learning specialists, learning-environment planners, and most importantly as diagnosticians. Within these roles, teachers must know how to plan, organize, and promote learning in a print-rich environment. They must also recognize the importance of a well-stocked, well-organized classroom, since an abundance of materials provides children with many opportunities to read and write independently for a large part of the day while teachers work with small groups and individuals.

Within this planned environment, the teacher promotes developmentally appropriate practice and learning, observes children, engages in ongoing assessment, and interacts with children and volunteers. In addition, teachers must make sure that they incorporate the following goals into all aspects of instruction:

- Focus on the learner.
- Immerse children in reading and writing.
- Model literacy.

Focus on the Learner

Effective teaching in the emergent literacy classroom focuses on the learner. Each learner brings strengths and weaknesses to the classroom, and teachers must realize that each child is a unique individual and that enormous variance exists within the normal range. Teachers must be flexible in their expectations about when and how children will acquire literacy. Their first responsibility is to promote children's learning so that children are active participants in the literacy process. Once children are participating in literacy experiences, teachers must become actively involved to increase literacy skills. During these experiences, teachers should

> intervene judiciously at any point in the process with suggestions for improving particular skills, and do so in some confidence that the suggestions—these being the main teaching factor—will be learned because they offer not skills in general but the specific skills needed right now by a particular learner (Walshe, 1985, p. 80).

Although children can learn many skills informally, direct instruction is also needed. Without this kind of intervention, real growth in literacy skills will not occur, since children need effective strategies to become independent learners—a key goal of schooling.

Immerse Children in Reading and Writing

In order to promote literacy growth, teachers need to immerse children in all forms of language—listening, speaking, reading, and writing. These four areas of the language arts should be integrated rather than taught as separate subjects. Within this context of integration, teachers will provide many opportunities for oral language (discussions, drama, role playing); for listening experiences (stories read aloud, listening center activities); for reading experiences (independent reading, shared reading with Big Books or charts, wall charts); and for writing experiences (journals, language experience, letter writing, writing center activities). Sometimes these immersion experiences are teacher controlled (directed), and at other times they are learner controlled (directed). An example of teacher-controlled aural immersion is when teachers reading to children saturate them with the cadences, rhythms, and sounds of written language (Cambourne, 1989). An example of learner-controlled (directed) visual and aural immersion is when teachers provide sufficient time and resources for children to choose books and read independently (Cambourne, 1988).

The literature-based units presented in this book provide numerous examples of how teachers can effectively immerse children in all forms of language.

Model Literacy

Literacy models provide the required experiences from which children can learn. For example:

- Guided reading in the shared language period enables children to practice reading strategies with teacher support. This is a necessary prerequisite to successful independent, silent reading.

- Reading aloud to children teaches them about reading and writing.

- Large-group language experience activities provide young learners with demonstrations of writing, how words are pronounced (grapho-phonemic correspondence), and how letters are formed. "These demonstrations are the raw data that young learners must use in order to tease out how the language they must learn is structured." (Cambourne, 1988, p. 34)

Such demonstrations can take two forms. They can be experiences provided by the teacher or experiences provided by the materials (charts, books). For example, when a child reads a book, the book demonstrates what a book is, how words form sentences, how the author develops the characters and plot, and so on. In essence, the book itself teaches how reading and writing works and helps the child build on prior knowledge gained from home and school. According to Cambourne, such demonstrations need to be demonstrations of language "wholes" and need to be repeated continually (1988). In conclusion, he notes that "classrooms need to provide a smorgasbord of contextually relevant demonstrations." A contextually relevant demonstration is one that is appropriate to a particular literacy task a learner is trying to complete.

How Can Teachers Effectively Structure Their Classroom Environments to Support Quality Teaching for Emergent Literacy?

The challenge for all teachers of young children is to provide a rich learning environment that supports optimum literacy development in developmentally appropriate ways. A well-planned, carefully organized, well-stocked classroom can contribute a great deal to the success of the instructional program as well to the children's continuous growth of literacy development. Such an environment must be print rich. It must have an abundance of good books and a wide range of easily accessible materials that promote purposeful reading and writing activities. It must also contain many examples of writing on the walls, on bulletin boards, and on interesting displays set up throughout the classroom. Such a classroom does not just happen. It must be carefully planned, organized, and structured by the teacher. It must also be well stocked with literacy materials if it is to meet the needs and interests of all the children. In addition, it must be visually appealing if it is to capture and sustain children's interest.

Many teachers working in such an environment like to organize all or part of their classroom space into a number of learning areas (centers) where children can work individually or in small groups on related learning experiences that have been designed to promote integrated learning. While the actual number and arrangement of such centers will vary according to the needs of children, certain centers are crucial. For example, it is very important to include a well-stocked library as well as a writing and publishing center. Other needed centers are a viewing and listening center for audiovisual materials (slides, films, story tapes, read-along tapes, and so on) and equipment, and a creative center (drama, puppets) where children can dramatize favorite stories they have read, heard, or written. In addition, teachers might want to include a math discovery center, a science and social studies center, a research center, a music center, and a construction center, as well as an area where the class can meet as a whole for shared language experiences.

References

Anderson, et al (1985). *Becoming a Nation of Readers: The Report of the Commission on Reading.* Washington, D.C.: The National Institute of Education.

Bissex, G. L. (1980). *GNYS at Work: A Child Learns to Read.* Cambridge, Mass.: Harvard University Press.

Butler, A., and J. Turbill (1984). *Towards A Reading-Writing Classroom.* Portsmouth, N.H.: Heinemann Educational Books.

Butler, D., and M. Clay (1979). *Reading Begins at Home.* Portsmouth, N.H.: Heinemann Educational Books.

Cambourne, B. (1988). *The Whole Story: Natural Learning and the Acquisition of Literacy in the Classroom.* Toronto: Scholastic–TAB Publications.

Calkins, L. M. (1983). *Lessons from a Child: On the Teaching and Learning of Writing.* Portsmouth, N.H.: Heinemann Educational Books.

Carbo, M. (1978). "Teaching Reading with Talking Books." *The Reading Teacher,* 32, 267–73.

Clark, M. M. (1976). *Young Fluent Readers.* Portsmouth, N.H.: Heinemann Educational Books.

Clay, M. M. (1966). *Emergent Reading Behavior.* Doctoral dissertation, University of Auckland.

——— (1975). *What Did I Write? Beginning Writing Behavior:* Auckland: Heinemann Educational Books.

——— (1988). *Writing begins at home.* Portsmouth, N.H.: Heinemann Educational Books.

——— (1989). Foreword to *Emerging Literacy: Young Children Learn to Read and Write,* D. Strickland and L. Morrow, Eds. Newark, Delaware: International Reading Association.

Durkin, D. (1966). *Children Who Read Early.* New York: Teachers College Press.

——— (1989). *Teaching Them to Read.* Boston: Allyn & Bacon.

Feitelson, D., B. Kita, and Z. Goldsteen (1986). "Effects of Listening to Stories on First Graders' Comprehension and the Use of Language." *Research in the Teaching of English,* 20, 339–56.

Ferreiro, E. (1978). "What is Written in a Written Sentence? A Developmental Answer." *Journal of Education,* 160, 25–39.

——— (1986). "The Interplay Between Information and Assimilation in Beginning Literacy." In W.H. Teale and E. Sulzby (Eds.), *Emergent Literacy: Writing and Reading.* Norwood, N.J.: Ablex.

Ferreiro, E. and A. Teberosky. (1982). *Literacy Before Schooling.* Portsmouth, N.H.: Heinemann Educational Books.

Goodman, K. (1986). *What's Whole in Whole Language?* Toronto: Scholastic–TAB Publications.

Graves, D. (1983). *Writing: Teachers & Children at Work.* Portsmouth, N.H.: Heinemann Educational Books.

Hillerich, R. L. (1976). "Toward an Assessable Definition of Literacy." *The English Journal,* 65, 29–31.

——— (1988). "Helping Emergent Literacy to Emerge." *Teaching K–8,* 18(7), 23–27.

Holdaway, D. (1980). *Independence in Reading.* Portsmouth, N.H.: Heinemann Educational Books.

——— (1982). "Stability and Change in Literacy Learning—the Early Eighties." *Reading Around,* A.R.A. 10, 3.

——— (1984). *Stability and Change in Literacy Learning.* London, Ontario: London University of

Western Ontario, Faculty of Education.

Jagger, A. (1980). "Allowing for Language Differences." In G. S. Penell (Ed.), *Discovering Language with Children.* Urbana, Ill.: National Council of Teachers of English.

Laughlin, C. E., and M. D. Martin (1987). *Supporting Literacy.* New York: Teachers College Press.

McVitty, W. (Ed.) (1985). *Children and Learning.* Rozelle, N.S.W.: Bridge Printery.

Pikulski, J. (1988). "Questions and Answers." *The Reading Teacher,* 42(1), 76.

Routman, R. (1988). *Transitions: From Literacy to Literacy.* Portsmouth, N.H.: Heinemann Educational Books.

Salinger, T. (1988). *Language Arts and Literacy for Young Children.* Toronto: Merrill.

Schickedanz, J. A. (1986). *More Than ABCs: The Early Stages of Reading and Writing.* Washington, D.C.: National Association for the Education of Young Children.

Schickedanz, J., et al. (1983). *Strategies for Teaching Young Children* (2nd ed.)

Englewood Cliffs, N.J.: Prentice Hall.

Schwartz, J. (1988). *Encouraging Early Literacy: An Integrated Approach to Reading and Writing in N–3.* Portsmouth, N.H.: Heinemann Educational Books.

Snow, C. E. (1983). "Literacy and Language: Relationships During the Preschool Years." *Harvard Educational Review,* 53, 165–89.

Strickland, D., and L. Morrow. (1988). "Emerging Readers and Writers: New Perspectives on Young Children Learning to Read and Write." *The Reading Teacher,* 42, 70–71.

————— (1989). *Emerging Literacy: Young Children Learn to Read and Write.* Newark: International Reading Association.

Taylor, D. (1983). *Family Literacy: Young Children Learning to Read and Write.* Portsmouth, N.H.: Heinemann Educational Books.

Teale, W. (1978). "Positive Environments for Learning to Read: What Studies of Early Readers Tell Us." *Language Arts,* 55, 922–32.

————— (1982). "Toward a Theory of How Children Learn to Read and Write Naturally." *Language Arts,* 59, 555–70.

Temple, C., and J. W. Gillet (1989). *Language Arts: Learning Processes and Teaching Practices* (2nd ed.). Glenview, Ill.: Scott, Foresman.

U.S. Department of Education. (1987) *What Works: Research About Teaching and Learning* (2nd ed.).

Vaughan, J. (1985). "Learning in School—What and How?" In W. McVitty (Ed.), *Children and Learning.* Rozelle, NSW: Bridge Printery.

Walshe, R.D. (1985). "Teaching Writing: Attend to Skills as Part of the Process." In W. McVitty (Ed.), *Children and Learning.* Rozelle, N.S.W.: Bridge Printery.

Wells, G. (1981). *Learning Through Interaction: The Study of Language Development.* London: Cambridge University Press.

————— (1985). *Language Development in the Preschool Years.* New York: Cambridge University Press.

SECTION

2

Developmental Program Overview

Introduction

The two volumes of *Favorites, Friendships, Food, and Fantasy* outline sequential daily plans for four popular literature-based themes (Old Favorites, Friendships, Food from the Farm, and Dragons from East and West) to be used in the early primary grades to enable children to explore and learn developmentally as well as experientially. Reading and writing are taught as an integrated whole as much as possible.

All four units contain numerous innovative yet developmentally sound learning activities and strategies that focus on implementation using carefully selected books and verses suitable for the emergent reader. The books contain meaningful stories that match a natural language flow with quality illustrations. Furthermore, they usually employ a rhyme or rhythmic quality in a repetitive or cumulative structure to make the learning experiences easy and rewarding. Not only are these books and verses used in the shared book experiences, but they are also used for guided reading when the teacher works directly with the children to develop their reading ability, and for self-selected reading during the school day and at home for independent practice and enjoyment. Some of these titles should also be made available as

Big Books, produced commercially, by teachers, or by the learners themselves. These strategies enable young learners to move more naturally from listening and speaking to emergent reading and writing.

Favorites, Friendships, Food, and Fantasy provides teachers with a field-tested Interactive Teaching/Learning Model based on sound research. Educators in New Zealand, the country with the highest literacy rate in the English-speaking world, have been employing literature to teach reading and writing for well over 20 years. This handbook also provides a framework for designing other integrated, literature-based units, and it has been used as successfully with linguistically different learners as it has with learners for whom English is their first language. Don Holdaway, who worked extensively with linguistically different learners, noted that children from different cultural and linguistic backgrounds often gain their first positive feelings about school through the use of literature.

Specifically, the four units have been designed to incorporate the following objectives and features:

■ to build on children's strengths

- to help teachers move to a total integrated literature-based reading and writing program

- to present teachers with new, up-to-date, child-centered ideas to expand their present programs

- to show teachers how to utilize brainstorming and group interaction to develop new vocabulary and concept development

- to promote the learning of key sight vocabulary needed by young emergent readers (Dolch words)

- to develop an early and enduring love of good literature in young children

- to develop independence and cooperative social skills in young children

- to provide teachers with a good bibliography of appropriate (narrative and expository) books and other teaching materials

- to provide teachers with effective assessment procedures to evaluate individual student growth

- to accommodate the varied learning styles of young children, including gifted children and those with disabilities

- to introduce children to story structure through a variety of activities—role playing, dramatization, puppets, story drama, feltboard stories, story mapping, and rhyme to prose

- to use children's cultural and linguistic backgrounds as a basis for curriculum development

- to develop critical thinking, problem-solving skills, and reasoning skills through the provision of suggested discussion questions focusing on higher-level thinking skills

- to provide teachers with practical ideas for independent, partner, cooperative-group, and small-group work for learning centers

- to provide teachers with a variety of blackline masters to complement unit plans

- to include a unit timetable grid presenting a short outline of each day's activities so that each unit can be viewed at a glance

- to include many more activities than one would use in one day allowing teachers to select the ones most appropriate to the age and needs of their children

- to provide teachers with a chart presenting an overview of the skills developed in each unit

- to include key wordlists specific to each theme for class and individual use as writing and spelling aids

- to present teachers with an Interactive Teaching/Learning Model as a planning tool for daily sessions and future unit development

Using the Interactive Teaching/Learning Model

The Interactive Teaching/Learning Model (see page 15) is based on the work of Don Holdaway (1979, 1984). It is comprised of four components: **Tune-In, Read Aloud, New Verse/Story,** and **Activity Time.** Each component will be discussed separately, though all are crucial to the overall success of the teaching and learning experience in some way and are closely linked to each other. The effectiveness of the model depends on the recommended sequencing of the four key components as well as on the selection of learning materials and strategies that are developmentally appropriate to the needs of the young learner. In order to complete all four components, teachers will need to set aside about 90 minutes for language arts (shared language time). This amount of large-group time could be shortened at the beginning of the school year or with younger children. Teachers could even spend more than one day on the listed daily group activities. This large group time is followed by one or more periods of center time—activity time—during which children work on activities independently or in small groups.

Each of the four components of the model is described below.

Tune In (8–10 minutes)

The focus of the first component of the model is the presentation of two or more warm-up activities consisting of number verses, choral verses, chants, songs, jingles, poems, action songs or verses, jump-rope rhymes, or echo chants. Those chosen for each unit were selected for their rhythmic quality as well as for their unit potential. They are usually chosen by student request after they have been introduced by the teacher.

Chanting simply means reading to a beat with speech alone or with clapping and finger snapping. This can be done either in unison, with the teacher and children chanting the words together, or as an echo, in which the teacher chants each line while pointing to the individual words, and then the children alone chant the same line as the teacher points to each word. The teacher then starts the beat, clapping or snapping fingers to the rhythm of the words. At times, the teacher or the children may wish to use musical instruments to beat out the rhythm.

Once everyone joins in the beat, the chanting of the words begins. Young children enjoy this activity and soon become totally involved in the material of the chant. The clapping or snapping are added only after the children have heard and read the same material several times. This rehearsal of the oral version imprints the language, helping children match their oral language to their written language (sight vocabulary), as well as introducing them to the sounds, rhythm, and flow of language. In essence, children are learning the relationship of oral language to written language.

It is only when the children are ready to match the oral language to written language that the reading material is written on charts, displayed with an overhead projector, or made into sentence strips for use on pocket charts, allowing children to enjoy the material visually as well as orally. At this stage, the teacher uses a pointer to point to each word as it is chanted. By following the pointer, the children begin to establish directional reading habits (left to right, top to bottom) as well as increasing their confidence in their own reading ability.

These repeated readings also help the children to develop oral reading fluency in an enjoyable manner as well as building on their listening, speaking, reading, and writing vocabularies. As the children become more comfortable with the reading material, they often enjoy taking the teacher's role of pointing during the Tune In component. Then, once the material has been learned, children enjoy repeating this procedure individually or in small groups during Activity Time. At this stage, send home individual copies of the material for children to share with their families. Some samples are provided as blackline masters at the end of each unit of this book. They can be reproduced as single sheets or as a small book.

It is important at this stage to provide emergent learners with easy, highly motivating, nonthreatening materials that allow them to participate at their own level of development. Even the children who are not responding orally with the group are following along visually and aurally as the teacher points to each individual word in the material. This is especially effective with linguistically different children and reluctant readers because it provides them with the necessary support needed at this beginning stage.

Finally, this beginning component of our model helps the children tune in to the topic of the day, since most of the material is related to the developing unit.

Read Aloud (10–15 minutes)

In *Becoming a Nation of Readers* the commission stressed the importance of reading aloud not only in the home but also at school. It noted that the practice should continue throughout the grades, findings supported by other leading researchers who have studied successful early readers. For example, Durkin's study showed that being read to frequently was the one common factor found in early readers (1989). In a fifteen-year study of children in England, Wells also concluded that their school success was directly related to the frequency to listening to stories read (1986). Cazden found that reading to children was a superior method in aiding language acquisition (1981). Numerous other reasons for reading or telling stories to emergent readers have been cited in early childhood literature, including some of the following:

- Reading to children strengthens and creates a positive attitude about reading and books.

- Reading to children helps to increase listening, speaking, reading and writing vocabulary. Children must hear words before they are able to speak and write words.

- Reading to children helps to familiarize them with story structure and the language of books.

- Reading to children introduces them to people, places, and experiences outside of their immediate environment, which aids in concept development.

- Reading to children nourishes their imagination. Glazer noted that imagination is a critical component of later reading comprehension; without imagining, readers experience difficulty mentally visualizing scenes, identifying with characters, and so on (1986). Wells also noted that children with rich, broad book exposure were able to narrate and describe scenes more vividly (1985). These are useful skills that support oral and written communication and enhance literacy development. In addition, young children often get ideas from these stories for use in imaginative play.

- Reading aloud increases listening comprehension, which is a prerequisite to the development of silent reading comprehension.

- Reading aloud presents emergent readers with a good oral reading model.

- Reading aloud develops and lengthens attention span as well as discussion skills.

- Reading to children establishes the connection between reading and writing.

A new book or verse is usually shared each day during the Read Aloud component. The readings should be a balance of literature (fiction and nonfiction), finger plays, number verses, and poetry. These should be carefully selected, since they are used to introduce key concepts required to develop higher-level thinking skills in listening and speaking, as well as to activate the learner's existing schema structure. In order to help teachers facilitate this process, numerous teaching suggestions to introduce material during the New Verse/Story component are included. Because the Read Aloud component is so closely linked to teaching the New Verse/Story component, both must be selected and used very carefully. In addition, care must be taken as to how the books are used. The following guidelines are provided to assist teachers in conducting the Read Aloud component.

Suggested Guidelines for the Read Aloud Component

- Become familiar with the book so that you can share it effectively.

- Select materials within the limits of your learners' attention span.

- Think about the story structure and pattern (whether it is cumulative, comparative, repetitive).

- Decide whether the story is best told or read.

- Use drama props (objects related to story content) and feltboard materials when appropriate.

- Tape the story as it is being read or told for later use in the listening center.

- For variety invite other people (principal, older students, parents) to read to children. Holdaway notes the importance of male models as well as female models.

- Allow time for discussion and children's questions at the end of the reading.

- Place materials in easily accessible areas for student use (books in the library center, tapes in the listening center).

New Verse/Story (20–30 minutes)

This component emphasizes using developmentally appropriate practices and quality literature to develop literacy. There are numerous valid reasons for using literature to teach the reading and writing processes.

- The purpose of reading is always for meaning and enjoyment. The literature selected for a literature-based program is usually predictable in structure and outcomes, so that it makes sense to the children and is easily read, talked about, and remembered. This leads to early reading success, which helps to promote confidence and positive attitudes toward reading in young readers.

- Through the use of literature children learn specific vocabulary and comprehension strategies in context. This enables early learners to view themselves as readers and writers from the beginning of the program.

- Using literature in teaching helps to develop a greater sense of story grammar. The notion of story grammar and story structure suggests that stories are organized in a specific manner (Mandler and Johnson, 1977). A well-structured story generally has a *setting* (beginning, time, place); *characters* (major and minor); *theme* (goal or main problem); *plot episodes* (events that take place in which characters endeavor to solve a problem or achieve a goal); and a *resolution* (the problem or goal the characters solved or achieved at the end). Throughout the four units, numerous opportunities for children to develop and expand their concept of story structure are provided. McGee and Richgels note that the children's concept of what a story is "is very important in learning to construct meaning from stories." (comprehension) (1990, p. 138). See pages 223-4 in Volume Two for story structure frames for teacher use.

- Since literature presents well-written stories as a whole, its use provides teachers with opportunities to demonstrate and strengthen children's understanding of what reading is all about. For example, while the teacher models how a book is read (beginning, middle, end, story structure/grammar, reading strategies, concept of authorship), children are developing metacognitive knowledge of how to approach reading tasks. According to Morrow, metacognition is one's awareness of how learning is taking place; it thus nurtures one's own learning (1988, p. 78).

- Literature promotes oral and written language development through the exposure of rich, varied vocabulary and sentence patterns. In addition, literature provides children with models of good language and story structure for their independent story and verse writing. Because the children are reading material over and over again as the teacher points to words or word groups or masks specific words, the children develop a visual sense of letter structure and standard spelling as they progress from the scribble stage. They also increase their sight vocabulary.

- Literature provides engaging content, thus providing teachers with excellent opportunities for designing higher-level questions. Examples of such questions appear in each of the four units.

- Literature introduces children to a variety of artwork styles and media through illustrations. Wordless books are especially useful, since they tell a complete story through pictures.

For the above reasons, literature is the principal material used in this program. The selected materials used in the New Verse/Story component provide the teacher with numerous opportunities to explore and model language in many different ways. Many books related to the four carefully developed themes have been selected for each unit because several books on a common theme can often enrich meaning more effectively than a single book (McGee and Richgels, 1990). In addition, information books have been listed throughout the units to extend and clarify the children's understanding of concepts, as well as to build on their prior knowledge. The verse or story used in the New Verse/Story component closely relates to the books and concepts discussed in the Read Aloud component. Many of the selections can be used in an enlarged format (charts, overhead transparencies, pocket charts, or Big Books).

The teaching emphasis is on *process*. Most children come to school with some basic understanding of story structure (Applebee, 1978; Bartlett, 1932). Teaching in this component is designed to expand and refine the prior knowledge of all children through Directed Listening Thinking Activities (DLTA). Research has shown that this type of teaching activity can increase the story comprehension of young listeners (Morrow, 1988). Emphasis is also directed to (a) creating awareness of the four cuing processes—prior knowledge, graphophonic, syntactic, and semantic; (b) developing oral language through discussion; (c) developing listening skills; (d) developing social and cooperative skills; and (e) developing higher levels of thinking (Barrett's Taxonomy).

Suggested Guidelines for the New Verse/Story Component

- Try to obtain as many of the materials as possible, especially the books. If possible, obtain Big Book versions of the recommended material to facilitate the teaching of process and provide a visual aid.

- Before teaching, read all the unit books several times to obtain a good understanding of their content as well as their story structure.

- Hunt for additional poems, books, and pictures related to the theme at your school library or public library—the more materials the better. Such materials can be placed in the centers for individual or small-group use.

Activity Time (30–45 minutes)

The Activity Time component provides numerous opportunities to teach something new; to further clarify a teaching focus (cuing systems, story grammar); to consolidate, expand, and refine reading and writing skills and strategies developed earlier. The focus is on integrating the four language areas with each other and with other subject areas.

The Activity Time component consists of two parts, whole group and individual or small groups. Both parts are necessary for reading and writing instruction and learning, since they are social processes that best flourish in a wide variety of settings. Make grouping patterns varied and flexible to ensure effectiveness.

Whole-Group Time

Activities for the whole group are mainly teacher directed with the emphasis on modeling process, procedure, or product. They precede individual or small-group time. Holistic learning with active learner participation in a positive, risk-free learning environment encourages all children to participate at their own level of development, thus eliminating the pressure of participating on a competitive level. A feeling of belonging and enhanced self-esteem can be fostered in this setting. Some examples of whole-group activities used in our model are listed below.

- Teaching original or published verses or songs
- Writing verse to prose
- Brainstorming to develop vocabulary or writing ideas
- Developing story maps
- Reading in unison (chanting, echo reading)
- Modeling, cuing strategies (prior knowledge, graphophonic, semantic, and syntactic)
- Coordinating art projects (murals, illustrating Big Books)
- Developing schema for story grammar
- Writing letters and poetry
- Developing sentence sense (open frames)
- Dramatizing verses or songs or stories (role play, story drama, puppets)

- Cooking and preparing for cooking (recipes, following directions, measurement)
- Producing cooperative books (Big Books, anthologies, little books)
- Producing cooperative language experience stories

Individual/Small-Group Time

Activities for individuals or small groups provide children with opportunities to extend what has been learned during the preceding components. Children are expected to work and play cooperatively or independently on meaningful activities or projects. Activities may be selected by the children themselves or planned by the teacher. Small-group activities should consume the greater part of the scheduled activity time as well as other center time during the day. Activities are changed frequently so that they are closely related to the whole-group teaching/learning activities that have taken place earlier in the day. Since the curriculum is integrated, centers related to other subject areas other than the four language arts strands are included in the teaching plans. Centers and their use will be discussed later in this section.

While the children are working throughout the classroom, the teacher circulates and interacts with them in order to sustain interest and provide help or guidance when the need arises. The teacher is also actively involved in observing and recording each child's progress at regular intervals, and individual reading and writing conferences are scheduled at appropriate times. These results are used to improve large- and small-group or individual instruction, and can be used during parent conferences. To help teachers in this important role, observation and conference forms are included in the Appendix. During small-group time it is important for the teacher to observe group dynamics as well as how the materials are being used. It is important for teachers to listen to children's observations about the groups in which they participate as well as to listen to children as they interact with each other.

Figure 1: Interactive Teaching/Learning Model

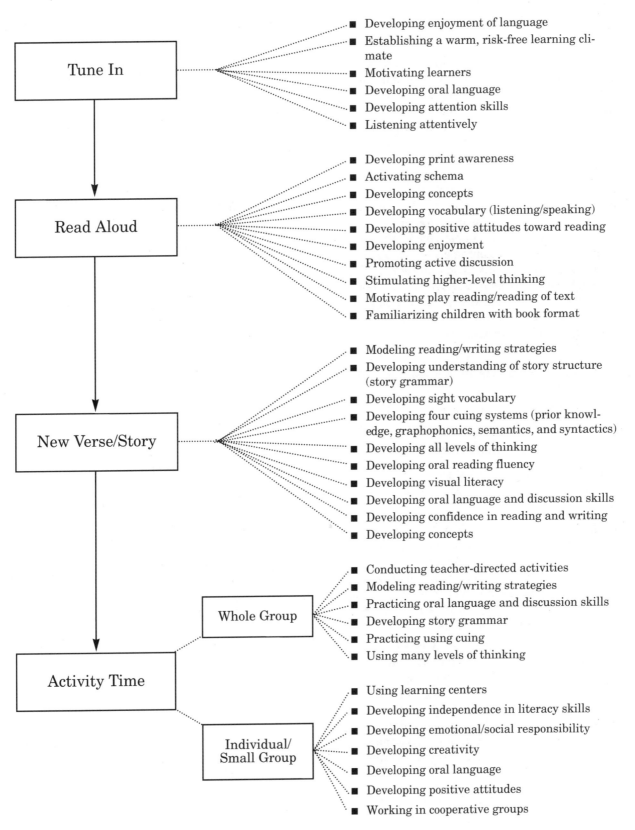

Tune In
- ■ Developing enjoyment of language
- ■ Establishing a warm, risk-free learning climate
- ■ Motivating learners
- ■ Developing oral language
- ■ Developing attention skills
- ■ Listening attentively

Read Aloud
- ■ Developing print awareness
- ■ Activating schema
- ■ Developing concepts
- ■ Developing vocabulary (listening/speaking)
- ■ Developing positive attitudes toward reading
- ■ Developing enjoyment
- ■ Promoting active discussion
- ■ Stimulating higher-level thinking
- ■ Motivating play reading/reading of text
- ■ Familiarizing children with book format

New Verse/Story
- ■ Modeling reading/writing strategies
- ■ Developing understanding of story structure (story grammar)
- ■ Developing sight vocabulary
- ■ Developing four cuing systems (prior knowledge, graphophonics, semantics, and syntactics)
- ■ Developing all levels of thinking
- ■ Developing oral reading fluency
- ■ Developing visual literacy
- ■ Developing oral language and discussion skills
- ■ Developing confidence in reading and writing
- ■ Developing concepts

Activity Time

Whole Group
- ■ Conducting teacher-directed activities
- ■ Modeling reading/writing strategies
- ■ Practicing oral language and discussion skills
- ■ Developing story grammar
- ■ Practicing using cuing
- ■ Using many levels of thinking

Individual/Small Group
- ■ Using learning centers
- ■ Developing independence in literacy skills
- ■ Developing emotional/social responsibility
- ■ Developing creativity
- ■ Developing oral language
- ■ Developing positive attitudes
- ■ Working in cooperative groups

Adapted from *The Foundations of Literacy* by Don Holdaway.
Toronto: Ashton Scholastic, 1979.

Developing Comprehension Strategies: Barrett's Taxonomy*

The essence of effective teaching is related to good questioning. Good questioning can awaken learner curiosity and interest, stimulate imagination, and invigorate the search for new knowledge. Effective teachers continually try to draw answers from children during comprehension discussion, working not to provide children with answers, but to provide the guidance necessary for children to come up with the right answer themselves. Sometimes it becomes necessary to paraphrase the question or break it into two or more easier questions for the children to answer. Developing good questions requires asking questions on different thinking levels. Several taxonomies have been developed to assist teachers in asking good questions in order to improve comprehension. The most frequently used is Barrett's Taxonomy (1979). It specifies four levels of comprehension:

- Literal Comprehension (Recognition and Recall)
- Inferential Comprehension
- Evaluative Comprehension
- Appreciative Comprehension

The following discussion describes what is required of the reader at each of the four levels of comprehension.

- **Literal Comprehension, Recognition** requires children to be able to find the answer to the question asked when the text is in front of them, and to identify words and chunks of words in response to the question asked. This task of identification requires the strategies of skimming and scanning.

- **Literal Comprehension, Recall** requires children to synthesize what they have listened to or read silently and respond to the questions asked. Sometimes children are asked to respond using the author's exact words to reinforce key concepts and literary style of presentation. In other instances, children are encouraged to respond to questions

in their own words, demonstrating that they have understood what they have listened to or what they have read.

- **Inferential Comprehension** is based on previous experiences, either vicarious or actual. Children are asked to utilize information obtained on the Literal Comprehension level to predict responses to questions or add information to what is already known.

- **Evaluative Comprehension** also requires children to utilize the information obtained on the Literal Comprehension level to state judgmental reasons based on criteria that may have been obtained vicariously or through actual experience.

- **Appreciative Comprehension** requires children to respond with feeling to a verse or story. At this level children might be asked to describe (a) how the author developed the setting or characters; (b) how the author used specific words or chunks of words; and/or (c) how they themselves feel about the verse or story.

It is important for teachers to realize that not all the subcategories within each level of comprehension must be represented in each lesson. Questions are based on a careful analysis of the verse or story. Quality rather than quantity becomes the benchmark in question design.

Each unit presents questions that develop different levels of comprehension and provides guidelines for teachers to model behaviors and questions for children to ask when reading and thinking on their own. For example, when discussing "Humpty Dumpty," the teacher might ask the children to think of reasons why Humpty Dumpty fell. This question is categorized as Inferential Comprehension (Cause-Effect). It requires the children to understand the rhyme (Literal Comprehension) and use their own ideas based on prior experiences (vicarious or actual). Children learn that their responses are important and essential to the activity-based discussion in the lesson. The teacher might also ask what else children would like to find out about Humpty Dumpty, modeling how to ask questions when reading independently.

Using Barrett's Taxonomy, Figures 2–5 show sample questions from the Old Favorites Nursery Rhyme section (NR) and a story from the Dragons from East and West unit (D), *The Paper Bag Princess*.

*Thomas C. Barrett, "Taxonomy of Reading," *Teaching Reading in the Middle Grades,* Richard J. Smith and Dale D. Johnson, eds. Reading, Mass.: Addison-Wesley Publishing Company, © 1979

Figure 2: Barrett's Taxonomy
Literal Comprehension: Recognition and Recall

(Note: Recognition questioning takes place with the text available to the reader. Recall questioning takes place with the text unavailable to the reader.)

- Who is the rhyme all about? (NR)
- Describe what Elizabeth looked like. (D)

·····

1.0 *Literal Comprehension.* This level requires recognition or recall of information and happenings that are explicitly stated in materials read and/or listened to. Recognition tasks ask children to locate or identify explicit statements in the reading selection itself. Recall statements require students to produce from memory explicit statements from a selection.

1.1 *Details.* The student is asked to produce from text/memory facts such as the name of characters, the time of the story, or the place of the story.

1.2 *Main Ideas.* The student is required to state a main idea of a paragraph or a larger portion of the selection from text/memory when the main idea is explicitly stated in the selection.

1.3 *Sequence.* The student is asked to provide from text/memory the order of incidents or actions explicitly stated in the selection.

1.4 *Comparisons.* The student is asked to provide from text/memory the likenesses and differences in characters, times, and places that are explicitly stated in the selection.

1.5 *Cause-and-Effect Relationships.* The student is requested to produce from text/memory explicitly stated reasons for certain happenings or actions in the selection.

1.6 *Character Traits.* The student is asked to call up from text/memory explicit statements about characters that illustrate the type of person they are.

- What happened in the beginning? Middle? End? (NR)
- Review what Elizabeth had the Dragon do. (D)

·····

- What happened to Humpty Dumpty? (NR)
- What happened to the dragon? (D)

·····

- How would you compare Elizabeth at the beginning of the story and after the dragon burned the castle? (D)

·····

- What type of a person was Little Miss Muffet? (NR)
- How does the author describe the dragon? (D)

Figure 3: Barrett's Taxonomy
Inferential Comprehension

2.0 *Inferential comprehension.* Inferential comprehension is demonstrated when the student uses the ideas and information explicitly stated in the selection, intuition, and personal experience as a basis for conjectures and hypotheses. Inferences drawn by the student may be either convergent or divergent in nature, and the student may or may not be asked to verbalize the rationale underlying inferences. Inferential comprehension demands thinking and imagination that go beyond the printed page.

2.1 *Inferring supporting details.* The student is asked to conjecture about additional facts the author might have included in the selection that would have made it more informative, interesting, or appealing.

2.2 *Inferring main ideas.* The student is required to provide the main idea, general significance, theme, or moral that is not explicitly stated in the selection.

2.3 *Inferring sequence.* The student may be requested to conjecture what action or incident might have taken place between two explicitly stated actions or incidents, or what would happen next if the selection had not ended as it did.

2.4 *Inferring comparisons.* The student is required to infer likenesses and differences in characters, times, or places. Such inferential comparisons revolve around ideas such as *here and there, then and now, he and he, he and she,* and *she and she.*

2.5 *Inferring cause-and-effect relationships.* The student is required to hypothesize about the motivations of characters and their interactions with time and place and may also be required to conjecture as to why certain ideas, words, characterizations, and actions appeared in the writing.

2.6 *Inferring character traits.* The student is asked to hypothesize about the nature of characters on the basis of explicit clues in the selection.

2.7 *Predicting outcomes.* The student is requested to read an initial portion of the selection and on the basis of this reading is required to conjecture about the outcome of the selection.

2.8 *Interpreting figurative language.* The student is asked to infer literal meanings from the author's figurative use of language.

- Where do you think the sheep were hiding? (NR)
- If you were Elizabeth what might you say to Arnold? (D)

- What do you think Jack and Jill will do next? (NR)
- What do you think Elizabeth will do now? (D)

- Why do you think Jack and Jill fell? (NR)
- Why do you think Arnold acted the way he did? (D)

- What kind of a boy was Little Boy Blue? Why? (NR)
- How do you think Elizabeth felt when Roland spoke to her that way? Why? (D)

- What do you think the princess will do? (D)

Figure 4: Barrett's Taxonomy
Evaluative Comprehension

■ Do you think a lamb could really go to school? Why or why not? (NR)

■ Could this type of a story take place today? Why or why not? (D)

■ Why couldn't the King's men put Humpty Dumpty together again? (NR)

■ Do you think it is possible for a princess to rescue a prince? Why or why not? (D)

3.0 *Evaluative Comprehension.* Purposes for reading and teacher's questions require responses that indicate that the student has made an evaluative judgment by comparing ideas presented in the selection with external criteria provided by the teacher, other authorities, or other written sources, or with internal criteria provided by the reader's experience, knowledge, or values. In essence, evaluation deals with judgment and focuses on qualities of accuracy, acceptability, desirability, worth, or probability of occurrence. Evaluative thinking may be demonstrated by asking the student to make the following judgments:

3.1 *Judgments of reality or fantasy.* Could this really happen? Such a question calls for a judgment based on the reader's experience.

3.2 *Judgments of fact or opinion.* Does the author provide adequate support for conclusions? Is the author attempting to sway your thinking? Questions of this type require the student to analyze and evaluate the writing on the basis of personal knowledge as well as to analyze and evaluate the intent of the author.

3.3 *Judgments of adequacy and validity.* Is the information presented here in keeping with what you have read on the subject in other sources? Questions of this nature call for the reader to compare written sources of information, with an eye toward agreement and disagreement or completeness and incompleteness.

3.4 *Judgments of appropriateness.* What part of the story best describes the main character? Such a question requires the reader to make a judgment about the relative adequacy of different parts of the selection to answer the question.

3.5 *Judgments of worth, desirability and acceptability.* Was the character right or wrong? Was the character's behavior good or bad? Questions of this nature call for judgments based on the reader's moral code or value system.

■ Is Elizabeth solving her problem? Why or why not? (D)

■ Do you think Pussy-cat did the right thing by frightening the mouse? Why or why not? (NR)

■ How do you feel about Elizabeth's decision at the end of the story? (D)

Figure 5: Barrett's Taxonomy
Appreciative Comprehension

- Which nursery rhyme did you like best? Why? (NR)
- How do you feel about Arnold? Why? (D)

- How would you feel if you were Little Miss Muffet? Why? (NR)
- How do you feel about the story? (D)

4.0 *Appreciative Comprehension.* Appreciation involves all the previously cited cognitive dimensions of reading, since it deals with the psychological and aesthetic impact of the selection on the reader. Appreciation calls for the student to be emotionally and aesthetically sensitive to the work and to have a reaction to the worth of its psychological and artistic elements. Appreciation includes both the knowledge of and the emotional response to literary techniques, forms, styles, and structures.

4.1 *Emotional response to the content.* The student is required to verbalize feelings about the selection in terms of interest, excitement, boredom, fear, hate, amusement, and so on. It is concerned with the emotional impact of the total work on the reader.

4.2 *Identification with characters or incidents.* Teachers' questions of this nature will elicit responses from the reader that demonstrate sensitivity to, sympathy for, and empathy with characters and happenings portrayed by the author.

4.3 *Reactions to the author's use of language.* In this instance the student is required to respond to the author's craftsmanship in terms of the semantic dimensions of the selection, namely, connotations and denotations of words.

4.4 *Imagery.* In this instance, the reader is required to verbalize feelings with regard to the author's artistic ability to paint word pictures that cause the reader to visualize, smell, taste, hear, or feel.

- What does the author tell us about Mary's feelings about her lamb? (NR)
- How would you illustrate your favorite part of the story? (D)

Figure 6: Sample Room Arrangement

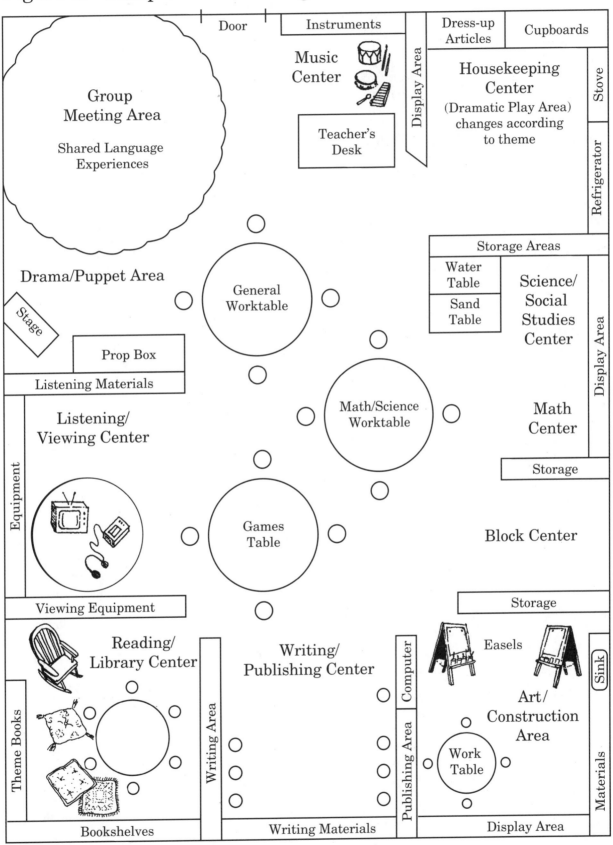

Concept of Integration

The integrated unit model provides the structure upon which our early childhood literature-based curriculum has been developed. It is based on the belief that reading, writing, speaking, and listening should be naturally integrated with each other and with all other subject areas of the curriculum whenever possible, thus providing children with opportunities to learn concepts as part of an integrated whole rather than as isolated bits of information under particular single-subject areas. In addition, the model allows teachers intentionally to integrate many single curriculum areas into a broader, interest-based curriculum in meaningful, natural ways. Through this process young children learn a great deal about literacy and how language works. This approach to learning has been consciously adapted to a literature-based program because topics of study developed through a literature base have the greatest potential for literacy growth. Once selected, the literature-based thematic unit provides children in the integrated classroom with focal points for the following:

- Inquiry
- Oral and written language
- Problem solving
- Integration with other subject areas
- Cognitive development (cuing system, comprehension)
- Social, physical, and emotional development
- Cooperative learning
- Use of varied multicultural, age-appropriate literacy materials
- Child-teacher interaction
- Development of self-esteem and positive feelings toward literacy growth
- Assessment of literacy growth
- Independent reading

The thematic unit provides a needed focus for the large, shared-language sessions, as well as for the small-group and individual activities taking place throughout the classroom. It also provides a framework for curriculum as language arts and content are integrated in meaningful, purposeful ways. The actual amount of integration possible will depend to a large degree on the selected topic, the age and background of the children, and the availability of literature and other sources. The actual time spent on each unit will vary depending on class interest in the topic. Each day of any of the five units can be shortened or expanded to meet individual class needs.

Designing the Learning Environment

The success of this program will depend to a large extent on how well the classroom learning environment is organized, designed, managed, and stocked. The environment should complement the entire program and provide children with many rich and varied opportunities to engage in activities that will contribute to their literacy growth. For many teachers, this can best be accomplished by arranging their classrooms into a number of clearly defined learning centers. Within each center, children are free to pursue tasks individually or in small informal groups, as they work with multilevel material appropriate to their ages and interests. Centers are places where teachers can initiate and reinforce learning, which is most effective when it has been linked to the particular unit being studied by the children.

In setting up various learning centers, teachers may need to arrange desks or tables into groups so that extra space can be created. Tables should be placed so that children can move freely and easily from center to center. Besides the centers, teachers will need to set aside a large area for whole-class meetings and activities. Figure 6 on page 21 presents a diagram of a sample room arrangement that would be appropriate for the early primary years.

The four learning centers that are critical to the integrated, literature-based classroom are described below.

The Reading/Library Center. The library center should be set off from the rest of the classroom by partitions or shelves and should contain comfortable seating (cushions, a rug, a soft chair). It should be well stocked with a variety of trade books (fiction and nonfiction) on different topics and at varying levels of difficulty as well as with Big Books, magazines, dual-language texts, and dictionaries that have been organized in some way, such as by subject, by level of difficulty, or by unit topic. It should be an attractive area containing stuffed animals, posters, and displays to encourage children to read independently. It should also be a place where stories can be shared with small groups of children. Keep original published books written by the children or the teacher or both at this center.

The Writing/Publishing Center. The writing/publishing center should be an attractive, inviting, well-stocked center where children can learn the skills of writing through active participation in the process. It should contain all kinds of paper varying in size, texture, color, and shape; an abundance of writing supplies such as crayons, markers, pencils, pens; and staplers and construction paper for making covers. Blank books in a variety of shapes, sizes, and colors can do much to attract the avid as well as the reluctant writer. While some of these books may have titles related to the present unit of study written on the cover, most should be left blank.

Keep at the writing center the children's journals and writing folders with decorated covers, as well as samples of books published by students. Display here children's writing as well as writing suggestions, alphabet models, good story titles, and spelling aids (theme words, high-frequency words). The center should accommodate four to five children and include a typewriter or computer for publishing writing. Directions and materials for binding books should also be included at this center.

The Listening/Viewing Center. The listening/viewing center should be a quiet, comfortable place where audiovisual materials (story tapes, read-along tapes, records, filmstrips, blank tapes) and equipment (record player, tape recorder, filmstrip projector) are made available. Tapes made by the children and the teacher should also be included. While some of the tapes can be made just for pleasurable listening, others can be made to allow children to read along with the tape while following in the book. Story maps or feltboard file folders with appropriate figures may also be used to promote attentive listening. If blank tapes are included in the center, children can record stories, songs, poems, and original research for others to hear. Children may want to view or review filmstrips related to individual interests and class units in this center.

The Drama Center. The focus in the drama center is on stimulating oral-language development. Here children meet to discuss matters of importance and to dramatize favorite stories. The center should be stocked with a variety of puppets, a puppet stage, costumes, props, simple masks, flannelboards, pictures, and enough space for a few actors to move about. Children use these materials to retell favorite stories or create new stories.

There are many possibilities for learning centers in addition to the four core centers mentioned above, including the following:

- Art
- Mathematics
- Science
- Social studies
- Cooking
- Blocks
- Housekeeping/Dramatic play
- Music

Stocking the Print-Rich Environment

The physical environment, if properly stocked, can be used effectively to support the literacy growth of young learners. It is very important that this environment be print-rich. In addition to a wide variety and range of books, display an abundance of reference charts, signs, labels, word lists, pictures with captions, samples of children's projects and writing, as well as numerous chants, songs, verses, and books produced in large print. Also display all kinds of key word lists (high-frequency words, theme words, spelling aids, alphabet word lists and so on) and published and children-made or teacher-made dictionaries throughout the classroom to help young beginning writers move more quickly to standard spelling forms. Teachers may also wish to promote the use of personal word banks in their classrooms.

In stocking their classrooms, teachers need to keep the following print materials in mind.

- picture books
- Big Books
- wordless books
- patterned books
- magazines
- nonfiction materials
- student-published books
- cookbooks, recipes, and menus

- poetry books and charts
- fiction books
- read-along books
- pocket charts with cut-up stories, poems, or songs
- posters
- newspapers
- alphabet letters
- song sheets

Grouping Patterns

Grouping in the early primary classroom must be flexible, allowing young children to work individually, in pairs, in small cooperative groups, and in whole-class groups. Whole-class activities help young children develop a sense of community (belonging) and provide teachers with time to teach new concepts and to model a process, procedure, or product. Whole-group time is also a time to share, to set rules, to enjoy musical activities, to brainstorm ideas, to play games, to hear poems and stories, to report on completed tasks, and to engage in all kinds of concrete experiences. These activities also provide support for children with limited English. Because whole-class grouping involves heterogeneous groups in which all children are given a chance to participate at their own level, competition is eliminated.

The use of small cooperative groups is also an effective way to group young learners. Ideally, such groups should range in size from three to six children. Some of the most frequently used patterns are interest groups, social (friendship) groups, special-needs groups, cooperative groups, and ability groups. Interest groups are formed when children group themselves according to an identified common interest in some topic materials, or child-originated interest. Social groups are formed when children choose to work on an activity together on the basis of friendship. These types of groups are usually formed during free play or learning center time. Special needs groups are formed only after direct observation by the teacher. They are used to review, reteach, or teach needed new skills. Once their purpose has been achieved, they are disbanded. Ability groups are not often used but are especially useful for gifted learners.

Pairs of children working together are yet another popular way of grouping young learners. A very common practice in primary classrooms is to use reading buddies (peers or older children) to share a favorite book. Buddies can take turns reading to each other, or they can read in unison. Using reading buddies with emergent readers offers learning gains to both buddies. In the same way, writing buddies can help each other during the writing process. Older writing buddies can write down the dictated stories of their younger buddies.

Finally, teachers must schedule time for children to work independently. Remember that comprehending, reading, and composing are essentially solitary acts. Children need plenty of time to play and to read and to write about things that interest them.

Unit Organization

Children in the early primary years are curious, active, and imaginative learners. They love to dance, beat out rhythms, explore, dramatize, role play, draw, construct, and chant their favorite songs and verses as well as talk about their world. Many children have been introduced to basic story structure through rhymes, songs or stories either read or told to them during the preschool years.

Therefore, the first unit in Volume One—Old Favorites: Nursery Rhymes and Favorite Tales (folktales)—has been designed to bridge the literature of the home with the literature of the school and to meet the many needs of young learners found in our multicultural society. Rhymes and folktales are found in cultures worldwide and are the most frequent form of literature heard by young children. They have been passed down from generation to generation. They provide insight into many cultures, reflecting the similarities as well as their unique characteristics.

Old Favorites. Nursery rhymes are the first part of the first unit because of their long oral tradition and the fact that they are found in many cultures. In many cases, children have already been introduced to nursery rhymes, either in English or in their own language, before they enter school. Because of their strong rhyme, rhythm, and singable quality, they are easily memorized. They tell a brief satisfying story that often features children or animals as main characters. Their brief story lines are a good introduction to story schema, and they lend themselves to repeated chanting or echo reading, providing numerous opportunities for children to develop sight vocabulary in context in a very enjoyable way. The extensive use of rhyming words also helps to lay the foundation for teaching graphophonics in context. For these reasons, they provide excellent material for emergent readers.

Favorite tales (folktales) naturally follow nursery rhymes because of the strong oral tradition and familiarity of the material. Many of the tales have appeared in many different versions and in many different languages. The stories develop the child's concept of story schema through more clearly defined main characters, more detailed settings, and more complicated plot lines than those found in nursery rhymes. Story lines are repetitive, predictable, and cumulative, making them ideal for emergent readers; simple plots easily lend themselves to retellings and dramatization using simple props, puppets, or feltboards. Dramatization is an excellent comprehension activity, providing numerous opportunities for children to develop oral language and have fun at the same time. In addition, children enjoy using the simple plots to write and illustrate their own versions of the same story.

Friendships. The second unit in Volume One emphasizes the classroom community. Children of primary age are becoming intensely interested in their peers, so the thrust of this unit is on the development of peer interaction and social and cooperative skills that provide a foundation for the many social competencies required for success later in life. Since an important component of friendship is getting to know each other, this unit provides a strong link to the appreciation of the culture of one's friends. In order to accomplish this, literature has been selected along with many cooperative classroom discussion experiences that focus on the following points:

- Understanding what a friend is
- Identifying activities children like to do with friends
- Solving problems that arise with friends
- Showing one's true feelings to friends
- Learning how to become a good friend
- Understanding that friends come in many sizes, ages, and shapes

This unit provides many good opportunities for large- and small-group discussions, brainstorming, and charting, as well as numerous opportunities for creative writing activities, role playing, and drama. The material chosen for the Read Aloud and New Verse/Story components of the unit provides continued learning experiences in relation to concept formation, story schema, and higher-level thinking skills. Numerous books are available on this theme topic for independent reading time.

Food from the Farm. The unit three (Volume Two) topic moves from the school to the larger work community, yet remains within the limits of the young child's world. It was chosen because food production is common to all cultures. Although eating is a commonplace activity, young children often do not understand where or how their food is produced. This unit provides children with the opportunity to see how food is produced and appreciate the role of the farmer in the process. This unit also introduces young children to the concept of a job. Not only can children read and write about these activities, but they can get actively involved in discovering the joy of planting seeds, taking care of plants, and then eating the harvest.

Furthermore, the unit increases children's understanding of our dependency on plants and animals, a concept that was first introduced through the nursery rhyme, "Little Boy Blue" and the story, *The Little Red Hen.* A wealth and variety of songs, verses, and good literature are available on food, from alphabet books to narrative and expository prose, stimulating independent natural writing. The wide range of materials allows the teacher to continue building on the cognitive processes developed throughout the earlier units (four cuing systems, story schema, and higher levels of thinking).

Dragons from East and West. The final unit (Volume Two) was chosen because of its potential to take children from the real world to the world of fantasy and make-believe. Young children love stories of dragons, castles, knights, and princesses that are widely found in traditional European tales. Large creatures, imaginative as well as real, have always fascinated young learners. Eastern dragons also have a special appeal because of the vital role they play in Asian cultures. Although dragons found in stories written for older children often appear as frightening, large creatures, most of the dragons found in the stories, poems, songs, and verses selected for this unit tend to be young, friendly, loving, and helpful. Several of the stories feature heroines rather than heros, providing excellent role models for young girls. Most of the stories selected for this final unit tend to have a more complicated story line than those used in the earlier units. Because of this factor, the main focus of this unit is on developing higher levels of thinking within the organizational structure of story schema as well as extending the cognitive processes of earlier units. These imaginative adventure stories provide young writers with rich content for story writing as well as dramatization.

In summary, these units have been designed to be developmentally appropriate, shaping the cognitive and social and emotional growth of the child. They have been carefully sequenced and have already been enjoyed by many children with varied backgrounds and experiences. In designing all four units, the key focus has been the integration of language arts (listening, speaking, reading, writing) with other subject areas (drama, social studies, mathematics, art, music, dance, health). Numerous field-tested teaching and learning activities suitable for use by individuals, small groups, or large groups have been developed for all four units. The Transactive Teaching/Learning Model provides the framework for the four units. Each of the components within the unit plans is discussed in detail, providing teachers with clear step-by-step teaching plans that describe how the units can effectively be implemented. Furthermore, many suggestions facilitate meeting the individual needs of the varied learners in the classroom. To indicate the degree of difficulty of the activities, easier activities or literature selections are marked with an open diamond ◇ and more challenging activities are marked with a double solid diamond ◆◆. All other activities are deemed suitable for all learners in the classroom and provide opportunities for children to engage in learning activities that are developmentally appropriate to them.

References

Applebee, A. N. (1978). *The Child's Concept of Story: Ages Two to Seventeen.* Chicago: University of Chicago Press.

Barrett, T. C. (1979). "Taxonomy of Reading Comprehension." In R. J. Smith and D. D. Johnson (Eds.), *Teaching Reading in the Middle Grades.* Reading, Mass.: Addison-Wesley.

Bartlett, F. C. (1932). *Remembering.* Cambridge, Mass.: Cambridge University Press.

Cazden, C. (Ed.) (1981). *Language in Early Childhood Education.* Washington, D.C.: National Association for the Education of Young Children.

Durkin, D. (1989). *Teaching Them to Read.* Boston: Allyn & Bacon.

Glazer, J. (1986). *Literature for Young Children* (2nd ed.). Columbus, Oh.: Merrill.

Holdaway, D. (1979). *The Foundations of Literacy.* Toronto: Ashton Scholastic.

——— (1984). *Stability and Change in Literacy Learning.* Portsmouth, N.H.: Heinemann Educational Books.

Mandler, J., and N. Johnson (1977). "Remembrance of Things Parsed: Story Structure and Recall." *Cognitive Psychology, 9,* 111–51.

McGee, L. M., and D. J. Richgels (1990). *Literacy's Beginnings: Supporting Young Readers and Writers.* Boston: Allyn & Bacon.

Morrow, L. M. (1988). *Literacy Development in the Early Years.* Englewood Cliffs, N.J.: Prentice Hall.

Salinger, T. (1988). *Language Arts and Literacy.* Columbus, Oh.: Merrill.

Wells, G. (1985). *Language Development in the Preschool Years.* New York: Cambridge University Press.

SECTION

3

Integrated Literature-Based Units to Promote Growth in Emergent Literacy

Old Favorites

Part One: Introduction to Nursery Rhymes

Nursery rhymes provide an excellent introduction to literature, and many young children entering elementary school already have been introduced to them at home or in preschool. Rhymes are found in the oral traditions of our culture as well as many cultures throughout the world, providing not only a link to the young child's home environment but also an introduction to children's literature.

The extensive use of rhyming patterns and flowing use of vowel sounds in rhymes provide young learners with a natural foundation of graphophonics—initial consonants, word families, phonograms, and so on. In addition, their repeated use of high-frequency words (Dolch and/or Kucera-Francis) provides the children with numerous opportunities to increase their sight vocabulary. An alphabetical Key Vocabulary list of all the words introduced during New Rhyme/Verse time is provided at the end of the section. These verses, ranging from sheer nonsense to little stories, also appeal to the child's auditory mode and promote listening skills, a prerequisite for beginning reading and writing. Because the rhymes are short and filled with action, they also provide the young learners with clear images and an introduction to the concept of story grammar (what makes up a story).

Nursery rhymes are also an excellent vehicle for introducing children to the Language Experience Approach (LEA), a widely used method of teaching beginning reading, especially for ESL learners. LEA begins with oral discussion of the subject and leads to story dictation, during which the teacher writes the children's own words on a chart. The dictation may be done by an individual or a group. When the story has been completed, the teacher reads the story aloud, pointing to each word as it is said. Then the large group or the inividual reads the story aloud. The completed chart is posted in a prominent place so that it can be read by individuals or small groups of children with or without teacher assistance. The story may be reproduced in a smaller format so that each child can have a personal copy. The Language Experience Approach is also used to support children's writing growth by modeling capitalization, punctuation, spelling, sentence formation, and so on.

From a teaching standpoint, rhymes are an excellent resource and provide opportunities to promote growth in emergent reading and writing. For example, the emphasis on the use of rhyming words introduces young learners to many of the sound-symbol relationships that they will need in the early stages of emergent reading and writing. After the rhymes have been introduced orally, they can be used during shared language time through the use of charts, Big Books, and overhead transparencies. In addition, nursery rhymes can help to develop the concept of story structure through problem solving, predicting, webbing, brainstorming, story sequence, and story retelling. Many of the activities lend themselves to the use of puppets, role playing, flannelboards, dramatization, and pantomime, which are activities well suited to young learners.

The rhyme part of the unit also introduces children to books at the primary grade level, since so many books of nursery rhymes are readily available. In fact, a volume of nursery rhymes is often the first book purchased by parents or grandparents for young children. The wide range of topics in nursery rhymes provide opportunities to explore

- New and varied vocabulary
- Concepts of prose and story
- The relationship between reading and writing
- An understanding of story structure
- An understanding of how books work and how readers read

Finally, nursery rhyme books provide an excellent addition to the library center since children individually or with friends are able to find their favorite verses to read over and over again.

 Reminder: Before starting this unit, send home a letter asking parents to send in any nursery rhyme books that could be shared with the class. (See page 96.)

Nursery Rhyme Web

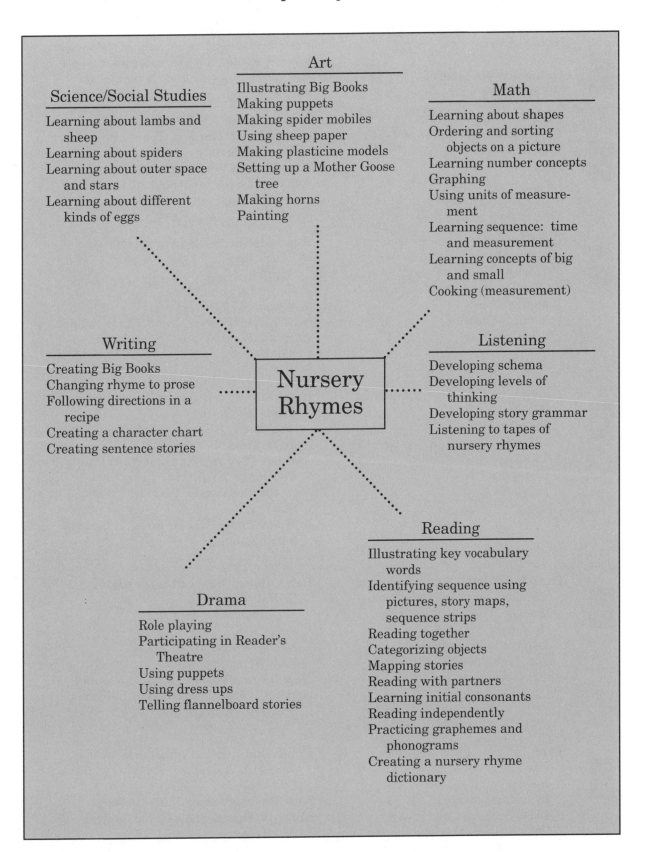

Art

Illustrating Big Books
Making puppets
Making spider mobiles
Using sheep paper
Making plasticine models
Setting up a Mother Goose tree
Making horns
Painting

Science/Social Studies

Learning about lambs and sheep
Learning about spiders
Learning about outer space and stars
Learning about different kinds of eggs

Math

Learning about shapes
Ordering and sorting objects on a picture
Learning number concepts
Graphing
Using units of measurement
Learning sequence: time and measurement
Learning concepts of big and small
Cooking (measurement)

Writing

Creating Big Books
Changing rhyme to prose
Following directions in a recipe
Creating a character chart
Creating sentence stories

Nursery Rhymes

Listening

Developing schema
Developing levels of thinking
Developing story grammar
Listening to tapes of nursery rhymes

Drama

Role playing
Participating in Reader's Theatre
Using puppets
Using dress ups
Telling flannelboard stories

Reading

Illustrating key vocabulary words
Identifying sequence using pictures, story maps, sequence strips
Reading together
Categorizing objects
Mapping stories
Reading with partners
Learning initial consonants
Reading independently
Practicing graphemes and phonograms
Creating a nursery rhyme dictionary

Outline for Nursery Rhymes

DAY 1

Introduction

Welcome to the Land of Mother Goose

Day One establishes the focus of the section through the use of pictures, books, songs, and verses about Mother Goose and her nursery friends.

DAY 2

Tune In: Mother Goose and class favorites

Read Aloud: *Bad Egg, The True Story of Humpty Dumpty*
New Rhyme/Verse: Humpty Dumpty
Activity Time: Whole Group, Individual/ Small Group

DAY 3

Tune In: Select from the following:
Hokey Pokey
This Old Man
If You're Happy and You Know It
Mother Goose
Humpty Dumpty
(Class favorite)

Read Aloud: Select from the following:
"Meg's Egg"
"Egg Thoughts"
Green Eggs and Ham
Scrambled Eggs Super
New Rhyme/Verse: Two Little Dicky Birds
Activity Time: Whole Group, Individual/ Small Group

DAY 4

Tune In: Select from the following:
Hokey Pokey
This Old Man
If You're Happy and You Know It
Two Little Dicky Birds
(Class favorite)

Read Aloud: Select from the following:
Goodnight Moon
After Dark
Papa, Please Get the Moon for Me
Where Does the Sun Go at Night?
Goodnight, Little One
New Rhyme/Verse: Twinkle, Twinkle, Little Star
Activity Time: Whole Group, Individual/ Small Group

DAY 5

Tune In: Select from the following:
Twinkle, Twinkle, Little Star
Wonder What It's Like to Be a Star
Goodnight
Two Little Dicky Birds
Star Light, Star Bright
The Cat and the Fiddle

Read Aloud: Select from the following:
Be Nice to Spiders
Spiders in the Fruit Cellar
Spiders
Anansi, the Spider
Zoe's Webs
New Rhyme/Verse: Little Miss Muffet
Activity Time: Whole Group, Individual/ Small Group

DAY 6

Tune In: Select from the following:
Itsy Bitsy Spider
Anansi
Little Miss Muffet
Class Book *If I were a Spider*
I'm a Little Spider
(Children's choice)

Read Aloud: Select from the following:
The Grass is Greener
Little Lamb
New Rhyme/Verse: Little Bo-Peep
Activity Time: Whole Group, Individual/ Small Group

DAY 7

Tune In: Select from the following:
- I'm a Little Spider
- Baa, Baa, Black Sheep
- Little Bo-Peep
- Going on a Lamb Hunt
- Little Lamb
- (Children's choice)

Read Aloud: Select from the following:
- *Nattie Parson's Good Luck Lamb*
- *Sheepchase*

New Rhyme/Verse: Mary Had a Little Lamb

Activity Time: Whole Group, Individual/ Small Group

DAY 8

Tune In: Select from the following:
- Mary Had a Little Lamb
- Baa, Baa, Black Sheep
- Mary Had a Little Farm
- A-Hunting We Will Go
- One Sheep, Two Sheep
- (Children's choice)

Read Aloud: Select from the following:
- *Charlie Needs a Cloak*
- *When Sheep Cannot Sleep*
- *Sheep in a Jeep*
- *Sheep on a Ship*

New Rhyme/Verse: Little Boy Blue

Activity Time: Whole Group, Individual/ Small Group

DAY 9

Tune In: Select from the following:
- Mary Had a Little Lamb
- Little Bo-Peep
- Baa, Baa, Black Sheep
- Blue Is the Sky
- A-Hunting We Will Go
- Little Blue Ben
- Little Betty Blue

Read Aloud: *In A Wishing Well*

New Rhyme/Verse: Jack and Jill

Activity Time: Whole Group, Individual/ Small Group

DAY 10

Tune In: Select from the following:
- A-Hunting We Will Go
- The Lamb Went over the Mountain
- Jack and Jill
- Jack Be Nimble, Jack Be Quick
- (Children's choice)

Read Aloud: Select from the following:
- *Amelia's Nine Lives*
- *So Many Cats!*

New Rhyme/Verse: Pussy-cat, Pussy-cat

Activity Time: Whole Group, Individual/ Small Group

DAY 11

Tune In: Select from the following:
- One Little, Two Little, Three Little Children
- Let's Do the Numbers Rumba
- Pussy-cat, Pussy-cat
- (Children's choice)

Read Aloud: Select from the following:
- *The Elves and the Shoemaker*
- *Puss in Boots*

New Rhyme/Verse: One, Two, Buckle My Shoe

Activity Time: Whole Group, Individual/ Small Group

DAY 12

Culmination: Mother Goose Day
Tune In: All the children's favorite verses
Activity Time: Whole Group

Presentation to Parents
- Games
- Display
- Wishing Well
- Party Time

Introduction

Tune In

So that the children's first introduction to the topic will be immediate, make a big sign to hang on the classroom door.

Welcome to the Land of Mother Goose

Below the sign, display pictures of Mother Goose and other nursery rhyme characters. This promotes immediate interest in the topic and prompts many questions: What does the sign say? Who is in the pictures? Who is Mother Goose? Why does she have a goose? The teacher should respond to questions immediately by inviting the children to come and sit down in the class meeting center, where a large number of nursery rhyme books can be displayed so that children can find out all about the land of Mother Goose.

Read Aloud

Read some favorite rhymes from few of these books. The books listed below are highly recommended:

- *Book of Nursery and Mother Goose Rhymes* by M. De Angeli
- *Mother Goose* by T. dePaola
- *The Random House Book of Mother Goose* by Arnold Lobel
- *Mother Goose* by J. Marshall
- *Sing a Song of Mother Goose* by B. Reid
- *Mother Goose* by B. Wildsmith

As you show each book, discuss pictures of Mother Goose. As you read each poem, ask children if they have heard the verse before. You could read "Mary, Mary, Quite Contrary," "Peter, Peter, Pumpkin Eater,"

"Old King Cole," "Hickory, Dickory, Dock," and "Little Jack Horner." See page 97 for a picture of Mother Goose that may be duplicated.

After reading a few favorites, point out to the children that most Mother Goose rhymes are from Great Britain. Also explain that nursery rhymes are a part of many cultures other than English-speaking cultures. Then introduce the children to a number of nursery rhymes from other cultures. These can be selected from the following sources:

- *Its Raining said John Twaining* by N. M. Brodecker
- *Prancing Pony: Nursery Rhymes from Japan* by C. DeForest
- *Dragon Kites and Dragonflies* by Demi
- *Tortillitas Para Mama and Other Nursery Rhymes* (in Spanish and English) by M. Griego et al
- *My Favorite Nursery Rhymes* by H. Offen
- *Chinese Mother Goose Rhymes* by R. Wyndham

The two Chinese nursery rhyme books are highly recommended. Wyndham's *Chinese Mother Goose Rhymes* contains an appealing collection of authentic rhymes, riddles, and games that are hundreds of years old. An important feature of the book is that these easy-to-read poems are written in Chinese as well as in English. They are especially suitable for reading to young children. The simple watercolor illustrations have been painted by an award-winning Chinese artist. The book starts with a delightful dragon verse followed by many other verses that describe items that are familiar to young children (ladybug, cricket, butterfly, rooster, chicken). In addition, many of the poems involve young children.

Demi's collection of 22 traditional nursery rhymes *(Dragon Kites and Dragonflies)* will also appeal to young children. The large book is filled with beautiful pictures of flying kites; children dancing, playing, and running; dragon boats; acrobats; and a young boy opening his own store. The children will be delighted with the watercolor illustrations that complement and enhance the text. Together they introduce the young reader to Chinese folklore.

Griego's dual language text, *Tortillitas Para Mama,* is also worth purchasing for the classroom. This collection of Latin-American nursery rhymes has also been passed down from generation to generation in the oral tradition. Many of the verses can be taught as finger plays. The verses cover a wide range of topics (family life, food, nature). The beautiful paintings provide children with an insight into Latino culture.

In addition to reading the verses, select some of the children's favorites for later rereading on charts or overhead transparencies. Charts should be put up in the area where the nursery rhyme books and charts will be displayed.

After reading some verses from different cultures, go back to the original Mother Goose display and reread a few favorites. Invite the children to recite some of their favorites. Write the title of each book with the words *Mother Goose* highlighted in red on a word card and display it above each book. Then ask, 'What do you notice about all the titles on the books?" Word cards can be placed on the chalk tray or in a pocket chart as each book is shown. Elicit that all the titles contain the words *Mother Goose*. Tell the children the following verse about Mother Goose and then reread it from a chart or pocket chart.

• • • • • • • • • • • • • • • • • •

Mother Goose

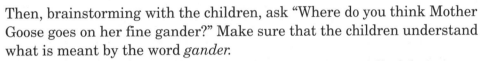

Old Mother Goose

When she wanted to wander

Would ride through the air

On a very fine gander.

• • • • • • • • • • • • • • • • • •

Then, brainstorming with the children, ask "Where do you think Mother Goose goes on her fine gander?" Make sure that the children understand what is meant by the word *gander*.

Record children's suggestions on chart paper. Accept all of their suggestions, then explain, "Mother Goose was a make-believe person, but she was supposed to have written all the rhymes that we call Mother Goose rhymes. Parents told these rhymes to their children and the children loved them so much that they were finally put into a book. Because this happened a long, long time ago, the people in the pictures are dressed in what we now call old-fashioned clothes." Show a variety of pictures and discuss how the clothes are different from today. Record the comparisons in a chart.

After completing the chart, read *Mother Goose and the Sly Fox* by Chris Conover. Explain that this mother goose is a real goose, and she has seven little goslings.

Young children enjoy singing nursery rhymes as well as saying them. Four excellent books containing nursery songs are listed below:

■ *Sing Hey Diddle, Diddle* by B. Harrop

■ *Mother Goose* by Sharon, Lois, and Bram

■ *Songs from Mother Goose* by N. Larrick

■ *The Mother Goose Songbook* by Glazer and McPhail

Of the four books listed, Larrick's book is our first choice. In this delightful collection, an easy-to-play musical arrangement accompanies each of the 56 verses. Many of the songs and verses used in this unit are included, along with interesting background information about each verse or song.

Activity Time

Whole Group

Teach some of the following songs: "Old Mother Goose" from *The Mother Goose Songbook,* p. 53; "Mother Goose Lullaby" from *Mockingbird Flight,* p. 19; "Where is Your Goose?" (first verse) from *The Funny Song Book,* p. 15.

Have children paint their favorite nursery rhymes and display their pictures in the room. Pictures could be grouped by rhyme. On each child's picture, add the following sentence: "_____'s favorite nursery rhyme is '_____.'"

Think of other animals or objects Mother Goose could ride. Record children's responses in a chart.

Individual/Small Group

• • • • • • • • • •

 Reading/Library Center

Display nursery rhyme books that the children can explore.

Put the Big Book version of *Sing a Song of Mother Goose* by Barbara Reid in the center, along with nursery rhyme posters (verses).

Make a blank book for each child, using newsprint for the pages and construction paper for the cover. Write "Mother Goose Family Album" on each child's book, along with his or her name. Children can decorate the cover and add the Mother Goose character to the first page. This will become a growing book for the entire unit. On subsequent days, the children will add new nursery rhyme characters as they are introduced. They may wish to add a few words or a sentence about each picture.

Set up a "Mother Goose tree," using a branch spray-painted white. Place the branch in a large can filled with dirt. During the unit, small pictures or objects (a small horn for Little Boy Blue, small pail for Jack and Jill, and so on) can be hung on the branch to depict nursery rhymes covered in the unit. Display the branch on the last day of the unit.

Humpty Dumpty

Tune In

Reread favorites from the charts along with the verse "Mother Goose." Then ask which verse children liked best and why. After listening to several responses, have children decide the class favorites. This could be done by having each child place a sticky square on the chosen nursery rhyme title. Once this activity has been completed, point out that each verse described someone special. Referring back to the Mother Goose chart, ask the children to name the character in this verse. After naming the character, ask, "What did the character do in the rhyme?" Record answers on a character chart:

Nursery Rhyme	Characters	What the Character Did	Why
Mother Goose	Mother Goose	Rode through the air on a gander	
	gander	Gave Mother Goose a ride	

The "Why" response is open-ended, providing opportunities for some creative thinking. All answers should be accepted.

Add to the chart as each nursery rhyme is introduced throughout the unit.

Read Aloud

Read *Bad Egg, the True Story of Humpty Dumpty,* by Sarah Hayes. Tell the class that this is a story about someone they may have heard of.

New Rhyme/Verse

Tell the class that you are going to read a nursery rhyme about Humpty Dumpty for them to listen to.

• •

Humpty Dumpty

Humpty Dumpty sat on a wall,

Humpty Dumpty had a great fall;

All the King's horses and all the King's men

Couldn't put Humpty together again.

• •

After saying the verse once, introduce the character by showing a poster or picture of Humpty from one of the class nursery rhyme books. After showing and discussing the pictures, read the verse again, using sentence strips in a pocket chart to track each word. Highlight *Humpty Dumpty, wall* and *fall* in red.

Invite children to say the verse as you track each word. Following this third reading of the printed verse, discuss the questions below.

■ Who is the new character in the rhyme? (Literal Comprehension— Details, Character Identification) (This new character can be added to the character chart.)

■ What is Humpty Dumpty? (Literal Comprehension—Details, Description)

■ What happened to Humpty Dumpty? (Literal Comprehension— Details, Cause and Effect)

■ Can you think of some other reasons why Humpty Dumpty fell? (Inferential Comprehension—Cause and Effect)

Use the chart to record children's responses to the following questions:

■ What happened when Humpty Dumpty fell? (Inferential Comprehension—Cause and Effect)

■ Why couldn't the King's men put Humpty Dumpty together again? (Evaluative Comprehension—Fact or Opinion)

Following this discussion, have the class chant the verse again while tracking the words. After this rereading, point out that two words in the verse sound and look very much like each other. Display the two words, *wall* and *fall* on word cards or write them on the chalkboard. Ask for volunteers to cup their hands around the part of the word that looks the same. As the volunteer cups the part of the word that looks the same, have everyone chant the word part *-all*. This activity not only introduces rhyming words but also focuses on the visual component and the oral sound-symbol relationship of the phonogram *-all* (word families). The children should then be asked to suggest other words that end with the same phonogram. Record responses and then read them. Explain that these words are called *rhyming words.*

Now that the concept of rhyming words has been introduced, begin a chart of words ending in *-all* that includes words and pictures (*wall, fall, ball, call*).

Activity Time

Whole Group

Tell the children that you know another nursery rhyme about an egg, but this verse is a Chinese verse. Using a chart or overhead transparency, read the following verse from Wyndham's *Chinese Mother Goose Rhymes.*

• • • • • • • • • • • • •

Come and see!

Come and see!

A black hen has laid

A white egg for me!

• • • • • • • • • • • • •

Chart body parts of Humpty Dumpty and have children compare the number of each to their own body parts (math activity). Then pairs of children could trace each other, adding the body parts discussed as well as other features.

Have children paint a picture showing why Humpty Dumpty fell from the wall. (This is an extension from the brainstorming done during the discussion.) The completed pictures could be stapled together to form a Big Book entitled *Why Humpty Dumpty Fell*. First graders can write a story to go with their picture, with or without teacher help. For kindergarten students, the writing activity is optional.

Brainstorm ways to put Humpty Dumpty together again.

Use charts to teach children the action songs, "Hokey Pokey" and "This Old Man" (in Raffi, *The 2nd Raffi Song Book*, p. 29).

Individual/Small Group

• • • • • • • • • • •

Art Center
Have each child make Humpty Dumpty from construction paper and use it to dramatize the verse.

Writing/Publishing Center

Have children make and illustrate -*all* books.

Have children add Humpty Dumpty to their *Mother Goose Family Album.*

Reading/Library Center

Illustrate key vocabulary words on word cards (*wall, king, Humpty Dumpty, fall, horses*). These can be stored in a Key Word box for later use by individuals during writing. This activity aids in developing sight vocabulary.

You may want to develop a *Big Book Nursery Rhyme Dictionary* comprised of key vocabulary from this unit.

Have children work in pairs to put together a Humpty Dumpty puzzle and chant the rhyme.

Using pictures for each line, children work in pairs to put the pictures in sequence and tell the story of Humpty Dumpty orally. Stories can be taped and placed in the listening center for use with this activity.

Display the nursery rhyme books listed below.

The Fox's Egg, by I. Isami

Sing a Song of Sixpence, by T. C. Pearson

Listening/Viewing Center

Tape a number of nursery rhymes that have been introduced. Individual small booklets for each child containing the verses are recommended so that the children can follow along with the tape. Booklets can then be taken home at the end of the unit. Include only rhymes that have been introduced to date, adding a new verse as it is taught. Some of these are provided on blackline masters.

Reminder: Remind the children to bring an uncooked egg to class the next day. The eggs will be needed for making scrambled eggs and egg-salad sandwiches during the whole-group activity.

Two Little Dicky Birds

DAY 3

Tune In

Select from the following for unison chanting or singing.

Hokey Pokey

This Old Man

If You're Happy and You Know It (in Nielsen, Sucher and Garman, *Mockingbird Flight,* p. 63). Place body words and pictures on cards.

Mother Goose and class favorite verse graphed on Day Two.

Humpty Dumpty. Use class chart, tracking the words as they are chanted.

(Class favorite)

Read Aloud

Read one of the following selections.

"Meg's Egg," from *The Random House Book of Poetry for Young Children* by J. Prelutsky, p. 148

"Egg Thoughts," from *The Random House Book of Poetry for Young Children* by J. Prelutsky, p. 147

Green Eggs and Ham by Dr. Seuss

Scrambled Eggs Super by Dr. Seuss

New Rhyme/Verse

Have children identify the character they met yesterday. Recall what happened to Humpty Dumpty, then tell children that today they are going to learn about someone else. Ask them to predict who else they might find sitting on walls. Use a feltboard to introduce the following verse:

Two Little Dicky Birds

Two little dicky birds
Sitting on the wall;
One named Peter,
One named Paul.
Fly away, Peter!
Fly away, Paul!
Come back, Peter!
Come back, Paul!

Use a chart with the words *Peter* and *Paul* highlighted in red to help children chant the verse several times. Ask different children to take the roles of Peter and Paul. After several chantings, have the children identify the new characters (dicky birds). Write the two names on cards. Ask the children if they know any other names that start like *Peter* and *Paul*. (*Penny, Pepe, Polly, Patrick*). Write the names on a *P* chart. For first graders this chart can be expanded to include other words that begin with *P*. Add *Peter* and *Paul* to the character chart.

Activity Time

Whole Group

Write *sitting on the wall* on the chalkboard or on a strip of paper. Brainstorm other people or animals that might be *sitting* on the wall. Include the children's names in their responses and record them on a chart.

Example: Meg saw a *cat* sitting on the wall.

Billy saw a *bird* sitting on the wall.

Ann saw a *dog* sitting on the wall.

After each sentence has been written, read it to the children while pointing to each word. Then have them echo read it back to you.

Cooking Activity: Making Scrambled Eggs

This activity focuses on teaching children sequence. Before making the eggs, ask the children how they like their eggs cooked. Remind them about the poems read earlier. List the ways that eggs can be prepared. Graph the student responses. Have children participate in creating the recipe, explaining how to make scrambled eggs. Write out, step by step, the instructions elicited from the children. Then review each step, making sure that it is given in the right order. If possible, have small groups of children follow the steps to make scrambled eggs. (This activity requires supervision. Invite some parents to help.)

 Be sure to obtain permission before allowing children to eat foods prepared in the classroom in case of food allergies or other restrictions.

Individual/Small Group

Math Center
Make objects or pictures of objects in two sizes available for sorting (big bird, little bird). Children sort the objects into two boxes, Big and Little.

Have first graders sort three sizes of objects.

Add the following books:

> *Big and Little* by R. Krauss
>
> *How Big Is Big?* by H. Ziefert

Listening/Viewing Center
Add "Two Little Dicky Birds" to the nursery rhyme tape, along with the individual verse books.

Provide a tape of *Horton Hatches the Egg* by Dr. Seuss for enjoyable listening.

Provide a tape of *The Most Wonderful Egg in the World* by H. Heine.

Science Center
Post a sign that says "What comes from an egg?" in the science center. Display books related to different kinds of eggs and pictures for the dren to read and observe. Suggested book titles include the following:

> *Remarkable Egg* by A. Holl

Seven Eggs by M. Hooper. Seven different types and sizes of eggs are introduced through the use of pictures and one short sentence as each egg hatches (penguin, crocodile, ostrich, lizard, turtle, owl, and finally a chocolate egg). The author changes the size of the page to fit the size of the egg.

The Egg Book by J. Kent. This is a book without words.

All About Eggs by M. Selsam

Reading/Library Center

Provide sequence cards for "Humpty Dumpty" and "Two Little Dicky Birds."

Add the following books: *Scrambled Eggs Super, Green Eggs and Ham, and Horton Hatches the Egg,* all by Dr. Seuss.

Match a sentence strip with a picture.

Humpty Dumpty sat on a wall.

Two Little Dicky Birds

Writing/Publishing Center

Have children add "Two Little Dicky Birds" to their Mother Goose Family Album.

Reminder: Make certain you have enough eggs left to boil for egg-salad sandwiches tomorrow.

Twinkle, Twinkle, Little Star

DAY 4

Tune In

Select from the following for unison chanting or singing.

Hokey Pokey

This Old Man

If You're Happy and You Know It

Two Little Dicky Birds (Use class chart to track words.)

(Class favorite nursery rhyme)

Read Aloud

Read one of the following selections.

Goodnight Moon by M. Brown

After Dark by B. Budney

Papa, Please Get the Moon for Me by E. Carle

Where Does the Sun Go at Night? by M. Ginsburg

Goodnight, Little One by R. Krauss

New Rhyme/Verse

Tell the children that you are going to read another nursery rhyme for them to listen to. Explain that some of them will probably have heard it before.

● ●

Twinkle, Twinkle, Little Star

Twinkle, twinkle,

Little star.

How I wonder

What you are!

Up above the world

So high,

Like a diamond

In the sky.

Twinkle, twinkle,

Little star.

How I wonder

What you are!

• •

Repeat the verse, adding each line to the pocket chart as it is said. Repeat unison readings of the verse with the children chanting as you track the words. Once children seem familiar with the words, brainstorm other objects that the children might see in the sky (moon, plane, birds). You may wish to record responses on a chart.

Activity Time

Whole Group

Using the format of "Two Little Dicky Birds," rewrite the verse with other words and names. For example:

• • • • • • • • • • • • •

Two little kitty cats

Sitting on the fence,

One named Fluffy,

One named Spence.

Run away, Fluffy!

Run away, Spence!

Come back, Fluffy!

Come back, Spence!

• • • • • • • • • • • • •

Make egg-salad sandwiches. Discuss the steps needed and record the children's suggestions on chart paper. Have children follow their directions to make sandwiches (good for snack time).

 Be sure to obtain permission before allowing children to eat foods prepared in the classroom in case of food allergies or other restrictions.

Teach the children some of the following songs, using charts or overhead transparencies.

■ "Twinkle, Twinkle, Little Star" from *Songs from Mother Goose,* p. 32.

■ "Good Night" from *Mockingbird Flight,* p. 3.

■ "Jump, Jump, Jump!" from *Mockingbird Flight,* p. 39.

Individual/Small Group

Reading/Library Center

Add the following books:

In the Night by A. Bourassa and C. Klein

After Dark by B. Budney

At Night by H. Clark

Goodnight Owl by P. Hutchins

Three Blind Mice by J. W. Ivimey

Goodnight, Goodnight by E. Rice

Have children use the pictures and sentences about making scrambled eggs in sequence and then explain each step.

Display pictures of objects that can be sorted according to the categories *Day* and *Night.*

Encourage children to bring in other pictures to sort according to opposite categories.

Math Center

Display the following shape books:

Round and Round and Round by T. Hoban. This is a wordless book.

Shapes by J. Reiss

If You Look Around You by F. Testa

Have children sort shapes and match shapes.

• • • • • • • • • •

Science Center

Display simple books on outer space and pictures of night creatures.

What Is a Star? by C. Arvetis and C. Palmer

Animals of the Night by M. Banks

Stars by S. Simon

Dark Night, Sleepy Night by H. Ziefert

• • • • • • • • • •

Writing/Publishing Center

Have children draw and write about their favorite day or night activity.

Little Miss Muffet

DAY 5

Tune In

Select from the following for unison chanting or singing.

Twinkle, Twinkle, Little Star

Wonder What It's Like to Be a Star

Goodnight

Two Little Dicky Birds

Star Light, Star Bright

The Cat and the Fiddle

Read Aloud

Read one of the following selections:

Be Nice To Spiders by M. B. Graham

Spiders in the Fruit Cellar by B. M. Joose

Spiders (Macdonald Starter Books)

Anansi, the Spider by G. McDermott

Zoe's Webs by T. West

These Read Aloud books may be taped and placed in the Listening/Viewing Center.

New Rhyme/Verse

• •

Little Miss Muffet

Little Miss Muffet

Sat on a tuffet

Eating her curds and whey;

There came a big spider,

Who sat down beside her

And frightened Miss Muffet away.

• •

Introduce "Little Miss Muffet." Repeat the verse, adding each line to the pocket chart as it is read. Point out some words that are not often heard today: *tuffet, curds, whey.*

For each word ask, "Do you know what a tuffet is?" or "Have you ever heard this word?"

Show the class a picture of a tuffet. Continue discussion of other unknown words. Explain what curds and whey are. Demonstrate by mixing a tablespoon of lemon juice or vinegar into a glass of milk.

After adding Miss Muffet to the character chart, select children to participate in dramatizing the verse while you and the rest of the class chant the verse. Follow up with group chanting.

Stress the letter and sound of /m/ for first graders.

Activity Time

Whole Group

Change verse to prose (Big Book format).

Reread the verse using clothesline props. Stress that it tells a little story about Miss Muffet. Point out that there are three parts to the story, using the following questions.

■ What happened first? (Beginning)

■ What happened next? (Middle)

■ What happened last? (End)

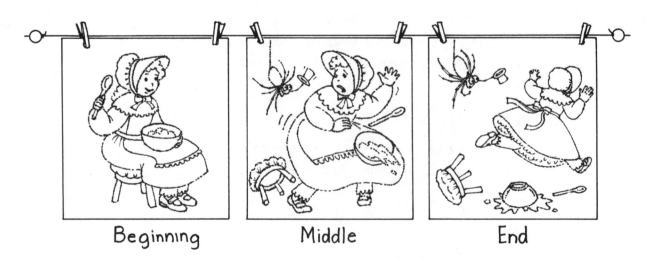

Beginning   Middle   End

After the discussion, tell the children that they are going to create a Big Book using their clothesline pictures. First ask the children, "What title would you like to put on the Big Book?" Once the title has been added to the cover, have children recall what happened in the first picture. Record their sentence(s) under the picture using the Language Experience Approach described on page 33. Repeat this procedure for the second and third pictures. Then have the children reread the story to see how it sounds as a whole. Finally, attach the covers to the pages and have the class reread the story several times for fun. Put the Big Book in the library center for later individual and group reading later on.

Discuss the following questions with the children and record their responses.

- What might Miss Muffet have done instead of running away? (Evaluative Comprehension)

- Would you have been frightened by the spider? (Create a graph of students' responses.)

  Have students work with a partner to discuss the following question:

- What makes you afraid? (Spend approximately five minutes on this part of the activity. After the students have shared their answers, record their responses under the following heading on a chart.)

> Things That Make Me Feel Afraid

Prepare a second group chart with the following heading and record children's responses:

> What I Do When I'm Afraid

Use charts to teach the children either of the following songs:

• •

I'm a Little Spider

(tune of "I'm a Little Teapot")

I'm a little spider,

Hanging from a vine,

Here is my mother,

Here is where I dine.

When we catch some insects

Then we meet,

Time for dinner

And time to eat.

• •

■ "Itsy Bitsy (Eency Weency) Spider" with finger play

Read *Spider Cat* by N. Bayley (first choice) or *I Love Spiders* by J. Parker.

Brainstorm with the children what they would do if they were spiders. Then have them draw a picture and complete the following sentence:

If I were a spider I would _____.

The drawings could be stapled together to make a Big Book, *If I Were a Spider.*

Individual/Small Group

• • • • • • • • •

Listening/Viewing Center

Provide tapes and the books suggested in Read Aloud.

• • • • • • • • • •

Reading/Library Center

Add "Little Miss Muffet" sentence strips to the center so that children can put them in order and read the poem.

Add the following books:

Spider Cat by N. Bayley

Little Miss Muffet by I. Beck

I Love Spiders by J. Parker

If I Were a Spider class Big Book

Miss Muffet class Big Book

• • • • • • • • • •

Math Center

Add more objects to the earlier collection so that children can sort them according to the categories *Big* and *Little*.

• • • • • • • • • •

Writing/Publishing Center

Using blank books, children can produce small books using the titles "Things That Are Big" and "Things That Are Small." They can also make their own book about Little Miss Muffet.

Have children add Little Miss Muffet to their Mother Goose Album.

Art Center

Children may paint pictures of Little Miss Muffet.

Children may construct spiders out of sections from an egg carton and strips of black construction paper or pipe cleaners. Use elastics to hang the spiders in the science center.

Children may make thumbprint spiders, adding legs and a web with crayons.

Science Center

Help children learn about spiders through observation, brainstorming, and discussion. Record children's ideas on a chart. Then have them make a web to show what they know about spiders.

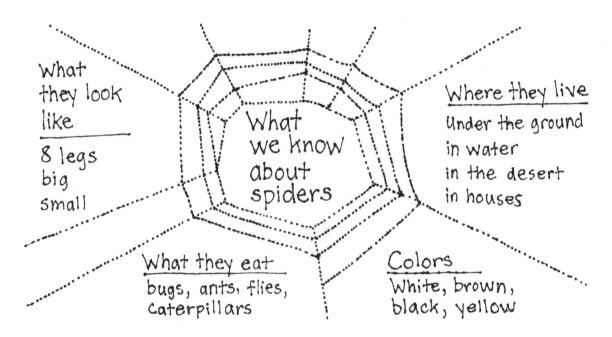

Provide books about spiders.

Spider Silk by A. Golden

Spiders Are Animals by J. Holloway and C. Harper

I'm a Spider by C. House

Spiders (MacDonald Starter Books)

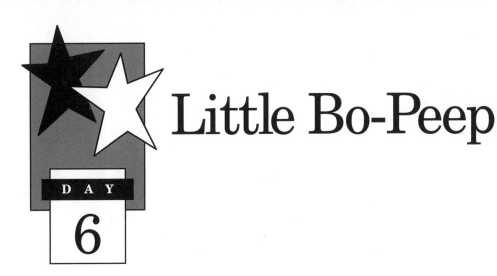

Little Bo-Peep

Tune In

Select from the following for unison chanting or singing.

Itsy Bitsy Spider

Anansi (in *The Raffi Singable Songbook,* p.8)

Little Miss Muffet

I'm a Little Spider

Class Book, "If I Were a Spider"

(Children's choice of nursery rhyme)

Read Aloud

Read one of the following selections.

The Grass is Greener by J. Alborough

Little Lamb by J. Dunn

After reading the story to the children, show pictures of sheep and lambs. Ask children to share information about sheep and lambs by filling out the chart below. Read *Sheep on the Farm* by Tessa Potter and Donna Bailey if more information is needed.

What they look like	Where they live	Why people keep them
soft, fluffy	barn, barnyard	for pets
white, black, brown	meadow	for wool
little balls	farm	for food
clouds	hills	
bubbles	zoo	

New Rhyme/Verse

● ●

Little Bo-Peep

Little Bo-Peep has lost her sheep;

And can't tell where to find them;

Leave them alone, and they'll come home,

And bring their tails behind them.

● ●

Read the rhyme to the children. Reread the rhyme using a chart or sentence strips:

Little Bo-Peep has lost her sheep

Reread the rhyme several times, and have the children chant with you. Stress the phonogram /ēp/. Then ask the following questions:

- Who is the rhyme about? (Literal Comprehension—Details)
- Who was lost? (Literal Comprehension—Details)
- Where do you think they went? (Inferential Comprehension—Details)
- Why do you think they ran away? (Inferential Comprehension—Cause/Effect)
- Where do you think they are hiding? (Inferential Comprehension—Details)
- Why do you think Little Bo-Peep is sure that they will come home? (Evaluative Comprehension—Cause/Effect)

Add Little Bo-Peep to the character chart.

Activity Time

Whole Group

Remind children of the story they wrote about Little Miss Muffet using clothesline props. They might even want to reread it as a group. Then discuss how stories usually begin. Chart the children's responses.

Use the following questions to develop the concept of schema structure/story grammar for Little Bo-Peep:

- Who is in the story? (Characters)

- Where does the story take place? (Setting)

- What do the sheep do in the story? (Problem)

- What happens to the sheep? (Solution)

Record the children's responses on a chart. Then have the children change verse into prose by writing the rhyme as a Language Experience story. For example:

How does the story begin?	Who is in the story?	Where does it take place?	What do the sheep do?	What happens to the sheep?
Once upon a time	Little Bo-Peep sheep	field farm barnyard	run away get lost	they come back

Develop sentence sense. Ask "Where do you think the sheep went?" List the children's suggestions on a chart.

● ● ● ● ● ● ● ● ● ● ● ● ● ● ● ● ● ● ● ●

The sheep went   over the hill.

                     under the bridge.

                     over the wall.

                     behind the barn.

● ●

The completed answers should be read and chanted with the children.

Using the sentences created during the previous activity, create a Big Book entitled *Where Did the Sheep Go?*

Teach the children "Spider on the Floor" from the songbook *The Raffi Singable Songbook,* p. 84.

Teach children the following verse about clouds for a choral speech.

● ● ● ● ● ● ● ● ● ● ● ● ● ● ● ● ●

White sheep, white sheep,

On a blue hill,

When the wind stops

You all stand still.

When the wind blows

You walk away slow.

White sheep, white sheep,

Where do you go?

        (author unknown)

● ● ● ● ● ● ● ● ● ● ● ● ● ● ● ●

Individual/Small Group

Art Center

Have children paint illustrations for the class Big Book. Make a cover with a title such as *Where Did the Sheep Go?*

Have children paint illustrations of Little Bo-Peep.

Have children make pictures of sheep, using cotton.

Have children add drawings or cutout pictures for a class book about items made from wool.

Writing/Publishing Center

Have children add Little Bo-Peep to their Mother Goose Family Album.

Using small blank books, have first graders create /sh/ books. Have all children create /l/ books.

Have children illustrate key words from the Key Word box, such as *wall, sheep, spider, bird, star, egg.*

Science Center

Have children learn about sheep. *Put Sheep on the Farm* by Potter and Bailey in the center.

Reading/Library Center

Add the books read during Read Aloud time, along with the following titles:

Six Sleepy Sheep by J. R. Gordon

Counting Sheep by B. McGee

Add the class Big Book (Language Experience story for Little Bo-Peep).

Mary Had a Little Lamb

DAY 7

Tune In

Select from the following for unison chanting or singing.

I'm a Little Spider

Baa, Baa, Black Sheep

Little Bo-Peep

Going on a Lamb Hunt (patterned after Going on a Lion Hunt)

Little Lamb. This new verse provides a lead-in to the story in Read Aloud called *Sheepchase*. It should be taught using overhead transparencies or charts.

(Children's choice)

• • • • • • • • • • • • • • • • • • •

Little Lamb

Little Lamb, Little Lamb,
Where did you hide?
At the country fair
On a fast ride.

Little Lamb, Little Lamb,
What did you do?
I tried to hide from my shepherd
And all of you.

• • • • • • • • • • • • • • • • • • •

Read Aloud

Read one of the following selections:

Nattie Parsons' Good-Luck Lamb by L. Campbell

Sheepchase by P. Rogers. In this story Flossie the sheep runs away to the fair. Jack, her shepherd, tries to catch her.

First graders might map the story events (See sample story maps on pages 223–224 or chart the sequence of events.)

New Rhyme/Verse

The American rhyme, "Mary Had a Little Lamb" is best introduced to the children using the book by Sarah Josepha Hale, published by Holiday House. The illustrations are by Tomie dePaola.

Show the children the cover of the book and introduce the title. Then ask the following questions:

- Who do you think is in the story? (Characters)

- When do you think this story takes place? (Time. Stress the fact that we know it took place long ago because of how the children are illustrated.)

- Where do you think this story takes place? (Setting)

Before starting to read the book, have the children look at the picture on page 1 to decide whether their predictions were right. The picture shows Mary with her lamb and the lamb's mother on a farm. Mary's father is also shown working. Use pictures from the first page to develop concepts of farm life and Mary's role on the farm.

Once the setting has been clearly established and concepts developed, read the rhyme, stopping at appropriate illustrations. Tomie dePaola's pictorial interpretation of the rhyme will help children discuss and predict. For example:

Show the picture of the lamb in the classroom.

- What other trouble might the lamb get into? (Inferential Comprehension—Details)

Show the picture of the lamb waiting for Mary.

- What does this tell us about Mary's feeling for the lamb? (Appreciative Comprehension—Imagery) How do you think the lamb felt? Do you think this could really happen? Why or why not?

Upon completing the discussion of Sarah Hale and Tomie dePaola's book, tell the children that you have another book version of "Mary Had a little Lamb" that you are going to read to them. As you read the contemporary version of Hale's "Mary Had a Little Lamb" photo-illustrated by Bruce McMillan, have the children look at the pictures carefully to see if they can find ways this book is different from the one illustrated by Tomie dePaola. Then show the children the covers of the two books. Ask, "How are the two pictures of Mary different from each other?" (The children should realize that one is a modern version of the story.) Read the verse from beginning to end, showing the pictures and stopping at appropriate times to extend the discussion. After completing the book, discuss the differences between the two versions of the verse (male teacher/female teacher, modern dress/old-fashioned dress, use of photographs/use of drawings, and so on). Record children's responses on a chart if you wish.

After the discussion, bring out the complete verse on chart paper so that the children can chant it with you.

• •

Mary Had A Little Lamb

Mary had a little lamb,

Its fleece was white as snow,

And everywhere that Mary went

The lamb was sure to go.

It followed her to school one day,

Which was against the rule;

It made the children laugh and play

To see a lamb at school.

• •

Before chanting the verse several times, discuss the meanings of the words *fleece* and *rule*.

Add Mary and the Little Lamb to the character chart.

Activity Time

Whole Group

Create a class Big Book, asking children to complete the sentence, "If I had a lamb I would _____."

Teach the children the song "Mary Had a Little Lamb." The music can be found in Hale's book.

Sing some of the old favorites from this unit.

Make graphs. Graph responses to the following questions:

■ Would you like to own a lamb?

■ Would you rather live on a farm or in a city?

Children could dramatize "Mary had a Little Lamb," taking parts of the characters—Mary, Teacher, Classmates, Father, Mother, and Lamb in the following situations:

■ Mary explains to the teacher why her lamb is in school. Teacher responds to Mary's comments.

- Mary explains to her parents what happened at school. Parents respond to Mary's comments.
- Mary scolds her lamb for coming to school. The lamb then tells Mary why she followed her to school.

Individual/Small Group

Drama Center

Provide feltboard figures or stick puppets for children to use as they retell the story. (See page 106.)

Art Center

Have children paint or draw their favorite part of the nursery rhyme.

Have children create small individual books entitled *Things That Are White* or *Things That Are Black*.

Reading/Library Center

Add the following books:

    The Naughty Lamb by A. Blanchard

    The Little Lamb by J. Dunn

    Big by J. Mesler

    Little by J. Mesler

    What Is Little? by J. Mesler

    City Mouse – Country Mouse by M. Parry

    Class Big Book

Science Center

Have children create little booklets about sheep.

Add the following book:

    Lamb by D. Roberts

Writing/Publishing Center

Introduce *If I Had a Sheep* by M. Inkpen. Then have children develop their own book using that title.

Have children add Mary and the Little Lamb to their Mother Goose Family Album.

Little Boy Blue

Tune In

Select from the following for unison chanting or singing.

Mary Had a Little Lamb

Baa, Baa, Black Sheep

Mary Had a Little Farm. Adapt from Old McDonald Had a Farm; have children suggest animals for the song.

Little Lamb

A-Hunting We Will Go; One Sheep, Two Sheep. These two new verses focus on sheep, because sheep continue to play a key role in the day's program.

(Children's choice)

• •
A-Hunting We Will Go

(adaptation)

A-hunting we will go,

A-hunting we will go,

We'll catch a little sheep

And take him home to keep;

A-hunting we will go.

• •

• •
One Sheep, Two Sheep

One sheep,

Two sheep,

Three sheep,

Four;

Five sheep,

Six sheep,

Seven sheep,

More.

• •

Read Aloud

Read one of the following selections.

Charlie Needs a Cloak by T. dePaola

When Sheep Cannot Sleep by S. Kitamura. This is a counting book.

Sheep in a Jeep by N. Shaw

Sheep on a Ship by N. Shaw

Discuss how yarn is made from wool and list items that can be made of wool. Record children's responses on a chart if you wish.

New Rhyme/Verse

• • • • • • • • • • • • • • • • • • • •

Little Boy Blue

Little Boy Blue,

Come blow your horn,

The sheep's in the meadow,

The cow's in the corn.

Where is the boy

Who looks after the sheep?

He's under a haystack

Fast asleep.

• • • • • • • • • • • • • • • • • • • •

Present the verse to children. Repeat it several times, using a chart. Then ask the following questions.

■ Should the cows be in the cornfield? Why do you think so? (Evaluative Comprehension—Fact/Opinion)

■ How do you think Little Boy Blue will get the cows out of the cornfield? (Inferential Comprehension—Details)

- What should Little Boy Blue have been doing instead of sleeping? (Evaluative Comprehension—Fact/Opinion)

- What kind of a job did Little Boy Blue have? (Literal Comprehension—Details)

- What does a shepherd do? (Inferential Comprehension—Details)

- Do you think Little Boy Blue did a good job? Why or why not? (Evaluative Comprehension—Fact/Opinion)

- What do you think will happen to Little Boy Blue because he didn't do his job? (Inferential Comprehension—Cause/Effect)

- What kind of a boy was Little Boy Blue? Why? (Inferential Comprehension—Character Traits)

Emphasize words with the initial sound /b/, compound words, and words containing the phonogram /ēp/.

Add Little Boy Blue to the character chart.

Activity Time

Whole Group

- Have class produce a poem patterned after the poem "Bugs" by M. A. Hoberman in *A House Is a House for Me*.

● ● ● ● ● ● ● ● ● ● ● ● ● ●

I Like Sheep

I like sheep

White sheep

Black sheep

● ● ● ● ● ● ● ● ● ● ● ● ●

- Change verse to prose (Big Book format). Using the teaching technique presented on Day Six with the verse Little Bo-Peep, have children complete a chart focusing on the story grammar of "Little Boy Blue."

Who?	When?	Where?	What happened?

Then have the children work cooperatively to write the story.

As a group, have children write a letter inviting their parents.

Individual/Small Group

Art Center

In small groups, have children illustrate the Big Book created in changing rhyme to prose.

Using a collection of large cardboard tubes, let children experiment making horns. One end must be covered with tissue paper and secured with a rubber band.

Create a special bulletin board to display pictures of favorite blue objects. Captions may be added to each picture.

Blue is

Deshon's new cap

Anna's new dress

Kim's car model

Ted's Book

Cooking Center

Make haystack cookies.

You will need: a large pot, can opener, wax paper

Ingredients: 1 T smooth peanut butter

1 C roasted peanuts

1 3-oz can fried chow mein noodles

1 6-oz package butterscotch chips

Directions: Melt peanut butter and butterscotch chips together in the large pot over low heat. Add noodles and peanuts to mixture. Mix until the noodles are well coated. Form little clusters on wax paper and set in refrigerator to harden. Makes 24 haystacks.

 Be sure to obtain permission before allowing children to eat foods prepared in the classroom in case of food allergies or other restrictions.

Reading/Library Center

Add the following books to the center, along with the Read Aloud books:

Each Peach Pear Plum by J. Ahlberg and A. Ahlberg

The Color Wizard by B. Brenner

What Is Little? by J. Mesler

Class Big Book

Math Center

Create graphs:

Have each child place the appropriate color sticky square above the name of her or his favorite color. Children can compare totals to determine which color is the class favorite.

Have children graph the number of children wearing blue compared to the number not wearing blue and tell the results.

Add *Jeanne-Marie Counts Her Sheep* by J. Francoise to the Math Center.

Writing/Publishing Center

Have children create books on *Blue* things and *B* things.

Have children add Little Boy Blue to their Mother Goose Family Album.

Science Center

Referring to *Charlie Needs a Cloak* by Tomie dePaola, make picture cards to tell "The Story of Wool." Use real fleece samples if possible. Children can then sequence the picture cards.

Have children use watercolors to experiment with mixing different colors, using the following book as a resource.

Making Colors by H. Hart

Listening Center

Tape record *The Color Wizard* by B. Brenner so that children can read along with the story. You may also want to include your Read Aloud book.

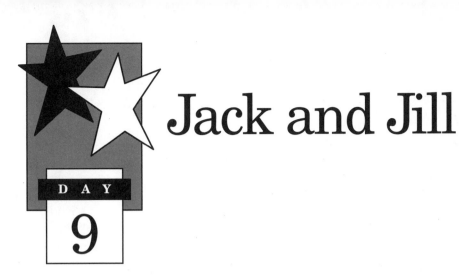

Jack and Jill

Tune In

Select from the following for unison chanting or singing:

Mary Had a Little Lamb

Little Bo-Peep

Baa, Baa, Black Sheep

Blue Is the Sky

A-Hunting We Will Go

Little Blue Ben

Little Betty Blue

Present the following verse using a flannelboard. Repeat the verse, having children echo the phrases and participate in the presentation.

● ●

Little Blue Ben

Little Blue Ben, who lives in the glen,

Keeps a blue cat and one blue hen,

Which lays of blue eggs a score and ten;

Where shall I find the Little Blue Ben?

● ●

Make a chart for the following verse.

● ●

Little Betty Blue

Little Betty Blue

Lost her holiday shoe;

What can Little Betty do?

Give her another

To match the other

And then she may walk out in two.

•••••••••••••••••••••••••••

Read Aloud

Read *A Dream in a Wishing Well* by R. Van Allen.

Read the entire story to the children. This story ends with ten pennies. Ask, "Can we buy much with one or two pennies? Can we buy something with ten pennies?" Show first graders ten pennies, two nickels, and a dime.

Use one of the following charts to brainstorm ideas.

•••••••••••••••••••••••••••••••••••

If I Had Ten Pennies

I would buy

_____

_____

_____

_____

•••••••••••••••••••••••••••••••••••

•••••••••••••••••••••••••••••••••••

If I Found a Wishing Well

I would wish for

_____

_____

_____

_____

•••••••••••••••••••••••••••••••••••

Construct a little wishing well in the classroom using a large ice-cream container. Children can write their wishes out on paper and place them in the well during the day. Materials for writing wishes can be provided in the writing center.

New Rhyme/Verse

●●●●●●●●●●●●●●●●●●

Jack and Jill

Jack and Jill

Went up the hill,

To fetch a pail of water;

Jack fell down

And broke his crown,

And Jill came tumbling after.

●●●●●●●●●●●●●●●●●●

Say the verse. Repeat the verse several times, using a chart or sentence strips. Have children chant the verse. Discuss the meaning of *fetch* and *crown* (Vocabulary Development) before starting group chanting. Once children have completed group chanting, stress the initial sound of /j/ and the phonogram /il/. Then discuss the following questions:

- Who is in the verse? (Literal Comprehension—Details)

- Where did they go for the water? (Literal Comprehension—Details)

- Why do you think they needed the water? (Inferential Comprehension—Details. You may wish to record children's responses on a chart.)

- Why do you think Jack fell? (Inferential Comprehension—Cause/Effect. You may wish to record children's responses on a chart.)

- Why did Jill fall too? (Inferential Comprehension—Cause/Effect)

- What do you think will happen to Jack and Jill? (Evaluative Comprehension—Details)

- What do you think they will do next? (Inferential Comprehension—Predicting Outcomes)

Add Jack and Jill to the character chart.

Activity Time

Whole Group

Change verse to prose (Big Book format). After the children are familiar with the verse, have pairs act it out while the group repeats it. Once the story of the verse is well known, have children determine the sequence for changing the verse to prose. For example:

Beginning   One day Jack and Jill walked up the hill to get some water.

Middle   Jack tripped and rolled down the hill, breaking the crown of his head.

End   Jill rolled down the hill with him.

Create a class *Big Wish Book.* Use children's wishes to write a book as a group project.

Individual/Small Group

Writing/Publishing Center

Have children add Jack and Jill to their *Mother Goose Family Album.*

Have children write their wishes on special wish paper.

My Favorite Nursery Rhyme
Felicity

Jak And Jell Went Up
The Hell to Feeg
A Peal Of Weater
Jak Fall Don And Bork
His corun Al And Jell CaIm
tumdallen After.

Art Center

In small groups, make illustrations for the Big Book created by the whole class.

Make wishing wells in a craft center.

Have children make collages using magazine pictures of things they wish for.

Reading/Library Center

Add the following books to the center:

What Comes Down? by June Mesler

A Dream in a Wishing Well by R. Van Allen

Class Big Book

Using small blank books, have children create books of words that begin with *J*, words that rhyme with *hill*, and words that rhyme with *down*.

Have children put three pictures in sequence and then retell the story of Jack and Jill into the tape recorder, using their name in the title (e.g., "Rebecca's story of Jack and Jill").

Use picture cards to have children categorize things that go up and things that go down. This activity promotes vocabulary development as well as math concept development.

Math Center

Set up a class store so that children can buy small articles ranging in price from one cent to ten cents. Each child has ten cents of play money to spend.

Pussy-cat, Pussy-cat

Tune In

Select from the following for unison chanting or singing.

A-Hunting We Will Go

The Lamb Went Over the Mountain (adapt The Bear Went Over the Mountain)

Jack and Jill

Jack Be Nimble, Jack Be Quick

(Children's choice)

Read Aloud

Read one of the following selections about cats who like to wander. Tape the selection for use in the listening center.

Amelia's Nine Lives by L. Balian

So Many Cats! by D. S. de Regniers

New Rhyme/Verse

• • • • • • • • • • • • • • • • • • •

Pussy-cat, Pussy-cat

"Pussy-cat, pussy cat,
Where have you been?"
"I've been to London
To visit the Queen."
"Pussy-cat, pussy-cat,
What did you do there?"
"I frightened a little mouse
Under the chair."

• • • • • • • • • • • • • • • • • • •

Before reading the verse, explain that you are going to read a verse about a pussy-cat who went to a very different place. Point out where London is on a globe or world map. Then say the verse. Repeat the verse several times, using a chart or story strips in a pocket chart. At first the teacher could ask the questions and have the children respond. Then one half of the class could ask the questions and the other half could respond. Stress the phonogram /at/.

Discuss the following questions:

- Who is the main character? (Literal Comprehension—Details)

- Who do you think might be asking the cat about its adventure? (Inferential Comprehension—Details)

- How do you think the queen felt when the cat frightened the little mouse? (Inferential Comprehension—Inferring Character Traits)

Activity Time

Whole Group

Change verse to prose (Big Book format).

Have children work cooperatively to create a Big Book. Begin by discussing parts of the verse with the children. Use the following guidelines:

- How should our story begin?

- Who is in our story?

- What happened in the story?

- How would you like the story to end?

Individual/Small Group

Reading/Library Center

Create sequence strips using the same format as in Day Nine.

Add the following books:

My Cat Maisie by P. Allen

Have You Seen My Cat? by E. Carle ◇

Rich Cat, Poor Cat by B. Waber ◆◆

Math Center

Create sets of cat pictures for children to sort and categorize.

Have children order by size magazine pictures of cats.

Art Center

Have children paint pictures of their favorite cat story or the new verse.

Writing/Publishing Center

Make a small class book of different kinds of cats. The pictures can be drawn by the children or cut from magazines. The children can also make individual books of their own.

Have children add the Pussy-cat to their Mother Goose Family Album.

Have children write individual cat stories on cat-shaped paper. Some possible titles are, "My Lost Kitten," "If I Owned a Cat," "My Cat _____," and "If I Were a Cat."

Listening/Viewing Center

Place the Read Aloud book along with the tape in the center.

Related Reading

If I Were a Cat I Would Sit in a Tree by E. Cutler.

This is a delightful read-aloud number book which starts with a verse about a single cat and ends with a verse about twelve cats. Once the book has been read, it should be placed in the math center.

One, Two, Buckle My Shoe

Tune In

Select from the following for unison chanting or singing.

One Little, Two Little, Three Little Children

Let's Do the Numbers Rumba (in *The 2ndRaffi Songbook,* p. 60)

Pussy-cat, Pussy-cat

(Children's choice)

Read Aloud

Read one of the following selections.

The Elves and the Shoemaker by F. Hunia

Puss in Boots by P. Galdone

New Rhyme/Verse

• • • • • • • • • • • • • • • • • •

One, Two, Buckle My Shoe

One, two,

Buckle my shoe;

Three, four,

Knock at the door;

Five, six,

Pick up sticks;

Seven, eight,

Lay them straight;

Nine, ten,

A good fat hen.

• • • • • • • • • • • • • • • • • •

Introduce the verse using sentence strips and pictures.

Kindergarteners could use a rebus, and first graders could use words plus pictures of the objects.

Have the children chant and clap the verse several times. Once they are familiar with the words, actions can be added.

Activity Time

Whole Group

Have children play a game in which they must follow orders by doing the correct action:

buckle your shoe

knock at the door

pick up sticks

mend your shoe

pick up the hen

Brainstorm with the children chores they do at home. Write the chores on word strips to make a new version of the original. For example:

1, 2, set the table.

3, 4, pick up your clothes.

5, 6, make your bed.

7, 8, brush your teeth.

9, 10, go to sleep.

Individual/Small Group

Math Center
Have children match shoeprints for 1 to 10.

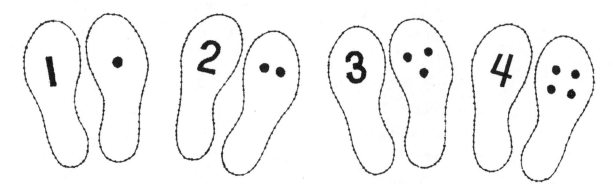

Use a shoe length to measure the room. How many shoe lengths does it take? Record results in a chart, as shown below.

Child	Length	Width
Gloria	26	20
Deshon	28	18
Ms. Kamita		

First graders could measure the hallway.

• • • • • • • • • •

Writing/Publishing Center

Have children use pictures to create their own small booklet.

1, 2, _____.

3, 4, _____.

• • • • • • • • • •

Reading/Library Center

Add the Read Aloud books to the library center, along with the following books:

Big Shoe, Little Shoe by D. Cazet

Puss In Boots by J. Poole

One Two by B. Randell

My Shoe Book by M. Silverman

Using story strips plus pictures, have the children put the strips in sequence and chart the verse, "One, Two, Buckle My Shoe."

• • • • • • • • • •

Listening/Viewing Center

Have children use puppets to act out *Puss in Boots*.

Provide tapes of the Read Aloud books.

Mother Goose Day (Culmination)

DAY 12

Tune In

Have the children chant all of their favorite verses.

Verses are all on charts that have been put together to form one Big Book. The teacher could come dressed as Mother Goose and the children as their favorite nursery rhyme characters. Children who are dressed like their favorite characters might want to dramatize the verse. The booklet of nursery rhyme favorites collected by the children can be taken home at the end of the day, along with their *Mother Goose Family Albums*.

Activity Time

Whole Group

For the presentation to parents, have the class dramatize some of their favorite nursery rhymes.

Have the class sing some of their favorite songs.

Have children play the following games:

- Hide the Egg (Use plastic eggs.)

- Lost Sheep

- Egg Relay

Display all of the children's work for the parents to see.

Parents and children can add their wishes to the well.

Party Time

Children and guests may end the day with a party. The menu could be pink lemonade, egg-salad sandwiches made by the children in the morning, and peanut haystack cookies. To make peanut haystacks, follow the recipe given in Day Eight.

Be sure to obtain permission before allowing children to eat foods prepared in the classroom in case of food allergies or other restrictions.

Key Vocabulary Introduced During New Rhyme/Verse Time

A
a
above
*after
*against
air
*all
alone
*an
*and
*another
*any
*are
*as
asleep
*at
*away

B
*back
behind
Bo-Peep
beside
Betty
*big
birds
blow
*blue
boy
broke
*bring
buckle

C
*come
*can
can't
catch
children
*come
corn
couldn't
country
cow's
crown
curds

D
*day
diamond
Dicky
*did
*didn't
dine
dinner
*do
door
Dumpty
down

E
*eat
eating
everywhere

F
four
*fall
*fast
fat
fell
fetch
*find
fine
*five
fleece
fly
followed
*for
*four
frightened
*from

G
gander
*gave
*give
*go
goose
*great

H
*had
hanging
*has
haystack
hen
*her
*here
he's
*hide
high
hill
*him
*his
*home
holiday
horn
horses
*how
Humpty
hunting

I
*I
I'm
*in
insects
is
*it
*its

J
Jack
Jill

K
*keep
king's
knock
*know

L
lamb
land
*laugh
lay
leave
*like
*little
lived
looks
lost

M
*made
*many
Mary
match
*may
meadow
meet
*men
Miss
*more
Mother
Muffet
*my

N
named

O
*of
*on
*one
*other
*out

*Included on Dolch Basic Sight Word List and/or Kucera-Francis Word List

---

Special Note:

- Of the 110 Easier Dolch Basic sight words, 54% are introduced in the Nursery Rhyme section of this unit.

- Of the 40 Pre-Primer Basic Dolch Sight words, 67% are introduced in the Nursery Rhyme section of this unit.

- Of the 41 First Grade Basic Dolch Sight words, 56% are introduced in the Nursery Rhyme section of this unit.

Key Vocabulary (continued)

P

pail
Paul
Peter
*pick
*play
*put

R

*ride
rules

S

sat
*school
*see
*seven
*she
sheep
sheep's
shepherd
shoe
sitting
*six
sky
snow
*so
*some
spider
star
sticks
straight
sure

T

tails
*take
*tell
that
*the
*their
*then
*them
*there
they'll
three
*through
*time
*to
*together
tried
tumbling
twinkle
*two

U

*under
*up

V

very
vine

W

*walk
wall
wander
wanted
*was
*water
*we
welcome
we'll
*went
*what
*when
*where
whey
*which
*white
*who
*will
*without
wonder
*world
*would

Y

*you
*your

References

Adams, A. (1975). *This Old Man.* New York: Grosset and Dunlap.

Ahlberg, J. and A. Ahlberg (1978). *Each Peach Pear Plum.* London: Puffin Books.

Alborough, J. (1987). *The Grass is Greener.* London: MacMillan.

Allen, P. (1990). *My Cat Maisie.* New York: Viking.

Arvetis, C. and C. Palmer (1988). *What Is a Star?* Chicago, Ill.: Children's Press.

Balian, L. (1986). *Amelia's Nine Lives.* Nashville, Tenn: Abingdon Press.

Banks, M. (1990). *Animals of the Night.* New York: Charles Scribner's Sons.

Bayley, N. (1984). *Spider Cat.* London: Walker Books.

Beck, I. (1988). *Little Miss Muffet.* Oxford: Oxford University Press.

Blanchard, A. (1989). *The Naughty Lamb.* New York: Dial Books.

Bourassa, A. and C. Klein (1984). *In the Night.* Toronto: Gage.

Brenner, B. (1986). *The Color Wizard.* Toronto: Byron Press.

Brown, M. W. (1947). *Goodnight Moon.* New York: Scholastic.

Brown, M. (1952). *Puss in Boots.* New York: Charles Scribner's Sons.

Budney, B. (1975). *After Dark.* New York: Lothrop, Lee & Shephard.

Burns, D., and Scholten (1989). *Here's to Ewe.* Minneapolis, Minn.: Lerner Books.

Campbell E. L. (1990). *Nattie Parson's Good-luck Lamb.* New York: Puffin Books.

Carle, E. (1986). *Papa, Please Get the Moon for Me.* New York: Scholastic.

———— (1991). *Have You Seen My Cat?* New York: Scholastic.

Cazet, D. (1984). *Big Shoe, Little Shoe.* New York: Bradbury Press.

Clark, H. (1977). *At Night.* Wellington, New Zealand: Dept. of Education, Schools Education Branch.

Conover, C. (1989). *Mother Goose and the Sly Fox.* New York: Farrar, Strauss & Giroux.

Cutler, E. (1985). *If I Were a Cat I Would Sit in a Tree.* Plattsburgh, N.Y.: Tundra Books of Northern New York.

Delton, J. (1982). *The Goose Who Wrote a Book.* Minneapolis, Minn.: Carolrhoda Books.

dePaola, T. (1974). *Charlie Needs a Cloak.* Englewood Cliffs, N.J:. Prentice Hall.

———— (1981). *The Comic Adventures of Old Mother Hubbard and Her Dog.* New York: Harcourt, Brace, Jovanovich.

———— (1985). *Tomie dePaola's Mother Goose.* New York: Putnam.

de Regniers, B. S. (1985). *So Many Cats!* New York: Clarion Books.

Dunn, J. (1977). *The Little Lamb.* New York: Random House.

Eisler, C. (1988). *Cats Know Best.* New York: Dial Books.

Fischer, H. (1959). *Puss in Boots.* New York: Harcourt Brace, Jovanovich.

Francoise, J. (1951). *Jeanne-Marie Counts Her Sheep.* New York: Charles Scribner's Sons.

Galdone, P. (1983). *Puss in Boots.* New York: Clarion Books.

Ginsburg, M. (1981). *Where Does the Sun Go at Night?* New York: Greenwillow Books.

Graser, T. (1990). *The Mother Goose Songbook.* Toronto: Doubleday.

Golden, A. (1964). *Spider Silk.* Toronto: Fitzhenry and Whiteside.

Gordon, J. R. (1991). *Six Sleepy Sheep.* Honesdale, Penn.: Boyds Mill Press.

Graham, M.B. (1967). *Be Nice to Spiders*. New York: Harper & Row.

Hale, S. (1984). *Mary Had a Little Lamb*. New York: Holiday House.

————— (1990). *Mary Had a Little Lamb*. New York: Scholastic.

Hart, H. (1977). *Making Colors*. Don Mills, Ontario: Addison-Wesley.

Hawes, J. (1972). *My Daddy Longlegs*. New York: Crowell-Collier.

Hayes, S. (1987). *Bad Egg, the True Story of Humpty Dumpty*. Boston, Mass.: Little, Brown.

Heine, H. (1983). *The Most Wonderful Egg in the World*. New York: Atheneum.

Hoban, T. (1974). *Circles, Triangles and Squares*. New York: MacMillan.

————— (1976). *Shapes, Shapes, Shapes*. New York: MacMillan.

————— (1978). *Is it Larger? Is it Smaller?* New York: MacMillan.

————— (1983). *Big Ones, Little Ones*. New York: Greenwillow Books.

————— (1983). *Round and Round and Round*. New York: Scholastic.

Hoberman, M. A. (1978). *A House Is House for Me*. New York: Viking Press.

Holl, A. (1968). *Remarkable Egg*. New York: Lothrop, Lee & Shepard.

Holloway, J. and C. Harper (n.d.). *Spiders Are Animals*. Richmond, Ontario: Scholastic-TAB Publications.

Hooper, M. (1985). *Seven Eggs*. London: Patrick Hardy Books.

House, C. (1981). *I'm a Spider*. Toronto: Addison-Wesley.

Hunia, F. (1978). *The Elves and the Shoemaker*. Auburn, Me.: Ladybird Books.

Hutchins, P. (1972). *Goodnight Owl*. New York: MacMillan.

Inkpen, M. (1988). *If I Had a Sheep*. Boston, Mass.: Little, Brown.

Isami, I. (1990). *The Fox's Egg*. Minneapolis, Minn.: Carolrhoda Books.

Ivimey, J. W. (1987). *Three Blind Mice*. New York: Clarion Books.

Joose, B. M. (1983). *Spiders in the Fruit Cellar*. New York: Alfred A. Knopf.

Kent, J. (1975). *The Egg Book*. New York: MacMillan.

Kitamura, S. (1986). *When Sheep Cannot Sleep*. New York: Sunburst.

Krauss, R. (1972). *Goodnight, Little One*. New York: Dutton/Springfield.

————— (1987). *Big and Little*. New York: Scholastic.

Lewis, R. (1987). *Friska, The Sheep That Was Too Small*. New York: Farrar Strauss, & Giroux.

Littendays, F.(1975). *The Elves and the Shoemaker*. New York: Four Winds Press.

Lobel, A. (1987). *Gregory Griggs and Other Nursery Rhyme People*. New York: Mulberry Books/ MacMillan.

MacDonald Starter Books (1986). *Spiders*. London: MacDonald.

Mesler, J. (1972). *What Comes Down?* London: Methuen Educational.

————— (1972). *Big*. London: Methuen Educational.

————— (1972). *Little*. London: Methuen Educational.

————— (1972). *What Is Little?* London: Methuen Educational.

McDermott, G. (1972). *Anansi, the Spider*. New York: Holt, Rinehart and Winston.

McGee, B. (1991). *Counting Sheep*. Charlotte, Vt.: Camden House.

McGovern, A. (1971). *Stone Soup*. New York: Scholastic.

McNulty, F. (1986). *The Lady and the Spider*. New York: Harper & Row.

Offen, H. (1984). *A Treasury of Mother Goose*. New York: Simon and Schuster.

Parker, J. (1988). *I Love Spiders*. Richmond Hill, Ontario: Scholastic-TAB Publications.

Parry, M. (1970). *City Mouse – Country Mouse*. Toronto: Scholastic.

Pearson, T.C. (1985). *Sing a Song of Sixpence*. New York: Dial Books.

Pool, J. (1988). *Puss in Boots*. Chicago, Ill.: Children's Press.

Potter, T. and D. Bailey (1979). *Sheep on the Farm.* Texas: Steck-Vaughn.

Prelutsky, J. (Ed.) (1986). *Read-Aloud Rhymes for the Very Young.* New York: Alfred A. Knopf.

Randell, B. (1980). *One Two.* London: Methuen Educational.

Reiss, J. J. (1974). *Shapes.* New York: Aladdin.

Rice, E. (1983). *Goodnight, Goodnight.* New York: Penguin Books.

Roberts, D. (1980). *Lamb.* New Zealand: Methuen Educational.

Rogers, P. (1988). *Sheepchase.* London: Puffin Books.

Selsam, M. (1952). *All About Eggs.* Reading, Mass.: Addison-Wesley.

Selsam, M., and J. Hunt (1983). *A First Look At Spiders.* New York: Walker.

Sendak, M. (1965). *Hector Protector and As I Went Over the Water: Two Nursery Rhymes.* New York: Harper & Row.

Seuss, Dr. (1940). *Horton Hatches the Egg.* New York: Random House.

——— (1953). *Scrambled Eggs Super.* New York: Random House.

——— (1960). *Green Eggs and Ham.* New York: Random House.

Silverman, M. (1987). *My Shoe Book.* New York: Golden Books.

Simon, S. (1989). *Stars.* New York: Mulberry Books.

Shaw, N. (1986). *Sheep in a Jeep.* Boston, Mass.: Houghton Mifflin.

——— (1989). *Sheep on a Ship.* Boston, Mass.: Houghton Mifflin.

Testa, F. (1983). *If You Look Around You.* New York: Dial Books.

Ungerer, T. (1964). *One, Two, Where's My Shoe?* New York: Harper & Row.

Van Allen, R. (1985). *A Dream in a Wishing Well.* Texas: DLM Teaching Resources.

Waber, B. (1963). *Rich Cat, Poor Cat.* New York: Scholastic.

West, C. (1987). *A Moment Rhyme.* New York: Dial Books.

West, T. (1990). *Zoe's Webs.* Auckland: Ashton Scholastic.

Ziefert, H. (1988). *Dark Night, Sleepy Night.* New York: Puffin Books.

——— (1989). *How Big Is Big?* New York: Puffin Books.

Music Books

Glazer, T. (1990). *The Mother Goose Songbook: Forty-five Favorite Rhymes for Piano.* New York: Doubleday.

Harrop, B. (1983). *Sing Hey Diddle Diddle.* London: A & C Black.

Larrick, N. (1989). *Songs from Mother Goose.* New York: Harper & Row.

Nelson, E. (1984). *The Funny Song Book.* New York: Sterling.

Nielsen, P., F. Sucher, and C. Garman (1982). *Mockingbird Flight.* Oklahoma City: The Economy Company.

Raffi (1987). *The Raffi Singable Songbook.* New York: Crown.

——— (1987). *The 2nd Raffi Songbook.* New York: Crown.

Sharon, Lois, and Bram (1985). *Mother Goose.* Vancouver, B.C.: Douglas and McIntyre.

Wiess, N. (1987). *If You're Happy and You Know It.* New York: Greenwillow Books.

Poetry

Dowell, R. (1987). *Move Over, Mother Goose! Finger Plays Action Verses and Funny Rhymes.* Mt. Rainier, Md.: Gryphon House.

Hopkins, L. B. (1989). *Still as a Star.* Boston, Mass.: Little, Brown.

Lee, D. (1983). *Jelly Belly.* Toronto: Macmillan of Canada.

Prelutsky, J. (1983). *The Random House Book of Poetry for Children.* New York: Random House.

——— (1986). *Read-Aloud Rhymes for the Very Young.* New York: Alfred A. Knopf.

English Nursery Rhymes

De Angeli, M. (1954). *Book of Nursery and Mother Goose*

Rhymes. New York: Doubleday.

dePaola, T. (1985). *Tomie dePaola's Mother Goose*. New York: Putnam.

Fowke, E. (1970). *Sally Go Round the Sun: Three Hundred Children's Songs, Rhymes and Games (K–6)*. New York: Doubleday.

Fujikawa, G. (1968). *Mother Goose*. New York: Grosset and Dunlap.

Hague, M. (1984). *Mother Goose: A Collection of Classic Nursery Rhymes*. New York: Holt, Rinehart and Winston.

Lobel, A. (1986). *The Random House Book of Mother Goose*. New York: Random House.

Mackay, D., B. Thompson, and P. Schaub (1970). *Sally Go Round the Sun and Other Nursery Rhymes*. London: Longman.

Marshall, J. (1979). *Mother Goose*. New York: Sunburst/Farrar, Strauss, & Giroux.

Reid, B. (1987). *Sing a Song of Mother Goose*. New York: Scholastic. (Available as a Big Book and as a little book).

Voake, C. (1985). *Over the Moon: A Book of Nursery Rhymes*. New York: Crown.

Warne, F. (1984). *Beatrix Potter's Nursery Rhyme Book*. Middlesex, England: Penguin.

Wildsmith, B. (1987). *Mother Goose—A Collection of Nursery Rhymes*. Oxford: Oxford University Press.

Wright, B. (1978). *The Real Mother Goose*. Chicago, Ill.: Rand McNally.

Nursery Rhymes from Other Countries

Brodecker, N. M. (1973). *It's Raining Said John Twaining: Danish Nursery Rhymes*. New York: Aladdin/Antheneum.

DeForest, C. (1967). *Prancing Pony: Nursery Rhymes from Japan*. New York: Walker/Weatherhill.

Demi (1986). *Dragon Kites and Dragonflies*. New York: Harcourt Brace Jovanovich.

Griego, M. C., et al. (1981). *Tortillitas Para Mama and Other Nursery Rhymes*. New York: Holt, Rinehart and Winston.

Offen, H. (1987). *My Favorite Nursery Rhymes*. New York: Simon and Schuster. (A collection of 150 of the best-loved nursery rhymes from around the world.)

Wyndham, R. (1989). *Chinese Mother Goose Rhymes*. New York: Philomel Books.

Nursery Rhyme Blackline Masters

Sample parent letter

Mother Goose picture

Humpty Dumpty sequence pictures

Humpty Dumpty verse

I'm a Little Spider

Little Miss Muffet sequence pictures

Mary Had a Little Lamb stick puppets

Little Lamb, Little Lamb

Jack and Jill sequence pictures

Greenwood Elementary School
325 West 12th Avenue
Sun City

Dear Parent or Guardian,

Our class will be starting a unit on Nursery Rhymes in one or two weeks. In preparation for this unit, I am looking for nursery rhyme books in any language to share with the children.

If you have any books you feel that the children would enjoy, please drop them off at the school or send them with your child.

In addition, if you would like to read any of your favorite rhymes to the children, we would love to have you come in and share your books and rhymes with them.

Yours sincerely,

Nursery Rhymes / Day 2 / Humpty Dumpty

Humpty Dumpty sat on a wall,

Humpty Dumpty had a great fall;

All the King's horses and
all the King's men

Couldn't put Humpty together again.

I'm a Little Spider

I'm a little spider,
Hanging from a vine,
Here is my mother,
Here is where I dine.
When we catch some insects
Then we meet,
Time for dinner
And time to eat.

Nursery Rhymes / Day 5 / Little Miss Muffet

Little Lamb

Little Lamb, Little Lamb,
Where did you hide?
At the country fair
On a fast ride.

Little Lamb, Little Lamb,
What did you do?
I tried to hide from my
    shepherd
And all of you.

Part Two: Introduction to Favorite Tales

Like nursery rhymes, favorite tales with familiar themes are found in many cultures and have been handed down from generation to generation, first orally and later in written form. Most of the original authors of these old favorites are unknown. Because of their popularity and simple story lines, old favorite tales continue to attract the attention of new authors and illustrators. As a result, one is able to find many versions of the same tale at various levels of reading difficulty.

The collection of old favorites selected for this part of the unit consists of both rhyme and prose. The part starts with rhyme, since the main teaching component in the preceding section dealt only with verse and rhymes. However, the two new selections, *The House that Jack Built* and *The Cake that Mack Ate,* are much longer than the rhymes introduced in the previous section. In addition, both selections are very predictable and cumulative in nature, a pattern also found in four of the books presented early in this section of the unit (*Henny Penny, Gingerbread Man, The Little Red Hen,* and *The Farmer and the Turnip*).

Before they hear the four cumulative tales, children are introduced to prose through a very simple story (*The Teeny Tiny Woman*) that has a very simple plot. It contains a large number of high-frequency words that are repeated often,

helping children practice their sight vocabulary. The four cumulative tales are followed by three very well-known old favorites, *The Three Billy Goats Gruff, Goldilocks and the Three Bears,* and *The Three Little Pigs.* All these stories contain repetitive refrains and patterns that can easily be chanted and remembered by the children. The three animal characters in each story have similar roles and relationships. The last four tales selected for this part of the unit (*Little Red Riding Hood, Stone Soup, The Magic Pot,* and *The Magic Fish*) vary in their format and story line. They introduce the children to other elements such as magic commonly found in old folktales. These last four stories also have more varied story lines and provide more challenge.

These old favorite tales present children with a better understanding of story structure (setting, characters, problem, resolution), as evidenced by the following factors:

- The characters are simple and fairly predictable.

- The settings are common and familiar.

- The simple, predictable plots are easily remembered by the children for writing, drama, and reading.

- Basic story structure formula is followed: characters and problems are introduced, obstacles are overcome, and resolutions are achieved.

Finally, favorite tales were selected because of their wide availability, allowing teachers to purchase multiple copies for guided and independent reading at a reasonable cost. They are available in many versions, in many languages, and at varied reading levels.

In this section of the unit, more time is spent with each book, allowing you to place more emphasis on developing the reading and thinking process during guided and independent reading. Two days are devoted to teaching each new rhyme or story. On the first day, the new story or verse is introduced and discussed during Read Aloud. On the next day, New Story/ Verse is devoted to extensive teaching of process. Related books should be read aloud for whole-class enjoyment at other times during the day.

Since the books in this unit often vary in difficulty, the code discussed in Section Two will be used to identify easy ◇ and more difficult ◆◆ material to aid teachers in the selection of developmentally appropriate material for their children.

Favorite Tales Web

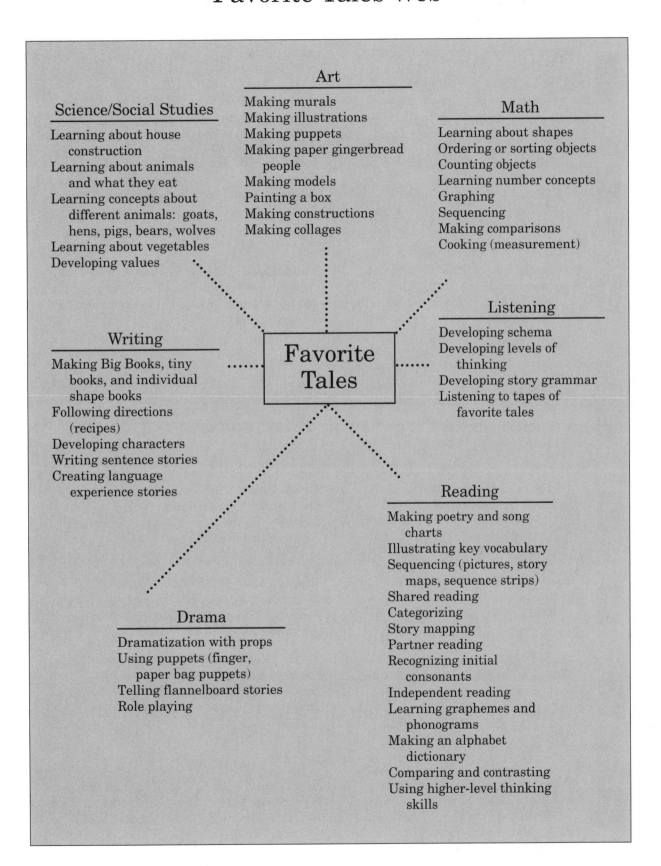

Art
Making murals
Making illustrations
Making puppets
Making paper gingerbread people
Making models
Painting a box
Making constructions
Making collages

Science/Social Studies
Learning about house construction
Learning about animals and what they eat
Learning concepts about different animals: goats, hens, pigs, bears, wolves
Learning about vegetables
Developing values

Math
Learning about shapes
Ordering or sorting objects
Counting objects
Learning number concepts
Graphing
Sequencing
Making comparisons
Cooking (measurement)

Writing
Making Big Books, tiny books, and individual shape books
Following directions (recipes)
Developing characters
Writing sentence stories
Creating language experience stories

Favorite Tales

Listening
Developing schema
Developing levels of thinking
Developing story grammar
Listening to tapes of favorite tales

Reading
Making poetry and song charts
Illustrating key vocabulary
Sequencing (pictures, story maps, sequence strips)
Shared reading
Categorizing
Story mapping
Partner reading
Recognizing initial consonants
Independent reading
Learning graphemes and phonograms
Making an alphabet dictionary
Comparing and contrasting
Using higher-level thinking skills

Drama
Dramatization with props
Using puppets (finger, paper bag puppets)
Telling flannelboard stories
Role playing

Outline for Favorite Tales

Tune In: Select from the following:
Hugh, Hugh
Peter, Peter, Pumpkin Eater
(Class favorite nursery rhymes)

Read Aloud:
A Very Special House
The House That Jack Built
Activity Time: Whole Group, Individual/
Small Group

Tune In: Select from the following:
Pussy-cat, Pussy-cat
Peter, Peter, Pumpkin Eater
I Like Cake
(Children's choice)

Read Aloud: *The Cake That Mack Ate*
New Story/Verse: *The House That Jack Built*
Activity Time: Whole Group, Individual/
Small Group

Tune In: Select from the following:
Pussy-cat, Pussy-cat
This is the Way We Build Our House
I Like Cake
Cabin in the Woods
The Alphabet Song

Read Aloud: *The Teeny Tiny Woman*
New Story/Verse: *The Cake That Mack Ate*
Activity Time: Whole Group, Individual/
Small Group

Tune In: Select from the following:
Thumbelina
The Alphabet Song
Old MacDonald Had a Farm

Read Aloud: *Henny Penny*
New Story/Verse: *The Teeny Tiny Woman*
Activity Time: Whole Group, Individual/
Small Group

Tune In: Select from the following:
The Alphabet Song
Old MacDonald Had a Farm
Hickety, Pickety, My Black Hen

Read Aloud: *The Gingerbread Man*
New Story/Verse: *Henny Penny*
Activity Time: Whole Group, Individual/
Small Group

Tune In: Select from the following:
Gingerbread Boy
Baking a Gingerbread Man

Read Aloud: *The Little Red Hen*
New Story/Verse: *The Gingerbread Man*
Activity Time: Whole Group, Individual/
Small Group

Tune In: Select from the following:
Baking a Gingerbread Man
I Like Cake
Hickety, Pickety, My Black Hen
I Had a Little Hen

Read Aloud: *The Farmer and the Beet*
New Story/Verse: *The Little Red Hen*
Activity Time: Whole Group, Individual/
Small Group

Tune In: Select from the following:
I Had a Little Hen
This is the Way She Made the Cake
Old MacDonald Had a Farm
(Children's choice)

Read Aloud: *The Three Billy Goats Gruff*
New Story/Verse: *The Farmer and the Beet*
Activity Time: Whole Group, Individual/
Small Group

DAY 9

Tune In: Select from the following:
The Bear Went over the Mountain
The Farmer and the Beet
Baby Bear

Read Aloud: *Goldilocks and the Three Bears*
New Story/Verse: *The Three Billy Goats Gruff*
Activity Time: Whole Group, Individual/
Small Group

DAY 10

Tune In: Select from the following:
The Bear Went over the Mountain
Baby Bear, Baby Bear, Turn Around
To Market, to Market

Read Aloud: *The Three Little Pigs*
New Story/Verse: *Goldilocks and the Three Bears*
Activity Time: Whole Group, Individual/
Small Group

DAY 11

Tune In: Select from the following:
Pease Porridge Hot
To Market, to Market
Ten Little Bears
Porridge Song

Read Aloud: *Little Red Riding Hood*
New Story/Verse: *The Three Little Pigs*
Activity Time: Whole Group, Individual/
Small Group

DAY 12

Tune In: Select from the following:
Alphabet Song
To Market, to Market
This Little Pig Went to Market
Grandma and Grandpa

Read Aloud: *Stone Soup*
New Story/Verse: *Little Red Riding Hood*
Activity Time: Whole Group, Individual/
Small Group

DAY 13

Tune In: Select from the following:
Pease Porridge Hot
Grandma and Grandpa
Red Hood's Song
I Like Soup

Read Aloud: *The Magic Porridge Pot*
New Story/Verse: *Stone Soup*
Activity Time: Whole Group, Individual/
Small Group

DAY 14

Tune In: Select from the following:
Pease Porridge Hot
Porridge Song
I Like Soup
Stone Soup Song

Read Aloud: *The Magic Fish*
New Story/Verse: *Strega Nona*
Activity Time: Whole Group, Individual/
Small Group

DAY 15

Culmination: Favorite Tales Day
Tune In: Whole Group presentation
of favorite verses and songs
using props

Shared Language
I Caught a Fish Alive
The Fisherman's Chant
The Magic Fish
Activity Time: Whole Group
Presentations to parents of favorite old
tales using props
Display of children's projects
Party time

Introduction

DAY 1

Tune In

Using charts or overhead transparencies, chant the following verses that were introduced in Nursery Rhymes.

Class Favorite Nursery Rhymes

Pussy-cat, Pussy-cat

Hugh Hugh (from *Jelly Belly* by Dennis Lee)

Introduce the children to the verse "Peter, Peter, Pumpkin Eater" using a chart or overhead transparency. Then have the class chant it several times.

• •

Peter, Peter, Pumpkin Eater

Peter, Peter, pumpkin eater,

Had a wife and couldn't keep her;

He put her in a pumpkin shell

And there he kept her very well.

• •

Read Aloud

The focus of this lesson is to expand on the children's concept of home and the construction of houses. Display pictures of all kinds of homes (apartments, townhouses, cabins) along with a few books about home building such as *Building a House* by B. Barton. Include pictures of houses from other cultures. Point out that people from all over the world have homes, and that these homes vary in type, material, and size.

Invite the children to tell what kind of a home they live in. Chart their responses using the following format:

● ●

Tran lives in a townhouse.

Ella lives in an old brick house.

Joe lives in an apartment on the second floor.

● ●

Explain that most places people live have already been designed by architects and built by construction workers. Point out that people could have someone build their home for them, or that in some cases they might build their own home.

Ask the children if they would like to build a special house for themselves when they grow up. Have a few of them describe how their special house might look.

Read *A Very Special House* by R. Krauss without stopping for discussion. After reading the story, point out to the children that the little boy's very special house is an imaginary house he would like to have if he could build a house for himself.

Introduce *The House That Jack Built*. This book has been illustrated by a number of illustrators. Select one that you think will appeal to your class. Some possible choices include the following:

The House That Jack Built by E. Falconer (a rebus book)

The House That Jack Built by A. Frasconi

The House That Jack Built by B. Lewish

The House That Jack Built by J. Stevens

This Is the House That Jack Built by L. Underhill (a pop-up book)

The House That Jack Built by N. B. Westcott (a pop-up book)

Read the rhyme in its entirety, sharing the pictures with the class and ensuring that the children know the meaning of the words—*malt, maiden, priest,* and *cock*. Then read the rhyme a second time, using charts or a pocket chart.

Activity Time

Whole Group

Teach the children the following song:

● ●

This is the Way We Build Our House

(tune: Here We Go Round the Mulberry Bush)

This is the way we build our house, build our house, build our house,

This is the way we build our house

Early in the morning.

> This is the way we dig a hole . . .
>
> This is the way we pour the cement . . .
>
> This is the way we saw the wood . . .
>
> This is the way we hammer the boards . . .
>
> This is the way we shingle the roof . . .
>
> This is the way we paint the house . . .

• •

Actions can be added once the words have been learned from a chart.

Create a class Big Book using the following title: *These Are the Houses That Our Class Built.*

Teach the letter and sound of /p/ to first graders.

Individual/Small Group

Children can either paint or draw their imaginary special house for the class Big Book described above. They should also write something about their special house to go with the drawing.

• • • • • • • • • •

 ## Reading/Library Center

Provide as many versions of *This is the House That Jack Built* as possible along with *A Very Special House* by R. Krauss.

• • • • • • • • • •

 ## Writing/Publishing Center

Provide the children with small blank books. On the cover write, "My Little Book of *P* Things."

Related Reading

Percy and the Five Houses by E. H. Minarik

Building a House by B. Barton

DAY
2

The House That Jack Built

Tune In

Using charts or overhead transparencies, chant the following verses:

Pussy-cat, Pussy-cat

Peter, Peter, Pumpkin Eater

(Children's choice)

Introduce the children to the verse "I Like Cake," using a chart or overhead transparency.

• •

I Like Cake

I like to eat cake.

   Soft sponge cake,

   Dark chocolate cake,

   Orange carrot cake,

And cake with red-colored sprinkles on top!

I like to eat cake.

   Very spicy cake,

   Tasty white cake,

   Fancy fruit cake,

And cake with sticky pink icing on top!

I like to eat cake.

   Big cakes,

   Little cakes,

   But, best of all . . .

I like birthday cake with bright candles on top!

• •

After introducing the verse, have children chant it several times.

Ask the children whether they like to eat cake. Have them tell their favorite kind. Record responses using a Language Experience approach:

Ron likes strawberry shortcake.

Flora likes carrot cake.

Ann likes Black Forest cake.

Keiko likes all kinds of cake.

Read Aloud

Tell the children that today's story is about a very special cake that Mack ate. Show them the cover of *The Cake That Mack Ate* by R. Robart and M. Kavalski. Ask, "What kind of a special cake is it? How many people do you think are coming to the party?" Tell students that today's story is written in rhyme, like *The House That Jack Built*. Read the rhyme in its entirety, showing pictures and text. The reading could be taped and later placed in the listening center. Read the rhyme a second time, using a teacher-made Big Book or pocket chart with pictures.

New Story/Verse

Recall with the children the title of the story read to them on Day One, *The House that Jack Built*. Retell the story, using a pocket chart with words and pictures for *house, malt, rat, cat, dog, cow, maiden, man, priest, cock,* and *farmer*. Print the first letter of each word in red. Also write the phrase, "That lay in the house that Jack built" in red. See pages 195–198 for pictures of key vocabulary.

Reread the rhyme several times with the children, having them chant as much of the rhyme as they can.

After several readings, children could take turns using stick puppets to dramatize the story while the class chants with the teacher. The backs of the stick puppets should be numbered to assist children in putting the events of the rhyme in sequence.

Activity Time

Whole Group

Teach the action song "Cabin in the Woods" from *The All New Elephant Jam,* by Sharon, Lois, and Bram, p. 39.

Sing "The Alphabet Song" using large alphabet letter cards set up along the chalk tray. Point to each letter as it is being sung.

Create a class Big Book using the title: *The World's Best Cakes.*

Brainstorm with the children all the words they can think of that rhyme with *cake*. Post the list for easy access.

Teach the sound /ak/.

Use the alphabet cards for "The Alphabet Song" to make a set of 26 cards, one for each letter, for key vocabulary developed throughout this section of the unit. Put the eleven key vocabulary words developed in the rhyme on the appropriate cards:

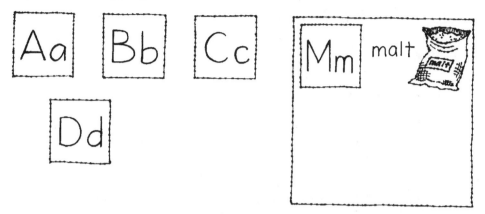

Add key vocabulary words to cards as the unit progresses. These cards will help children remember sight vocabulary and can also be used as a spelling aid during writing.

Individual/Small Group

Drama Center

Using the stick puppets (see blackline master sheets), children can dramatize *The House That Jack Built* or use the puppets to make up their own version.

Writing/Publishing Center

Have children start their own personal alphabet book using their own name in the title. *Albert's Alphabet* by L. Tyron provides a good model. Children should be encouraged to add their own words to their alphabet books throughout the unit. The words will provide reminders of sight vocabulary and help in spelling.

Provide children with sheets of paper in the shape of a house on which is written the following incomplete phrase:

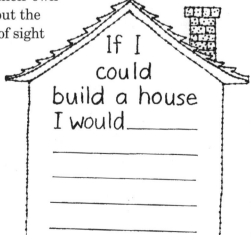

Reading/Library Center

Add the following books:

Stop Those Painters! by R. G. Gelman

This Is the House Where Jack Lives by J. Heilbroner

The Cake That Mack Ate by R. Robart and M. Kovalski

The Little Red House by N. J. Sawicki

Art Center

Children can either paint or draw their favorite cake. The cake can be real or imaginary. Children could add one or two sentences about the cake or write a recipe for how to make it.

Children can illustrate their favorite part of the story.

Using small boxes and construction paper or paint, have children design a house they would like to build. Display these with a sign in front that includes the child's name: "This is the house that Emily built."

Block Center

Children build houses with blocks.

Related Reading

The World That Jack Built by R. Brown ◆◆

Benedict Finds A Home by C. L. Demarest ◇

A New House by C. Gagnon and D. Labrasse ◆◆

The Big Orange Splot by D. M. Pinkwater. If you read this book, invite the children to paint their dream house during activity time.

The Cake That Mack Ate

Tune In

Select from the following for unison chanting or singing.

Pussy-cat, Pussy-cat

This Is the Way We Build Our House

I Like Cake

Cabin in the Woods

The Alphabet Song

Read Aloud

For the last few days the children have been listening to stories in rhyme, but today they will hear a favorite old tale. Show the cover of *Teeny Tiny* ◇ by J. Bennett or *The Teeny Tiny Woman* ◆◆ by P. Galdone or *The Teeny Tiny Woman* ◆◆ by B. Seuling and tell the class the title as you print it on the board. Then, through discussion, develop the concepts *tiny* and *teeny tiny*. Have children guess how tall the woman might be. Ask the children if they have heard any other stories about very tiny people (Tom Thumb, Thumbelina). Before starting to read the story, point out that old tales often start with "Once upon a time." Read the story in its entirety, showing the pictures as you read. If you wish, tape the story for use later in the listening center.

New Story/Verse

Hold up the book and remind children of the story title *The Cake That Mack Ate*. Reread the story using a pocket chart with words and pictures for *cake, egg, hen, corn, seed, farmer, woman, candles,* and *Mack*. Print the first letter of these words in red, as well as the repeated phrase, "That went into the cake that Mack ate."

Reread the rhyme several times with the children, having them chant as much of the rhyme as they can. After several readings, children could take turns using stick puppets to dramatize the verse while the class chants with the teacher. The backs of the stick puppets should be numbered to assist the children in putting the events of the verse in sequence. You might wish to provide first graders with a simplified printed version of the verse that they could illustrate and take home to read to their parents. (Use the pictures on pages 200–202 to make the puppets as well as the pocket chart cards.)

Activity Time

Whole Group

Teach the children the song "Thumbelina" from *The 2nd Raffi Song-Book,* p. 41.

Have children brainstorm things that are tiny and things that are big. Record their responses.

Have children brainstorm all the words they can think of that rhyme with *cake.* Post the list for easy access.

Add the key vocabulary that was introduced with pictures to the class alphabet cards.

Teach the letter and sound of /m/ to first graders.

Individual/Small Group

Cooking Center

Make a birthday cake for Mack from a cake mix. The children can decorate the cake with icing and sprinkles. It could be eaten as an afternoon snack, during which children can sing "Happy Birthday to Mack."

Be sure to obtain permission before allowing children to eat foods prepared in the classroom in case of food allergies or other restrictions.

Drama Center

Add the stick puppets made for *The Cake That Mack Ate* (pages 200–202) to the center.

Art Center

Provide folded paper for the children to make birthday cards for Mack. Encourage them to write a short note to him.

Writing/Publishing Center

Have children add key words plus pictures to their personal alphabet books.

Listening/Viewing Center

Place the tape of *The House That Jack Built* and *The Cake That Mack Ate* alongside the books.

Math Center

Children sort pictures or objects into two boxes, one marked "Tiny Things," the other marked "Big Things."

Reading/Library Center

Add any books you have read aloud to the children, along with a copy of *The Cake That Mack Ate.*

Related Reading

Arabella: the Smallest Girl in the World by M. Fox

The Teeny Tiny Woman

DAY 4

Tune In

Using charts or overhead transparencies, chant or sing the following:

Thumbelina

The Alphabet Song

Old MacDonald Had a Farm, using picture cards labeled with each animal's name from the Henny Penny story.

• •

Old MacDonald Had a Farm

Chicks (cheep, cheep)

Ducks (quack, quack)

Geese (honk, honk)

Turkeys (gobble, gobble)

• •

Read Aloud

Explain that today's story takes place in a farmyard, and the main character is a silly hen called *Henny Penny*. Show the hen's name on a word card, and tell the children that her name is also the title of the book.

Show the cover of either *Henny Penny* by H. W. Zimmermann ◇ or *Henny Penny* by P. Galdone ◆◆.

Then read the first part of the story without stopping until Cocky Locky asks Henny Penny where she is going. Ask the children to predict what Henny Penny will say to Cocky Locky (Inferential Comprehension—Details). Read to find out whether their predictions were correct.

Continue reading until Ducky Lucky asks Henny Penny where she is going. Again, have the children make predictions. Continue this same pattern for Goosey Loosey and Turkey Lurkey. Read until they meet Foxy Loxy. Then have the children predict what will happen next (Inferential Comprehension—Sequence). Finish reading the story to check children's predictions.

New Story/Verse

Hold up the book *Teeny Tiny Woman* and remind children of the title. Reread the story using a Big Book version or a pocket chart and sentence strips. Make certain that the sentences GIVE ME MY BONE! and TAKE IT! are in huge print. After several readings, give the children a copy of the story that they can illustrate and later read at school with an older buddy or at home with a relative. Suggest that partners read along with children to provide them with support at this early stage in emergent reading.

Activity Time

Whole Group

Develop the concept of teeny tiny books. Provide several samples of very small books (approximate size 3 1/2-by-3 1/2 inches). They are readily available in bookstores. Read one or two to the class. Show the children some small blank books that you have prepared for them from newsprint.

Have children brainstorm what they might write about in a teeny tiny book. Record their ideas on a chart or on the chalkboard. Tell the children that you are going to put a pile of these blank books in the writing center for those who want to produce a teeny tiny book. Remind them that they must write the title on the cover along with a picture. Also tell them to write their names at the bottom of the cover.

Teach the children the singing game, "The Farmer in the Dell."

Teach the letter and sound of /t/ and the sound of /el/.

Individual/Small Group

Reading/Library Center

Provide as many versions of *The Teeny Tiny Woman* as you can find, along with the Read Aloud books from the previous day.

Listening/Viewing Center

Provide a taped version of *The Teeny Tiny Woman* along with the book.

Writing/Publishing Center

Provide the children with small blank books. On the cover of each one, write, "My Little Book of *T* Things."

Provide the children with blank teeny tiny books so they can write stories on the topics they brainstormed.

Give children folded paper with the following open frame-sentences.

If I were a teeny tiny person I would	If I were a great big person I would
_____	_____
_____	_____
_____	_____
_____	_____
_____	_____

After drawing a picture of themselves being teeny tiny and great big, children could write a Language Experience story (see page 33) with the frames provided. Older writing buddies could write dictated stories for younger children.

Have children add key words plus pictures to their alphabet books.

Art Center

Using paper bags and construction paper or paint, have children make a puppet of their favorite character from *Henny Penny*. Post a list of the characters found in the book.

Science Center

Provide any books or pictures that you can find about foxes and wolves. The emphasis should be on obtaining books with good, clear pictures and simple text. Respond to any questions the children might ask. These books should be displayed in the science center throughout the entire unit.

Related Reading

At a later time, use a wordless Big Book to tell the children the old favorite tale, *The Elves and the Shoemaker*. You may want to tape the story for use in the listening center. A beautiful wordless version of this story is published by Addison-Wesley. *Thumbelina* (Hans Christian Andersen), adapted by A. C. Darke, could also be used.

The Big Book, along with the smaller versions of the book, should be placed in the reading/library center. Children could retell the story to each other using the version of their choice.

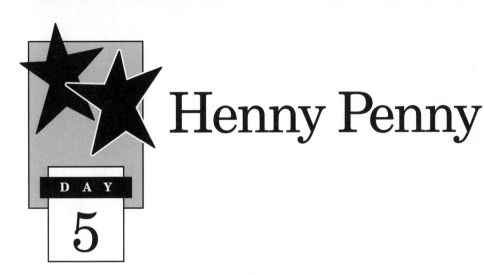

Henny Penny

Tune In

Select from the following for unison chanting or singing:

The Alphabet Song

Old MacDonald Had a Farm

Introduce the children to the verse "Hickety, Pickety, My Black Hen," using a chart or overhead transparency.

● ●

Hickety, Pickety, My Black Hen

Hickety, pickety, my black hen;

She lays eggs for gentlemen;

Gentlemen come every day,

To see what my black hen doth lay.

● ●

Read Aloud

Today the children will hear another well-known cumulative tale, *The Gingerbread Man.* Addison-Wesley publishes both a Big Book version and a smaller size of this tale. Like the previous story, this one also takes place in the country.

The main character of this story is a gingerbread man. The book has an easily memorized refrain.

Run, run, run,

As fast as you can

You can't catch me,

I'm the !

The Addison-Wesley edition is easy to read because it uses rebuses and a limited number of words. Also, the refrain is introduced on page 5 and repeated by itself on pages 7 and 9. This feature promotes the rapid acquisition of sight vocabulary. The children will start chanting almost immediately.

Tell the children that like the story of Henny Penny, the name of the main character (the Gingerbread Man) is also the title of the book. Then show students the cover of the Big Book and tell them the title. The following questions could be used to facilitate the development of story schema (grammar).

■ Who do you think is the main character in the story? (Literal Comprehension—Details) Why do you think so? (Inferential Comprehension—Character Traits)

■ Where does the story take place? (Literal Comprehension—Details)

Begin reading the story, pointing to each word as it is read. During the reading of the story, the following pattern is suggested.

Read pages 1 and 3.

■ What do you think the Gingerbread Man did? (Inferential Comprehension —Sequence) Why? (Inferential Comprehension—Details)

Read pages 4 and 5.

■ What do you think will happen next? (Inferential Comprehension—Predicting Outcomes)

Read pages 6 and 7 and discuss what happens next.

Read pages 8 and 9 and then have the children focus their attention on the large picture on page 10.

■ Which character does the Gingerbread Man meet next?

Have children predict what the Gingerbread Man will do next. Record responses on the chalkboard.

Continue reading pages 12 and 13, pointing to each word as it is said. Immediately after this reading, check the children's predictions.

Focus the children's attention on the picture on pages 12 and 13.

What will the crocodile do now that he has the Gingerbread Man on his nose and is far from the shore? (Inferential Comprehension—Predicting Outcomes)

Turn the page and finish reading the story.

New Story/Verse

Remind children of the story of Henny Penny.

■ Ask the children to recall where the story took place.

■ Recall who was in the story. As each character is recalled, show the children a picture with the name of the character underneath. Pictures of these characters can be found on pages 203–204.

Henny Penny   Cocky Locky   Ducky Lucky

Have students repeat the name with you as you display the picture card.

- Ask children to recall what happened to Henny Penny one day when she was eating corn in the farmyard. What did she think the acorn was?

Point out to the children that Henny Penny has a problem because she thinks the sky is actually falling. Because she thinks the sky is falling, what does she decide to do? (Problem—Resolution)

- After the setting, characters, and the problem and resolution have been discussed, retell the story using a pocket chart with sentence strips:

The sky is falling!

The sky is falling!

I must go and tell the king.

Write "I" in red on a small card that can be exchanged for another small card that has "We" written on it in red.

Four identical sentence strips should be made for the animals' response.

May I go with you?

Display the pocket chart for use as the story is read. Invite children to join in when you get to the parts of the story illustrated in the pocket chart.

Henny Penny
The sky is falling! The sky is falling!
I must go and tell the king.
May I go with you?
May I go with you?
May I go with you?
May I go with you?
I will show you a shortcut.

We

Using the pocket chart and pictures, have the children retell the story with the aid of teacher prompts such as the following:

- What happened first in our story?
- What did Henny Penny say?
- Who did she meet first?
- Who did she meet next?

Continue in the above pattern until Henny Penny and her friends meet up with Foxy Loxy. Then ask one of the children to tell the ending of the story.

Activity Time

Whole Group

Using the picture cards presented earlier, have the children volunteer to take the parts of the characters from the story. The children can hold the cards in front of them to remind the audience which character they are portraying. You may wish to number the pictures to help the children remember the story sequence. Since this is a simple story, have two or three groups present it.

Teach the song "Gingerbread Boy" from the songbook *Joyfully Sing, Book One* by L. Zeddies, p. 109.

Teach the sound /an/.

Individual/Small Group

Writing/Publishing Center

Children could either write or dictate a story about Henny Penny.

Provide the children with small brown-covered books in the shape of a gingerbread man. On the cover write "Things That Are Brown." Inside, children can either paste pictures of brown things cut from magazines or draw pictures of their own. Encourage them to provide a caption for each picture.

Have children add key words plus pictures to their personal alphabet books.

Listening/Viewing Center

Provide a tape with the version of the Henny Penny used with the class. You may also include tapes of other Read Aloud books.

Art Center

Help children make special headbands for each of the characters from Henny Penny to use during dramatization. See pages 203–204 for pictures to use on the headbands.

Children ma y illustrate their favorite part of the Henny Penny story.

Using cutout gingerbread man shapes, children add features to create a special gingerbread man.

Reading/Library Center

Place *The Story of Chicken Licken* by J. Ormerod in the center.

Related Reading

Hattie and the Fox by M. Fox

Chicken Little by S. Kellogg. This is a modern, humorous version of Chicken Little, in which Chicken Little lives happily ever after.

Reminder: Bring ingredients and equipment required for making gingerbread cookies on Day Six. You will need 24 pie tins, or 1 for each child.

The Gingerbread Man

DAY 6

Tune In

Review *The Gingerbread Man* by chanting in unison or singing.

Then introduce the children to the verse "Baking a Gingerbread Man" (an adaptation of Pat-a-Cake, Pat-a-Cake) using a chart or overhead transparency:

● ●

Baking a Gingerbread Man

Pat-a-cake, bake-a-cake,

   baker's man,

Bake me a Gingerman

   as fast as you can,

Roll it and cut it,

   and mark it with G,

Put it in the oven

   for teacher and me!

● ●

Once children know the verse, have them clap as they read it.

Read Aloud

Today the children will hear another well-known cumulative tale, *The Little Red Hen,* adapted by P. Galdone, or the Addison-Wesley version. This story also takes place in the country. Tell the children that the Little Red Hen is the main character and is also the title of the book. Show them the title of the book and have them look at the picture very carefully. Ask the children the following questions:

■ What do you think the Little Red Hen is going to do? (The picture of the Little Red Hen shows her carrying a watering can, hoe, and rake. These should provide clues.)

- Where does this story take place?

Begin reading the story, stopping at "Who will plant this wheat?"

Have the children predict which character the Little Red Hen might ask. Continue reading, stopping at "Who will cut the wheat?"

Again have the children predict which character the Little Red Hen might ask. Continue reading, stopping at "Who will take this wheat to the mill?"

Again, have the children predict who the Little Red Hen will ask. This time ask the children, "What do you think the animal will say?" Continue reading, stopping at "Who will eat this cake?"

Ask children, "What do you think the animal will say? What do you think the Little Red Hen will say?" Read to the end of the story.

Other versions of the story appropriate for reading aloud:

- *The Little Red Hen* by B. McClintock
- *The Little Red Hen* by N. Sheehan
- *The Little Red Hen / La Pequeña Gallina Roja* by L. Williams
- *The Little Red Hen* by M. Zemach

New Story/Verse

Remind children of *The Gingerbread Man*.

Ask the children if they remember any other character in the story. As the names are mentioned, place each character's picture and name in a pocket chart or on the chalkboard. Prepare pictures in advance. They should correspond to the rebus pictures found in the Big Book. When all the characters have been presented, have the children repeat the names several times as you point to the picture.

Ask the children to recall where the story takes place—farm kitchen, country road, and river.

- After the characters and settings have been reviewed, show the children the Big Book, focusing on the cover. Ask them to read the title along with you as you point to the words.

Tell the children you are going to reread the story and invite them to join in. In most cases, children will respond to the rebus as well as the refrain.

Reread the story several times, helping the children join in as much as possible. Once they are familiar with the story, the children can take turns reading the Gingerbread Man's part while you and the others in the class chant the rest of the story.

Place the Big Book in the reading/library center so that the children can read it individually or in small groups during activity time. Children often like to take turns being the teacher when reading in small groups.

Activity Time

Whole Group

Teach the letter and sound of /h/ to first graders.

In preparation for the cooking activity, read *Ben's Gingerbread Man* by N. Daly. This delightful story is about a little boy, Ben, who makes some gingerbread men with his mom. It is told from a little boy's point of view.

Then tell the children you have a special surprise for them. Let them try to guess what it is, then tell them that you made them some gingerbread dough so that they can make their own gingerbread people during activity time. Enlist the help of a few parents.

Post the following recipe so that the children can see what was used to make the dough.

 Be sure to obtain permission before allowing children to eat foods prepared in the classroom in case of food allergies or other restrictions.

Gingerbread People

(Makes one big one or two dozen small)

1/2 C shortening
1/2 C brown sugar
1/2 C molasses
1 egg
1 T vinegar
2 1/2 C whole wheat flour
  (white flour can be used)
1 t baking soda
1/4 t salt
1 t ginger
1/2 t each of cinnamon and cloves

Icing
2 T soft butter or margarine
1/2 C confectioner's sugar
1/4 t vanilla
1 t milk
raisins, candies, and nuts
  for decoration

1. Blend shortening and sugar, then beat in molasses, egg and vinegar.

2. Stir the dry ingredients together, then mix them well with the egg-sugar mixture.

3. Divide the dough into 24 balls. Put them in the refrigerator and let them chill for 2 or 3 hours, or overnight.

4. Grease a pie tin. Form the gingerbread person on the pie tin by using a small ball for the head and a longer one for the body. Roll some dough into snakes for the arms and legs. Press the arms and legs into the body and flatten the shape down a little with your hand. Bake at 375° for about 20 minutes.

5. When your gingerbread person is done, let it cool for 15 minutes. Decorate with it with icing, raisins, candies, and nuts. Use the icing as glue to stick on the decorations. Don't let your gingerbread person get away!

Individual/Small Group

During activity time or at another time during the day, use the smaller versions of *The Gingerbread Man* with small groups for guided reading.

Writing/Publishing Center

Provide the children with small blank books. On the cover, write "My Little Book of *H* Things."

Cut an accordion-folded paper (one sheet folded in four) into the shape of a gingerbread person to make a blank book.

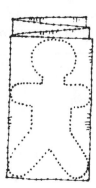 

(See directions for making accordion books on page 205.)

Have children write a story about a gingerbread man or woman, about making gingerbread people, or about the original gingerbread man.

Have children add key words and pictures to their alphabet books.

Reading/Library Center

Provide as many versions of *The Gingerbread Man* as you can find, along with the books read from the Related Reading from Day Five.

Math Center

Cut out paper gingerbread people of varying sizes. Have younger children order the figures by size. Make sets of gingerbread people (sets of 5, 10, 20, 50, and so on) for children to use in counting.

Listening/Viewing Center

Provide an audiotape along with the small book version of *The Gingerbread Man.*

Drama Center

Place children- or teacher-made stick or finger puppets for all characters in *The Gingerbread Man* for use in dramatizing the story.

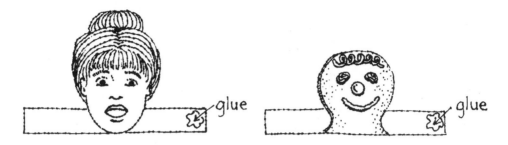

Cooking Center

Children may shape the teacher-prepared dough and then decorate their gingerbread people using raisins, colored candies, and nuts. Cookies can be baked in the staff kitchen with the help of adult volunteers.

Art Center

Children can make gingerbread men from play dough or another modeling medium.

Children can make stick puppets or finger puppets of their favorite character from *The Gingerbread Man.*

Related Reading

The Pancake by A. Lobel

The Gingerbread Rabbit by J. Randall. This is a Danish version of *The Gingerbread Man.*

Any other version of *The Gingerbread Man.*

Reminder: Bring canned beets as well as several fresh beets with leaves attached for developing concepts on Day Seven.

The Little Red Hen

Tune In

Select from the following for unison chanting or singing:

Baking a Gingerbread Man

I Like Cake

Hickety, Pickety, My Black Hen

Introduce the children to the verse "I Had a Little Hen," using a chart or overhead transparency.

• • • • • • • • • • • • • • • • • •

I Had a Little Hen

I had a little hen,

The prettiest ever seen,

She washed me the dishes

And kept the house clean;

She went to the mill

To fetch me some flour,

She brought it home

In less than an hour.

She baked me my bread,

She brought me my mail;

She sat by the fire

And told many a fine tale.

• • • • • • • • • • • • • • • • • •

Read Aloud

Today the children will hear another well-known cumulative tale called *The Farmer and the Beet,* a rebus Big Book published by Addison-Wesley that also comes in a smaller size. This tale is based on the Russian folktale, *The Turnip*. Tell children that this story has one main character, the farmer, and that his name is also in the title. Show them the title of the book and have them look at the picture carefully. Ask the children the following questions:

- What do you think the farmer is doing? Children's responses will vary. Accept all answers. If the children identify the beet, ask them how they knew it was a beet. If they do not know what the vegetable is, provide the word.

Show real beets to the children. Have the children examine and discuss aspects of beets (Concept Development). It is important that children understand that beets are vegetables; beets grow from seeds; the whole beet can be used for food; beets are usually cooked prior to eating; beets vary in size, but usually do not grow much larger than an apple or orange. Point out that the beet in the story is a giant beet.

- How would you describe the farmer? (Character Development) Record children's responses on a chart.

- Will the farmer be able to pull out the big beet? Why or why not? (Problem)

- What do you think the farmer will do? (Solution)

Begin reading the story. Point out that it starts with the words *Once upon a time*. Read to the end of page 3. Check to see whether any of the children's predictions were correct. (Problem)

- Why was the farmer pulling out the big beet? (Literal Comprehension—Details)

- Did the farmer have any trouble getting someone to help him? (Literal Comprehension—Details) Have children support their answers.

- Do you think the farmer will now be able to pull the beet with the horse's help? Why or why not? (Inferential Comprehension—Cause and Effect)

Continue reading, following the same questioning for each new character. Stop at the bottom of page 11 where the little mouse offers to help.

- What will happen next? (Inferential Comprehension—Cause and Effect)

Read pages 12 and 13 and check the children's predictions.

Before continuing to read the story, ask the children to predict how the story might end. Then read to the end of the story and check children's predictions as they look at the picture. Stress that the animals were successful because they used teamwork. Refer back to the children's responses about the farmer. Ask the children if they have learned anything new about the farmer. Elicit that he is kind and appreciative of the animals' help in pulling out the beet. Ask children to support their answers.

New Story/Verse

Recall with the children the name of the story that was read on Day Six (*The Little Red Hen*). Ask the following questions:

- Where did the story take place?

- Who was the main character in the story? Who else was in the story? (As the children name each character, show them a picture with the name of the character underneath.)

Little Red Hen   Cat   Dog

Have children repeat the name with you as you display the picture card. After all the characters have been recalled, ask the children if they can remember the order in which the animals were asked to help the Little Red Hen. Through discussion, display the pictures in order. Once the sequence has been established, number the pictures 1–5 on both the front and back of the cards. This will aid the children in retelling or dramatizing the story.

- What was the Little Red Hen's problem? Was she able to solve her problem? (Discuss. Elicit that none of the animals wanted to help at first. They wanted to sleep all day instead. Show the pictures to reinforce the facts. Elicit the fact that all three animals were lazy, and the hard-working Little Red Hen had to do all the housework herself. Discuss whether this is fair. Was the Little Red Hen ever able to solve the problem? Show the picture at the end of the story.)

Have the children use the following Circle Story Map to recall the events that led to the resolution.

The Little Red Hen

Characters: Little Red Hen, Cat, Dog, Mouse

Setting: Country

Problems:
- Who will help the hen plant the wheat?
- Who will cut the wheat?
- Who will take the wheat to the mill to be made into flour?
- Who will make a cake?
- Who will eat the cake?

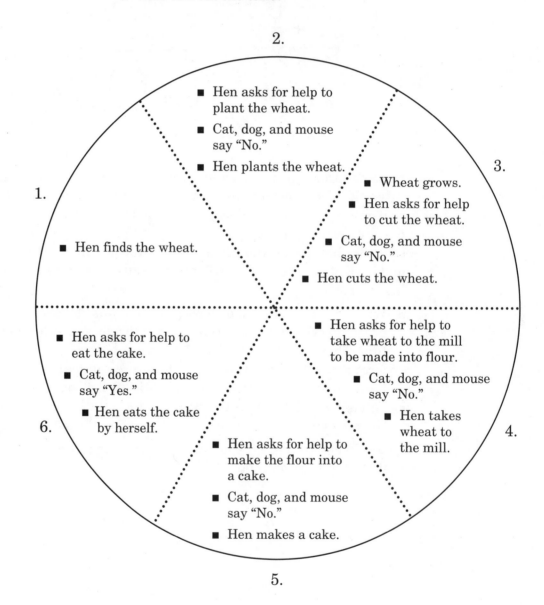

1.
- Hen finds the wheat.

2.
- Hen asks for help to plant the wheat.
- Cat, dog, and mouse say "No."
- Hen plants the wheat.

3.
- Wheat grows.
- Hen asks for help to cut the wheat.
- Cat, dog, and mouse say "No."
- Hen cuts the wheat.

4.
- Hen asks for help to take wheat to the mill to be made into flour.
- Cat, dog, and mouse say "No."
- Hen takes wheat to the mill.

5.
- Hen asks for help to make the flour into a cake.
- Cat, dog, and mouse say "No."
- Hen makes a cake.

6.
- Hen asks for help to eat the cake.
- Cat, dog, and mouse say "Yes."
- Hen eats the cake by herself.

Upon completing the Circle Story Map, have the children read the story along with you in unison, chanting on any parts they wish.

Activity Time

Whole Group

The Farmer and the Beet and *The Little Red Hen* deal with the concepts of helping others and social development. In one story, the animals willingly help the farmer without any thought of a reward. In the other story, the animals who lived together as a family are unwilling to help the Little Red Hen. This difference provides a unique opportunity to develop the thinking processes required to compare and contrast. The comparisons should be charted as follows:

Compare/Contrast Chart

Similarities	The Farmer and the Beet	The Little Red Hen
Beginning:	Once upon a time	Once upon a time
Animals (minor characters)	dog, cat, mouse	dog, cat, mouse
Setting:	country	country
Problem:	Farmer needs help; asks for help	Hen needs help; asks for help
Differences		
Animals' attitudes	helpful	lazy
Result of behavior	rewarded	not rewarded
Number of characters	five	three

After the chart has been completed, discuss the following questions.

- How do you feel about the farmer making a special feast for his helpers? Why?
- How do you feel about the Little Red Hen not sharing the cake with her friends? Why?
- What are some of the ways you can help at home or at school?

Record responses under the following headings.

Ways We Help At School	Ways We Help At Home

Teach the children the following song to the tune of "Here We Go Round the Mulberry Bush."

• •

This Is the Way She Made the Cake

This is the way she planted the wheat, planted the wheat, planted the wheat

This is the way she planted the wheat

Early in the morning.

This is the way she cut the wheat . . .

This is the way she delivered the wheat . . .

This is the way she made the cake . . .

This is the way she ate the cake . . .

• •

Actions can be added once the words have been learned from a chart or overhead transparency.

Arrange for a field trip to a bakery to see how cakes and other baked goods are made from flour.

Individual/Small Group

• • • • • • • • •

Writing/Publishing Center

Provide children with sheets of paper with the following open-ended sentence printed at the top:

If I had a little hen I would _____.

Staple the pages together to make a class book.

Have children add key words plus pictures to their alphabet books.

Reading/Library Center

Provide as many versions of *The Little Red Hen* as you can find, along with the books from the Related Reading section for Day Six.

Provide six pictures from the story (see pages 206–208) for children to put in order. Have children then use the pictures as clues to help them retell the story.

Listening/Viewing Center

Provide a tape of the version of *The Little Red Hen* used with the class. You may also wish to include tapes of Read Aloud books from Day Six.

Drama Center

Provide children with stick puppets of each character from *The Little Red Hen* for dramatization.

Art Center

Have children paint a picture of their favorite tale.

Related Reading

The Little Red Hen by L. McQueen. This is a modern humorous version of *The Little Red Hen.*

Who Said Red? by K. Narahashi

The Little Red Hen by M. Zemach

The Farmer and the Beet

DAY 8

Tune In

Select from the following for unison chanting or singing.

> I Had a Little Hen
>
> This Is the Way She Made the Cake
>
> Old MacDonald Had a Farm
>
> (Children's choice)

Read Aloud

Tell the children that the favorite tale that they will hear today was written long, long ago in Norway. Ask the class if anyone knows where Norway is. Locate Norway on a globe or map.

Show children the cover of Galdone's version of *The Three Billy Goats Gruff*. Ask children what they think the goats are doing.

- What do goats look like?
- What do goats eat?
- Where do goats live?

Show pictures of real goats.

Before beginning, to read, ask children what words might be used to introduce the story. (*Once upon a time . . .*) Read the first six pages, ending with ". . . who was mean as he was ugly."

- Where does the story take place?
- Who is in the story? What do you know about trolls?
- What do the goats want to do? How will they do it? Why do you think this might be hard to do?

Tell the children that you are going to continue reading to find out what the goats will do. Before reading, refer to the picture and ask the children which goat they think will be the first to cross the bridge. Have the children predict what will happen next.

Continue reading the next five pages, stopping where the troll says,

"Well then, be off with you."

- Were your predictions correct?

- What do you think will happen next?

Continue reading the next two pages, stopping where the troll says "Very well, be off with you." Check children's predictions and have them predict what will happen next.

Read to the end of the story.

- What did we learn about the Three Billy Goats Gruff?

- How did the three billy goats get to the meadow to get the green grass?

New Story/Verse

Model storytelling, using the feltboard cutouts for *The Farmer and the Beet*. (The patterns can be found on pages 209–210.) Follow the telling with several readings of the Big Book, pointing to the words and pictures as the children chant with you.

Activity Time

Whole Group

Have the children take turns dramatizing the story using the feltboard cutouts or simple props.

Teach the letter and sound of /f/ to first graders.

Sing "The Farmer and the Beet" to the tune of "The Farmer in the Dell."

• •

The Farmer and the Beet

The farmer in the garden

The farmer in the garden

Heigh-ho, the derry-o

The farmer in the garden

He grew a great big beet . . .

The animals came to help . . .

Out came the great big beet . . .

They had a great big feast . . .

• •

Provide children with the opportunity to taste canned beets if they would like to do so.

 Be sure to obtain permission before allowing children to eat foods prepared in the classroom in case of food allergies or other restrictions.

Individual/Small Group

Reading/Library Center

Provide as many versions of *The Farmer and the Beet* as you can find.

Provide the feltboard figures for *The Farmer and the Beet* so that children can use them to retell the story to each other.

Provide several small versions along with the Big Book of *The Farmer and the Beet* for individual, partner, or small-group reading. First graders may want to use the small books for guided reading.

Provide small blank books for children to use to create *F* books. Encourage children to label their pictures.

Writing/Publishing Center

Have children add key words plus pictures to their personal alphabet books.

Drama Center

Place props used in the large group retelling activity for children to use to act out *The Farmer and the Beet.*

Math Center

Put cutout figures of the six characters from *The Farmer and the Beet* (see pages 209–210) in order by size. Sets of each animal could also be used.

Art Center

Have children work in small groups to produce large pictures of characters from *The Farmer and the Beet.* The pictures should be arranged on a background created by the children.

Science Center

Provide children with two-piece puzzles so that they can match the animals with the appropriate foods.

Related Reading

The Turnip by J. Domanska. This is the original version of the old Russian folktale from which *The Farmer and the Beet* was adapted.

Elephant in a Well by M. J. Ets

The Turnip by P. Morgan. This version of the tale takes place in old Russia.

The Enormous Turnip by K. Parkinson. This book depicts a present-day family.

The Three Billy-Goats Gruff

Tune In

Select from the following for unison chanting or singing:

> The Bear Went over the Mountain
>
> The Farmer and the Beet
>
> Baby Bear (adaptation of the jump-rope rhyme "Teddy Bear")

• •

Baby Bear, Baby Bear, Turn Around

Baby Bear, Baby Bear, turn around

Baby Bear, Baby Bear, touch the ground.

Baby Bear, Baby Bear, show your shoe,

Baby Bear, Baby Bear, that will do.

Baby Bear, Baby Bear, go upstairs,

Baby Bear, Baby Bear, say your prayers.

Baby Bear, Baby Bear, switch off the light.

Baby Bear, Baby Bear, say good night.

• •

Read Aloud

Today the children will hear a favorite tale, *Goldilocks and the Three Bears.* If possible, read the version by J. Brett because of the beautiful, imaginative illustrations that accompany the text. Since this classic tale appears in so many different versions, find as many versions as possible to share with the group.

Show the children the cover of the book and ask the children if they can guess the title. Have individual children identify the characters. Ask the children where the three bears lived. Ask the children what words might begin the story.

Begin reading the story, allowing sufficient time for children to enjoy the pictures. Stop at the point where the bears go out for a walk in the woods and ask the children what they think will happen next. Accept all responses.

Continue reading until Goldilocks falls fast asleep. Ask the children if they know what happens next. Accept all responses.

Read to the point where the bears find Goldilocks sound asleep in baby bear's bed. Discuss with the children how each of the bears felt. Discuss how the children would feel if someone came into their home and did what Goldilocks did when she visited the bears' home.

After the discussion, show the picture of the three bears angrily looking at Goldilocks. Discuss how Goldilocks felt at that moment. Read to the end of the story.

New Story/Verse

The Three Billy Goats Gruff by Galdone can be reread or told to the children in its entirety. Afterward, recall with the children the three major events of the story. This can be done with the aid of story strips:

"TRIP! TRAP! TRIP! TRAP! TRIP! TRAP"

"WHO'S THAT TRIPPING OVER MY BRIDGE?"

"Oh, it's only I."

"Well then, be off with you."

When you come to the part in the story where one of the sentence strips can be used, invite the children to read with you.

After children have recalled the three major events of the story, have them read the four sentence strips together several times. This will facilitate instant recognition or memorization of the key words of the story.

Activity Time

Whole Group

Using masks or simple props, dramatize *The Three Billy Goats Gruff.*
Create a bridge using large construction blocks, chairs, or a large plank of
wood. The rest of the children can act as an audience, chanting "Trip,
trap, trip, trap, trip, trap" as each goat crosses the bridge.

Remind the children to use different voices for each goat and for the
troll.

Show the children pictures of different kinds of goats. Discuss the following questions:

- Why do people keep goats? (milk, cheese, wool)

- What do goats look like? Ideas will come from the Read Aloud story,
  the pictures, and the children's own experience.

Using the Language Experience Approach (see page 33), develop a class
story about goats.

Individual/Small Group

Writing/Publishing Center

Provide the children with crayons and paper. Have them illustrate and
write about their favorite part of *The Three Billy Goats Gruff.* Display the
pictures under the heading "The Adventures of The Gruff Brothers."

Have children add key words plus pictures to their personal alphabet
books.

Reading/Library Center

Provide as many versions of *The Three Billy Goats Gruff* as you can find.
The following are highly recommended.

Billy Goats Gruff by S. Blair. The illustrations are woodcut. ◇

The Three Billy Goats Gruff by M. Brown

The Gruff Brothers by W. Hooks. This is a rebus book. ◇

The Three Billy Goats Gruff by V. Southgate. ◇

The Three Billy Goats Gruff by J. Stevens. In this humorous version
the goats are dressed in modern dress and the troll has a pet frog. ◆◆

Science Center

Provide books and pictures of goats. Encourage children to work cooperatively to find out as much as they can about goats.

• • • • • • • • • •

 ## Listening/Viewing Center

Provide the tape made during Read Aloud time on Day Eight, along with Galdone's version of *The Three Billy Goats Gruff.*

• • • • • • • • • •

 ## Drama Center

Using stick puppets (see pages 211–212) and a small bridge made from blocks, have the children tell the story.

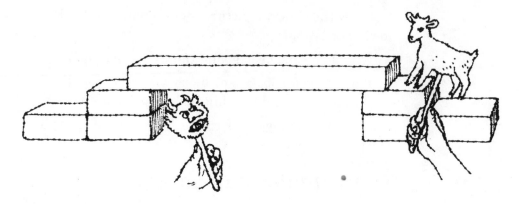

Related Reading

Anytime Mapleson and the Hungry Bears by M. Gerstein

Reminders:

Ask the children to bring their teddy bears to school for Day Ten.

Bring in ingredients for making porridge with the class.

Remember to invite a few parents to help in the cooking center for Day Ten.

Goldilocks and the Three Bears

DAY 10

Tune In

Select from the following for unison chanting or singing.

The Bear Went over the Mountain

Baby Bear, Baby Bear, Turn Around

Using an overhead transparency or chart, teach the following rhyme.

• • • • • • • • • • • • • • • • • • •

To Market, to Market

To market, to market

To buy a fat pig,

Home again, home again,

Jiggety-jig.

To market, to market,

To buy a fat hog,

Home again, home again,

Jiggety-jog.

• • • • • • • • • • • • • • • • • •

Read Aloud

The Three Little Pigs is a delightful English folktale, one of the best-loved beast tales, which appears in numerous versions. Paul Galdone's version of *The Three Little Pigs* presents the entire original folktale in clear text, and large colorful illustrations draw the listener into the story.

Show the children the cover and ask them if they can determine the title of the story. By now most children should be able to read the words *the* and *three* and be able to figure out the word *pig* from the picture clues. Ask the children where they think this story might take place. Finally, ask the children what words might begin the story.

Begin reading the tale. Make certain that sufficient time is spent looking at and discussing pictures. The discussion will enable young learners to develop the ability to interact with both the print and illustrations in comprehending the story on all levels. Read the first page and then focus on the picture.

- Who else is in the story? (Literal Comprehension—Details)
- How do you think the mother pig felt when her children were leaving home? Why? (Inferential Comprehension—Inferring Character Traits)
- How do you think the Three Little Pigs will seek their fortune? (Inferential Comprehension—Predicting Outcomes)

Explain the words *seek* and *fortune*.

- What do you think the pigs took with them in their knapsacks (point to them in the picture)? (Inferential Comprehension—Supporting Details)

Continue reading until the wolf tells the first pig that he will blow his house in.

- Were your predictions correct?
- Who else is in the story? (Literal Comprehension—Details)
- What do you think will happen next? (Inferential Comprehension—Predicting Outcomes)

Turn the page and read what happens. Check the children's predictions. Continue reading until the wolf tells the second pig that he will blow the house down.

- What do you think will happen next? (Inferential Comprehension—Predicting Outcomes)

Turn the page and read what happens. Check the children's predictions.

- What do you think the third pig will do? (Inferential Comprehension—Inferring Outcomes)

Continue reading to the end of the story. Check the children's predictions.

New Story/Verse

Hold up the Addison-Wesley Big Book version of *Goldilocks and the Three Bears,* along with Brett's version read as the Read Aloud selection on Day Nine. Recall the title with the children. Then ask children to name the four characters in the story. As the characters are named, place a sentence strip in the pocket chart with the character's picture and name:

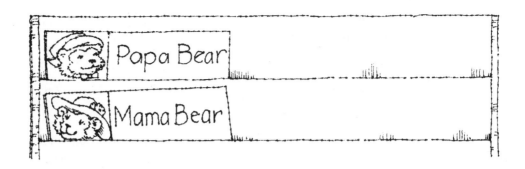

Read the story in its entirety, pointing to each word and picture as it is said.

Reread the story one or two more times. Encourage the children to chant as many words as they can.

After these readings, hold up the smaller versions of the Big Book and tell the children that these will be in the library center during activity time so that they can read them individually or with a friend.

Activity Time

Whole Group

Using headbands for the bears (see patterns, pages 213–214) and simple props, have children dramatize the story. Stress that children should use different voices for the characters.

The story props should be placed in the housekeeping/dramatic play center.

Using the Happily Ever After Wordless Book (Addison-Wesley Learning Through Literature Program), have the children create captions for the pictures. Captions can be written on sentence strips with a felt pen and attached to the Big Book with large paper clips. Have the children read their story several times.

The Big Book with the children's captions may be placed in the reading/library center to be enjoyed individually or with friends.

Recall with the children that the bears' favorite food was porridge. Using an overhead transparency or chart, teach the rhyme "Pease Porridge Hot."

● ● ● ● ● ● ● ● ● ● ● ● ● ● ● ● ● ●

Pease Porridge Hot

Pease porridge hot,

Pease porridge cold,

Pease porridge in the pot

Nine days old.

Some like it hot,

Some like it cold,

Some like it in the pot

Nine days old.

● ● ● ● ● ● ● ● ● ● ● ● ● ● ● ● ●

Prepare children for making porridge later in the cooking center. Ask, "How many of you have eaten porridge? Do you know how porridge is made?"

After the discussion, tell the children that you have brought a recipe for making porridge. Show the children a giant recipe card on which you have written the following recipe.

Three Bears Porridge

1 3/4 C water
1/4 t salt
1/4 C raisins or chopped apple
1 1/3 C quick rolled oats

1. Pour the water into a saucepan and turn the heat to high. While waiting for it to boil, add the salt and raisins. When the water starts to bubble hard, add the oats.

2. Turn the heat to low and cook the porridge until all the water is absorbed and the oats are soft (about 3–5 minutes).

3. Pour the porridge into three bowls and cover each with some milk.

Place the giant recipe card in the cooking center for later use.

Individual/Small Group

● ● ● ● ● ● ● ● ● ●

Cooking Center

With one or two parent helpers to supervise, have small groups of children make the porridge. Children can use individual spoons once each to sample the porridge.

Be sure to obtain permission before allowing children to eat foods prepared in the classroom in case of food allergies or other restrictions.

Writing/Publishing Center

Using paper cut in the shape of a chef's hat, have the children write about their cooking experiences.

Provide bear-shaped paper for children to write individual stories (see pattern on page 211). Suggested titles include "My Favorite Bear," "The Three Bears," "If I were a Bear," "Brown Bear," and "My Teddy."

Have children add key words plus pictures to their alphabet books.

Listening/Viewing Center

Place in the center the tape made during Read Aloud time on Day Nine, along with Brett's version of *Goldlocks and the Three Bears*.

Reading/Library Center

Provide as many versions of *Goldlocks and the Three Bears* as you can find. The following are highly recommended.

Addison-Wesley Big Book version and small books. These can be used for guided or for independent reading.

The Three Bears wordless Big Book with the children's captions ◇

Goldilocks and the Three Bears by L. Cauley

The Three Bears by P. Galdone

Bears by R. Krauss ◇

Goldilocks and the Three Bears by J. Marshall. This is a modern, humorous version with delightful illustrations. ◆◆

The Rebus Bears by S. Reit ◇

Make a display of alphabet books. Some suggested titles are:

Alphabears, An ABC Book by K. Hague

The Teddy Bear ABC by L. R. Johnson

Albert B. Cub and Zebra, An Alphabet Storybook by A. Rockwell

Housekeeping/Dramatic Play Center

Transform the housekeeping center into the home of the three bears with the props that were used in the whole-group activity. Children can act out the story using teddy bears or taking the parts of bears themselves.

Art Center

Have children make bears out of some type of modeling material.

Have children work together in small groups to paint the three pigs' houses on mural paper.

Science Center

Display books and pictures of bears in their natural habitat. Some suggested titles include the following:

A Book About Pandas by R. B. Gross

Animals in the Wild: Bears by M. Hoffman

Two Little Bears by Yila

Provide children with small blank books to record their facts about bears. Write a title, such as "All About Real Bears" on the front.

Have children sort bear pictures into two categories, "Make-Believe Bears" and "Real Bears."

Math Center

Have children order all the bears brought from home from smallest to largest. Let them place numbers in sequence in front of each bear. Kindergarteners will enjoy counting the bears.

Provide large numbers of small cutout bears for counting.

Collect a number of boxes that have a top opening. Decorate the front of each box to look like a house. Number the doors 1, 2, 3, and so on. Cut small bears from construction paper. Younger children can match sets with numerals; first graders can match number sentences with answers.

Place *Teddy Bears 1 to 10* by S. Gretz in the center. Encourage children to read the book and then write their own version in small blank books made from newsprint.

Place *10 Bears in My Bed* by S. Mack in the center for the children to read for enjoyment.

Related Reading

Bear in Mind: A Book of Bear Poems by B. Goldstein This is a poetry book.

Brown Bear, Brown Bear, What Do You See? by B. Martin, Jr.

Goldilocks and the Three Bears by J. McDonnell. This is a translation of an imaginative, humorous Spanish version of the old tale.

Deep in the Forest by B. Turkle. In this wordless picture book, the bear visits while the father, mother, and little girl are out for a walk.

 Reminder: Send home a newsletter telling about the work being done with favorite tales, and invite parents to Favorite Tales Day.

The Three Little Pigs

DAY 11

Tune In

Select from the following for unison chanting or singing:

Pease Porridge Hot

To Market, To Market

One Little, Two Little, Three Little Bears

Porridge Song (tune: "Here We Go Round the Mulberry Bush")

• •

Porridge Song

This is the way we made our porridge, made our porridge, made our porridge,

This is the way we made our porridge, early __(day)__ morning.

This is the way we poured the water . . .

This is the way we added the salt . . .

This is the way we added the spice . . .

This is the way we added the fruit . . .

This is the way we boiled the water . . .

This is the way we added the oats . . .

This is the way we stirred the porridge . . .

This is the way we ate the porridge . . .

• •

Read Aloud

Little Red Riding Hood is based on an original German tale called *Little Red Cap,* written by the Grimm Brothers. The version we recommend, by Galdone, is written in clear text accompanied by large colorful illustrations. This version, like the original version, has Red Riding Hood taking a basket with cake and wine to grandmother. You may wish to substitute something else to drink in place of the word *wine* when reading the story.

Show children the cover of the book. Write the title on the chalkboard and have children read it if they can. Ask the children who the little girl might be and tell them the book was named after her. Show the children the title page and ask the following questions.

■ Who else might be in the story? (Characters)

■ Where does this story take place? (Setting) Answers may vary.

■ Why do you think Little Red Riding Hood is in the forest? (Inferential Comprehension—Predicting Outcomes)

■ How do you think the story will begin? ("Once upon a time . . .")

Read the first page. After reading, ask the following question.

■ Who gave the little girl her red velvet cloak? (Literal Comprehension—Identifying Details)

Make certain the children know the meaning of the word *velvet* (show a piece of material or something made of velvet) and *cloak* (this is illustrated).

Continue reading, stopping at ". . . so she was not a bit afraid of him."

■ What is Little Red Riding Hood going to do now? (Inferential Comprehension—Predicting Outcomes)

Once the children have made their predictions, continue reading until the end of the page that shows Little Red Riding Hood picking flowers, stopping at "So she went deeper and deeper into the forest."

■ Check the children's predictions.

■ What do you think the wolf is doing? (Inferential Comprehension—Supporting Details)

■ What do you think will happen next? (Inferential Comprehension—Predicting Outcomes)

Read the next page to find out if children's predictions about the wolf were correct.

■ What do you think the wolf will do now? (Inferential Comprehension—Inferring Sequence)

Read until you reach the end of the page where Little Red Riding Hood reaches her grandmother's house, stopping at, "But she received no answer."

■ Were your predictions about the wolf correct? (Literal Comprehension—Details)

■ What do you think Little Red Riding Hood will do? (Inferential Comprehension—Predicting Outcomes)

Read to the end of the story and discuss the ending.

New Story/Verse

Using the Addison Wesley Big Book Level A edition, read the entire story of *The Three Little Pigs* to the children, pointing to each word as it is read. Then reread the story several times, inviting the children to join in.

After several readings of the Big Book, have the children complete a story map frame with you and post it as a reference. A sample of a completed story map frame follows.

Story Map Frame

Who is in the story?
1. first pig
2. second pig
3. third pig
4. wolf

Where does it take place?
at the pigs' houses

What is the problem?
The wolf wants to eat the pigs.

What happened in the story?
1. The wolf blew down the house of straw.

2. The wolf blew down the house of sticks.

3. The wolf couldn't blow down the house of bricks.

How did it end?
The wolf climbed down the chimney, fell in the soup, and then ran away forever.

Activity Time

Whole Group

Read the old Mother Goose favorite, *This Little Pig,* adapted by Lubin. Lubin's illustrations are unique and depict the pigs in British clothing of long ago.

Using masks, have children take turns dramatizing the story. Write the refrain on a chart and review it prior to dramatization. This is an excellent time to introduce the children to the concept of quotation marks to indicate dialogue.

● ● ● ● ● ● ● ● ● ● ● ● ● ● ● ● ●

"Little pig, little pig,

let me come in."

"No, no! Not by the hair

of my chinny chin chin."

"Then I'll huff, and I'll puff,

and I'll blow your house in."

● ● ● ● ● ● ● ● ● ● ● ● ● ● ● ● ●

The houses painted on Day Ten can be used as props for dramatization.

Have the children sing "One Little, Two Little, Three Little Pigs."

Read *If I Had a Pig* by M. Inkpen. Cut large sheets of paper in a pig shape. Write "If I Had a Pig . . ." on the title page to create a class Big Book.

Individual/Small Group

● ● ● ● ● ● ● ● ●

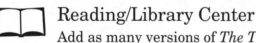 Reading/Library Center

Add as many versions of *The Three Little Pigs* as you can find. The following are highly recommended.

Addison-Wesley Big Book and small book versions. These can be used for guided or independent reading.

The Three Little Pigs by B. Gavin

If I Had a Pig by M. Inkpen ◇

This Little Pig by L. Lubin

The Three Little Pigs by M. Zemach ◇

Listening/Viewing Center

Provide the Addison-Wesley tape and small versions of *The Three Little Pigs.* ◇

Provide a teacher-made tape and Galdone's version of *The Three Little Pigs.* ◇

Writing/Publishing Center

Children can use paper cut in the shape of a pig (see page 214) to produce a page for the class Big Book, *If I Had a Pig.*

Have children add key words plus pictures to their personal alphabet books.

Art Center

Provide paint for the children who would like to paint a picture of their favorite part of the book. A caption could be written by the child or dictated to a buddy or teacher.

Block Center

Children construct houses using blocks or other types of building materials.

Drama Center

Using the story props from the whole-group activity, have the children dramatize the story of *The Three Little Pigs.*

Social Studies Center

Display books on how houses are made. One possible choice is *This Old New House* by S. McGraw.

Display a variety of materials:

Floor plans from realtors, architects, or building designers

Samples of building materials and supplies, including color charts, tiles

Pictures of all kinds of homes

Sale flyers from building suppliers

Math Center

Provide boxes of keys, nails, and so on for classification. Encourage children to decide their own classification system.

Cut out house shapes and write a number on the roof of each one. Cut out a door for each house and label it with dots or number sentences that correspond to the numbers on the houses. Children match doors and roofs.

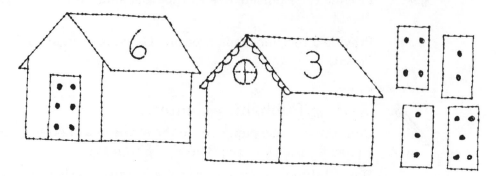

Related Reading

The Three Little Pigs by E. Blegvad. This version has beautiful illustrations by a distinguished artist, Blegvad, whose graphic art is appreciated by all ages.

The Three Little Pigs and The Fox by W. Hooks. This book is recommended for first graders because it has a higher reading level than most of the books introduced in this unit. This rendition of the old tale based on a number of oral versions has its origins in the Appalachian region of the United States. Although this version may not be familiar to the children, it is important for them to realize that many regions have their own versions of folktales, reflecting the areas in which they are told. Before reading the story, point out the Appalachian region of the United States on a map. Read the story in its entirety, stopping to clarify concepts presented in the story. Some of the vocabulary will not be familiar to the children and may need to be defined as the story is being read.

The Three Little Pigs by J. Marshall. Marshall's witty style of writing and illustrations provide a humorous version of the old tale.

The Three Little Pigs by J. McDonnell. This translation of a Spanish version of the old tale is imaginative and humorous.

The Three Little Pigs by M. Zemach. This beautiful visual interpretation of the classic tale is faithful to the traditional version.

Have children compare the similarities and differences of two versions of the story. Record their comparisons on a chart.

 Reminder: Bring a pot, stone, onion, carrot, picture of a chicken, picture of cut-up meat, salt and pepper, picture of butter, and some barley to class for Day Twelve.

Little Red Riding Hood

Tune In

Select from the following for unison chanting:

Alphabet Song

To Market, to Market

Using an overhead transparency or chart, teach the following rhyme.

● ●

This Little Pig Went to Market

This little pig went to market,

This little pig stayed home,

This little pig had roast beef,

This little pig had none,

This little pig cried, "Wee, wee, wee!"

All the way home.

● ●

Write the following verse on a chart or on sentence strips. Include actions to go with the words.

Grandma and Grandpa

Here is Grandma's paintbrush,	Here is Grandpa's baseball,
Here is Grandma's cap;	Here is Grandpa's mitt;
She's going to paint a picture	Here is Grandpa's lucky bat—
Of a kitty in my lap.	He's sure to get a hit.

Read Aloud

A number of versions of *Stone Soup,* originally a French folktale (*Une Drole de Soupe*), are available. McGovern's version, published by Scholastic, is written in plain language that is easy for children to comprehend.

Prior to reading the story, have the story props handy. Place the pot on one side of you and the bag of ingredients on the other. As the story unfolds, take the appropriate ingredients out of the bag and put them into the pot. This use of props helps children recall story sequence for retelling and aids in comprehension.

Show the children the cover of the book and explain that the title of the story is *Stone Soup.* Ask the following questions.

■ Who do you think is in the story?

■ Have any of you tasted stone soup?

■ How do you think stone soup is made?

■ Who do you think will make the stone soup? Why?

Begin reading the story, stopping at the end of page 6.

■ What do we find out about the young man? (Literal Comprehension—Identifying Details)

■ Where do you think the story takes place? (Inferential Comprehension—Inferring Details)

■ What do you think will happen next? (Inferential Comprehension—Predicting Outcomes)

Continue reading to page 11, stopping at "You cannot eat a stone!" Discuss the children's predictions.

■ What do you think will happen next? (Inferential Comprehension—Inferring Outcomes)

Continue reading to the bottom of page 16.

■ What other items will the young man ask the old woman to put into the soup pot? (Record responses in a chart.)

Continue reading to page 28, checking off the responses from the chart.

■ How do you think the story will end? (Inferential Comprehension—Predicting Outcomes)

Read to the end of the story. Discuss the children's predictions.

■ Why do you think the young man kept the stone? (Inferential Comprehension—Inferring Sequence)

New Story/Verse

Reread Galdone's version of *Little Red Riding Hood*. Review and list the names of characters on the board. Use the following Sequencing Events Model to review the story sequence.

Sequencing Events Model Chart

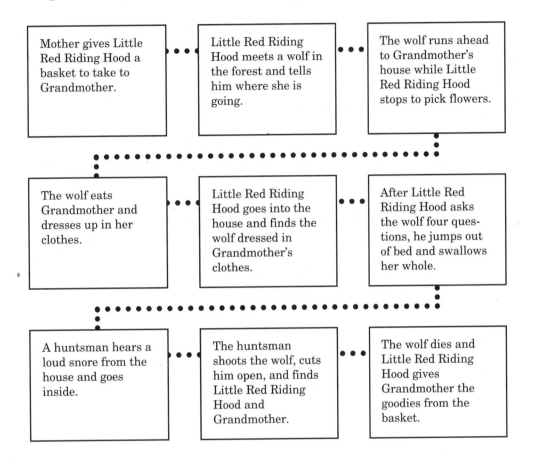

When the model has been completed, ask the children what lesson Little Red Riding Hood learned.

Activity Time

Whole Group

Use *Little Red Riding Hood* from Addison-Wesley's *Happily Ever After* Program.

Tell the children you have another version of Little Red Riding Hood, but in this version there are only pictures. Show the pictures in sequence and discuss what happens in this version. Have the children dictate appropriate sentences as you write them on blank sentence strips. These can be clipped to each page. After the children's story is completed, reread their version with them several times.

Teach "The Red Riding Hood Song" by Carmino Ravosa from *Story Songs.*

Brainstorm with the children which stories they would like to perform for their parents. Discuss what displays, materials, and projects they would like to show their parents.

Individual/Small Group

Reading/Library Center

Add as many versions of *Little Red Riding Hood* as you can find. The following are highly recommended.

Little Red Riding Hood: Addison-Wesley's *Happily Ever After* Program

Red Riding Hood by B. de Regniers. This version of the tale is in verse.

Little Red Riding Hood by T. S. Hyman. ◆◆

Little Red Riding Hood's Picture Puzzle Book by A. Morris ◇

Little Red Riding Hood by B. Watts

Lon Po Po: A Red Riding Hood Story from China by E. Young. In this version, the mother ventures to visit grandmother. Her three daughters remain at home, but are warned not to let anyone in the house. The wolf tries to trick the girls by taking the role of the grandmother.

Provide children with the pictures and sentences that were developed in the whole-group activity. Children working with partners or with an older buddy place the pictures in order. You may want to number the backs of the pictures in sequence for self-checking.

Listening/Viewing Center

Add a teacher-made tape of *Little Red Riding Hood* with Galdone's book.

Drama Center

Have children dramatize the events of the story using simple props:

blocks or chairs for Grandmother's bed (pillows, blankets)

cape (rectangles of red cloth fastened with a safety pin)

basket (any item can do for goodies)

Grandmother's clothes (shower cap, old plastic glasses, shawl)

Wolf (old fur hat or brown knit hat)

Writing/Publishing Center

Provide children with red paper cut in the shape of a hooded cape on which they can write about Red Riding Hood.

Science Center

Display books and pictures depicting wolves in their natural habitat.

Have children add key words and pictures to their alphabet books.

Related Reading

Little Red Cap by E. Crawford. The Grimm Brothers' version is the original on which all the other Red Riding Hood books have been based.

Little Red Riding Hood by T. Hyman. This version has beautiful illustrations that add to the enjoyment of the old tale.

Red Riding Hood by J. Marshall. This humorous modern version is highly recommended.

Little Red Riding Hood by J. Moncure. This is a translation of an imaginative and humorous Spanish version of the old tale.

Lon Po Po: A Red Riding Hood Story from China by E. Young. This book is recommended for first graders because it is written at a higher reading level and presents more difficult concepts. However, the author's dramatic, large, watercolor and pastel illustrations should assist in clarifying new concepts. Tell the children that this tale is similar to *Little Red Riding Hood* and is from China. It is thought to be over a thousand years old. If there are any children in the class from China, you may want to ask them if they know the story of Lon Po Po. Point out China on a world map. Read the story in its entirety, stopping to clarify concepts. After reading the story, have children compare it to *Little Red Riding Hood*. Record the similarities and differences on a chart.

Stone Soup

DAY 13

Tune In

Select from the following for unison chanting or singing:

    Pease Porridge Hot

    Grandma and Grandpa

    Red Hood's Song

Then introduce the children to the verse "I Like Soup," using a chart or overhead transparency.

• •

I Like Soup

I like to eat soup—

Tomato soup and vegetable soup,

Lentil soup and split pea soup,

Beet soup and green cabbage soup,

And delicious homemade soup!

I like to eat soup—

Chicken soup and French onion soup,

Potato soup and won ton soup,

Macaroni soup and hot Creole soup;

But best of all, STONE soup!

• •

Read Aloud

The following versions of *The Magic Porridge Pot* are recommended:

- *The Magic Porridge Pot* by Bernadette ◇
- *The Magic Porridge Pot* by V. Southgate ◆◆

Show students the book, and explain that it is another story originally written by the Grimm Brothers. Name some stories by the Grimm Brothers, such as *Little Red Riding Hood, Hansel and Gretel, The Bremen Town Musicians, Rumpelstiltskin, Snow White and the Seven Dwarfs.*

This tale differs from the other tales in the unit because it introduces the children to the concept of magic, a key element often found in old tales and fairy tales.

Write *The Magic Porridge Pot* on the chalkboard. Ask the children if anyone can read all or part of the title. Discuss with children what is meant by the word *magic.*

Tape the story as you read it so that it can be placed in the listening center.

Before reading the story, ask the following questions.

- What is a magic porridge pot?

- Would you like to have a magic porridge pot? Why or why not?

Read the entire story. When you have finished, discuss the questions again. Ask what kind of food children would like their magic pot to produce. Record responses in a chart.

New Story/Verse

Retell *Stone Soup,* using the props from Day Twelve.

Follow up by reading *The Soup Stone,* an American version of the same tale retold and illustrated by I. Van Rynbach, published by Greenwillow. Show the beautiful, detailed watercolors of New England colonial life in the post-Revolutionary War period as you read.

Use the following chart to help children compare the two versions of *Stone Soup.*

Comparing Stone Soup Tales

	Stone Soup	The Soup Stone
Setting	a big house in the country	a farmhouse on the edge of the village
Characters	a hungry young man a little old lady	a hungry soldier, farmer, his wife, their three children, and a cat
Problem	The hungry young man asks for food.	The hungry soldier asks for food and a place to sleep.

Soup Recipe	water, stone, onions, carrots, two fat chickens, beef bones, bit of pepper, handful of salt, butter, barley	water, soup stone, fistful of salt, carrots, a few potatoes, some salted beef, an onion, and some cabbage
Ending/Solution	The young man and old lady eat the soup. The young man takes the stone with him.	The family and soldier enjoy the soup. The soldier gives the farmer the soup stone and picks up a new stone.

After completing the chart, ask the children if they think the stone made the soup taste better. Discuss their answers. Make certain that the children are aware that the young man and the soldier tricked the other characters into making them free soup.

Activity Time

Whole Group

Read *Alphabet Soup* by K. Banks. In this delightful make-believe story, a little boy who doesn't want to eat dips his spoon into his soup and scoops up words *(bear, sword, boat, net, rope, tree, cage, house, bed)* that come to life. The book reinforces the concept of spelling and provides the children with motivation for the alphabet pasta activity that will be introduced on Day Fourteen.

Have children use the story props to dramatize a version of *Stone Soup.*

Tell the children that today they are going to write their own version of *Stone Soup.* Have them work together as a group to decide on the setting, characters, problem, soup recipe, and ending, using the chart to compare the two versions.

Teach the letter and sound of /s/.

Individual/Small Group

Listening/Viewing Center

Provide a copy of the teacher-made tape for McGovern's version of *Stone Soup* along with the book.

• • • • • • • • • •

Reading/Library Center

Add as many versions of *Stone Soup* as you can find. The following are highly recommended.

Stone Soup by M. Brown

The Soup Stone by I. Van Rynbach

• • • • • • • • • •

Housekeeping/Dramatic Play Center

Place the story props in the center so that children can dramatize the story.

• • • • • • • • • •

Writing/Publishing Center

Provide children with paper cut into the shape of a pot (see page 217). Have children use the paper to write their own recipe for making Stone Soup.

Have children add key words plus pictures to their personal alphabet books.

Provide the children with small blank books. On the cover write "My Little Book of *S* Things."

• • • • • • • • • •

Art Center

Have children paint illustrations for the Big Book created in the whole-group activity.

Related Reading

The following books may be read for enjoyment.

Stone Soup by J. Ross. This is a humorous modern version with animal characters.

Stone Soup by J. Stewig. This modern version has a heroine who uses the familiar ploy to find food.

Reminders:

Give the children a note requesting that they bring some pasta samples to school for Day Fourteen.

Bring in two packages of alphabet pasta.

Strega Nona

DAY 14

Tune In

Select from the following for unison chanting or singing:

Pease Porridge Hot

Porridge Song

I Like Soup

Using a Language Experience Approach (see page 33), have the children suggest original verses (ingredients) for the Stone Soup Song. Provide the children with the beginning two verses as follows:

● ●

Stone Soup Song

(tune: Here We Go Round the Mulberry Bush)

This is the way we make stone soup,

Make stone soup, make stone soup,

This is the way we make stone soup,

Early in the evening.

This is the way we boil the water . . .

This is the way we add the stone . . .

● ●

After singing the first three verses, use the children's suggestions for the remaining verses. Children can pretend to put each new ingredient into the pot as each verse is sung.

Read Aloud

Tell the children that today they will hear another old tale written by the Grimm Brothers. Like the story yesterday, this one also involves magic. Ask the children if they remember what object was magic in the story they heard yesterday (pot). Recall what the magic pot could do.

The Magic Fish by Littledale not only involves magic, but it will also help children review basic sight vocabulary.

Hold up the Big Book version of *The Magic Fish* and ask the children to read the title. Have the children look at the picture carefully and ask them who they think the story is about.

Before beginning the story, ask the children how this old tale might begin ("Once upon a time . . ."). Read the first six pages, stopping when the fisherman returns the fish to the water.

- Who is in the story? (Literal Comprehension—Identifying Details)

- Why did the fisherman return the fish to the water instead of taking it home? (Inferential Comprehension—Inferring Supporting Details)

- How do you think the wife will feel about this? Why? (Inferential Comprehension—Predicting Outcomes)

Read the next four pages to find out whether children's predictions about the wife were correct.

- Do you think that the fish will grant the wife the wish? Why or why not? (Inferential Comprehension—Predicting Outcomes)

Read the next six pages to find out whether children's predictions were correct.

- Do you think the fisherman's wife will be happy now? Why or why not? (Inferential Comprehension—Predicting Outcomes)

Read the next four pages to find out whether children's predictions were correct.

- Do you think the fisherman will go back a second time to ask for a castle? Why or why not? (Inferential Comprehension—Predicting Outcomes)

Read the next four pages and check the children's predictions.

- Do you think the wife will be happy now? Why or not? (Inferential Comprehension—Predicting Outcomes)

Read the next six pages to find out if children's predictions were correct.

- How do you think the story will end?

Read to the end of the story to see whether children's predictions were correct. Discuss the ending.

- How do you feel about the fish, the fisherman, and the end of the story? (Appreciative Comprehension—Identification with Characters or Incidents)

New Story/Verse

Recall *The Magic Porridge Pot*. Discuss with the children what was magic about the pot and what happened in the story.

Tell the children that today they will hear another story about a magic pot but that this pot does not make porridge.

Show the children the cover of *Strega Nona* by Tomie dePaola. Pronounce the title and tell them that Strega Nona lives in Italy. (Show the location on a globe.) She has a magic pot that makes her favorite food. Have the children predict what her favorite food might be. Record the children's responses on a chart.

Read the first nine pages, stopping at "My chance has come!" Show the pictures, which provide a wonderful addition to the story line. Check children's predictions about Strega Nona's favorite food.

■ What do you think Big Anthony will do now that he is left alone with the magic pot?

Read the next six pages, stopping at "the pasta . . . was coming out of the door!" Check the children's predictions.

■ What will happen to the pasta?

Read to the end of the story to find out whether the predictions were correct.

Activity Time

Whole Group

Record what happened in the story on a chart. Before completing the chart, discuss the *beginning, middle,* and *end* with the children. Write down the children's responses as they retell the story in their own words. Post the completed chart.

Have children brainstorm their favorite tales. Put results on a graph and post it on the bulletin board.

Practice drama presentations for parents for Favorite Tales Day.

Teach the letter and sound of /m/ to first graders.

Individual/Small Group

• • • • • • • • • •

Reading/Library Center

Add any version you can find of *The Magic Porridge Pot* along with *Strega Nona* and the following books.

Alphabet Soup by K. Banks. Provide a bowl of alphabet pasta letters to go with this book. Invite the children to use the letters to spell the words from the story along with any other words they wish to spell.

Oodles o' Noodles by M. Roc and A. Stomann. This delightful book illustrates all kinds of noodles.

Drama Center

All story props and other materials used throughout this unit should be made available for small-group activities.

Art Center

Have the children create collages using a variety of pasta.

Have children paint pictures of their favorite tales. Encourage the children to write descriptions to go with their pictures.

Writing/Publishing Center

Have children add key words plus pictures to their personal alphabet books. Have them use alphabet pasta to make any words of their choice.

Provide the children with small blank books. Write "My Little Book of *M* Things" on the cover.

Have children work with a buddy to create a story grid stressing beginning, middle, and end for a new magic porridge pot story. Remind children to refer to the Strega Nona chart made during the whole-group time. Have children use completed charts to write their story on magic-pot-shaped paper (page 217). Children can illustrate their books.

Listening/Viewing Center

Prepare tapes of *Strega Nona* and *The Magic Porridge Pot* for the children.

The Magic Fish (Culmination)

DAY 15

Since the focus of *The Magic Fish* was on developing sight vocabulary, it is an excellent book to end this unit. A short shared-language period can be presented during the first part of your teaching time, followed by the Favorite Tales Day for parents.

Shared Language Time

Using a chart or overhead transparency, teach the following rhyme to the children.

• • • • • • • • • • • • • • • • • •

I Caught a Fish Alive

One, two, three, four, five,

Once I caught a fish alive.

Six, seven, eight, nine, ten,

Then I let him go again.

Why did I let him go?

Because he bit my finger so.

Which finger did he bite?

The little one upon the right.

• • • • • • • • • • • • • • • • • •

Have the children recall the title of *The Magic Fish* and some of the events of the story.

Bring out the Big Book version of the story and read it in its entirety, pointing to each word as it is read.

Recall that the fisherman had to call the fish to come to him. Write the fisherman's chant on a chart.

• • • • • • • • • • • • • • • • • • • •

The Fisherman's Chant

"Oh, fish in the sea,

Come listen to me.

My wife begs a wish

From the magic fish."

• •

Read the chant with the children several times to familiarize them with each word.

Once the children are able to chant the verse, go back to the Big Book and reread it several times. The children should be encouraged to read as much of the story as possible as you point to each word.

Explain that *The Magic Fish* is a version of a Grimm Brothers tale called *The Fisherman and His Wife*. Put some copies of this old tale in the library/reading center.

- *The Fisherman and His Wife* by K. Brandt
- *The Fisherman and His Wife* by R. Jarrell
- *The Fisherman and His Wife* by E. Shub

Tune In

Have children chant or sing all of their favorite verses or songs. Provide props for children to use to accompany each selection.

Activity Time

Whole Group

Have children present to their parents a number of the favorite tales introduced during this unit through dramatization with props or puppets.

Provide parents with pink lemonade and some appropriate snacks, such as cake, gingerbread people, vegetables, and dip.

Display the children's work and have them present it to their parents.

You may also wish to invite the principal and classroom buddies to Favorite Tales Day.

References

Addison-Wesley (1991). *Happily Ever After: The Elves and the Shoemaker.* Menlo Park, Calif.: Addison-Wesley.

Addison-Wesley (1991). *Happily Ever After: Little Red Riding Hood.* Menlo Park, Calif.: Addison-Wesley.

Addison-Wesley (1991). *Happily Ever After: Goldilocks and the Three Bears.* Menlo Park, Calif.: Addison-Wesley.

Addison-Wesley (1989). *The Three Little Pigs, Level A (Big Book plus Little Books).* Reading, Mass.: Addison-Wesley.

Addison-Wesley (1989). *The Gingerbread Man, Level A (Big Book plus Little Books).* Reading, Mass.: Addison-Wesley.

Addison-Wesley (1989). *The Farmer and the Beet, Level A (Big Book plus Little Books).* Reading, Mass.: Addison-Wesley.

Addison-Wesley (1989). *Goldilocks and the Three Bears, Level A (Big Book plus Little Books).* Reading, Mass.: Addison-Wesley.

Addison-Wesley.(1989). *The Little Red Hen, Level B (Big Book plus Little Books).* Reading, Mass: Addison-Wesley.

Banks, K. (1988). *Alphabet Soup.* New York: Alfred A. Knopf.

Barton, B. (1981). *Building a House.* New York: Greenwillow Books.

Bennett, J. (1988). *Teeny Tiny.* Oxford: Oxford Press.

Bernadette (1978). *The Magic Porridge Pot.* Boston, Mass.: Little, Brown.

Bishop, G. (1989). *The Three Little Pigs.* New York: Scholastic.

Blair, S. (1963). *The Three Billy-Goats Gruff.* New York: Holt, Rinehart and Winston.

Blegvad, E. (1980). *The Three Little Pigs.* New York: Atheneum.

Brandt, K. (1969). *The Fisherman and His Wife.* London: The Bodley Head.

Brett, J. (1987). *Goldilocks and the Three Bears.* New York: Dodd, Mead.

Brown, R. (1990). *The World That Jack Built.* Toronto: Stoddart.

Brown, M. (1957). *The Three Billy Goats Gruff.* New York: Harcourt Brace Jovanovich.

———— (1975). *Stone Soup.* New York: Charles Scribner's Sons.

Cauley, L.B. (1977). *Pease-Porridge-Hot.* New York: G.P. Putnam's Sons.

———— (1981). *Goldilocks and the Three Bears.* New York: G.P. Putnam's Sons.

Crawford, E.D. (1983). *Little Red Cap.* New York: William Morrow.

Daly, N. (1985). *Ben's Gingerbread Man.* New York: Viking Kestrel.

Darke, A. C. (1991). *Thumbelina by Hans Christian Andersen.* London: Methuen Children's Books.

Demarest, C.L. (1982). *Benedict Finds a Home.* New York: Lothrop, Lee & Shepard.

dePaola, T. (1975). *Strega Nona.* Englewood Cliffs, N.J.: Prentice Hall.

de Regniers, B. (1972). *Red Riding Hood.* New York: Macmillan.

Domanska, J. (1969). *The Turnip.* New York: Macmillan.

Ets, M. J. (1972). *Elephant in a Well.* New York: Viking.

Falconer, E. (1990). *The House That Jack Built.* London: Heinemann.

Fox, M. (1986). *Arabella: The Smallest Girl in the World.* Brisbane: Ashton Scholastic.

———— (1986). *Hattie and the Fox.* New York: The Trumpet Club.

Frasconi, A. (1958). *The House that Jack Built* (written in English and French). New York: Harcourt, Brace & World

Gagnon, C. and D. Labrasse (1988). *A New House.* Toronto: McClelland and Stewart.

Galdone, P. (1968). *Henny Penny.* New York: Clarion Books.

——— (1970). *The Three Little Pigs.* New York: Scholastic.

——— (1972). *The Three Bears.* New York: Clarion Books.

——— (1985). *The Little Red Hen.* New York: Clarion Books.

——— (1973). *The Three Billy Goats Gruff.* New York: Clarion Books.

——— (1974). *Little Red Riding Hood.* New York: McGraw-Hill.

——— (1983). *The Gingerbread Man.* New York: Clarion Books.

——— (1986). *The Teeny-Tiny Woman.* New York: Clarion Books.

Gavin, P. (1989). *The Three Little Pigs.* New York: Scholastic.

Gelman, R. G. (1989). *Stop Those Painters!* New York: Scholastic.

Gerstein, M. (1990). *Anytime Mapleson and the Hungry Bears.* New York: Harper & Row.

Ginsburg, M. (1983). *The Magic Stove.* New York: Coward-McCann.

Goldstein, B. S. (1989). *Bear in Mind: A Book of Bear Poems.* New York: Trumpet Club.

Gretz, S. (1969). *Teddy Bears 1 to 10.* Chicago, Ill.: Follett Publishing.

Gross, R.B. (1980). *A Book About Pandas.* New York: Scholastic Book Services.

Hague, M. (1984). *Alphabears, An ABC Book.* New York: Henry Holt.

Haviland, V. (1990). *The Talking Pot.* Boston, Mass.: Little, Brown.

Heilbroner, J. (1962). *This Is the House Where Jack Lives.* New York: Harper & Row.

Hoffman, M. (1986). *Animals in the Wild.* New York: Scholastic.

Hooks, W.H. (1989). *The Three Little Pigs and the Fox.* New York: MacMillan.

——— (1990). *The Gruff Brothers.* New York: A Bantam Little Rooster Book.

Hyman, T. S. (1983). *Little Red Riding Hood.* New York: Holiday House.

Inkpen, M. (1988). *If I Had a Pig.* London: MacMillan Children's Books.

Jarrell, R. (1980). *The Fisherman and His Wife.* New York: Farrar, Straus & Giroux.

Johnson, L. R. (1982). *The Teddy Bear ABC.* London: Green Tiger Press.

Kellogg, S. (1985). *Chicken Little.* New York: Mulberry Books.

Krauss, R. (1948). *Bears.* New York: Scholastic.

——— (1953, 1990). *A Very Special House.* New York: Harper & Row.

Lewish, B. (1981). *The House That Jack Built.* New York: Four Winds Press.

Littledale, F. (1967). *The Magic Fish.* New York: Scholastic.

Lobel, A. (1978). *The Pancake.* New York: Greenwillow Books.

Lubin, L. B. (1985). *This Little Pig.* New York: Lothrop, Lee & Shepard.

Mack, S. (1974). *Ten Bears in My Bed.* New York: Random House.

Marshall, J. (1987). *Red Riding Hood.* New York: Dial Books.

——— (1988). *Goldilocks and the Three Bears.* New York: Dial Books.

——— (1989). *The Three Little Pigs.* New York: Dial Books.

McClintock, B. (1979). *The Little Red Hen.* New York: Random House.

Martin, B. Jr. (1967). *Brown Bear, Brown Bear, What Do You See?* Salt Lake City, Utah: Henry Holt.

McDonnell, J. (1988). *Goldilocks and the Three Bears.* Marikato, Minn.: The Child's World.

——— (1988). *The Three Little Pigs.* Elgin, Ill.:The Child's World.

McGovern, A. (1986). *Stone Soup.* New York: Scholastic Book Services.

McGraw, S. (1989). *This Old New House.* Willowdale, Ontario: Firefly Books.

McQueen, L. (1985). *The Little Red Hen.* New York: Scholastic.

Minarik, E.H. (1989). *Percy and the Five Houses.* New York: Greenwillow Books.

Moncure, J. (1988). *Little Red Riding Hood.* Elgin, Ill.: The Child's World.

Morgan, P. (1990). *The Turnip.* New York: Philomel Books.

Morris, A. (1987). *Little Red Riding Hood's Picture Puzzle Book.* London: Orchard Books.

Narahashi, K. (1988). *Who Said Red?* New York: Scholastic.

Ormerod, J. (1985). *The Story of Chicken Licken.* London: Walker Books.

Parkinson, K. (1986). *The Enormous Turnip.* Niles, Ill.: Albert Whitman.

Pinkwater, D. M. (1977). *The Big Orange Splot.* New York: Scholastic.

Raffi. (1987). *The 2nd Raffi Songbook.* New York: Crown.

Randall, J. (1964). *The Gingerbread Rabbit.* New York: MacMillan.

Ravosa, C. (1972). *Story Songs.* Philadelphia, Penn.: Shawnee Press.

Reit, S. (1989). *The Rebus Bears.* New York: A Bantam Little Rooster Book.

Robart, R. and M. Kovalski (1987). *The Cake That Mack Ate.* Waltham, Mass.: Little, Brown.

Roc, M. and A. Stomann (1987). *Oodles o' Noodles.* Great Britain: Picture Knight.

Rockwell, A. (1977). *Albert B. Cub and Zebra, An Alphabet Storybook.* New York: Harper & Row.

Ross, J. (1988). *Stone Soup.* London: Beaver Books.

Sawicki, N. J. (1989). *The Little Red House.* New York: Lothrop, Lee & Shepard.

Serfozo, M. (1988). *Who Said Red?* New York: Scholastic.

Seuling, B. (1976). *The Teeny Tiny Woman.* New York: Viking Press.

Sharon, Lois, and Bram (1989). *The All New Elephant Jam.* New York: Crown

Sheehan, N. (1979). *The Little Red Hen.* New York: Dandelion Press.

Shub, E. (1978). *The Fisherman and His Wife.* New York: Greenwillow Books.

Southgate, V. (n.d.). *The Magic Porridge Pot.* Leicestershire, England: Ladybird Books.

————— (n.d.). *The Three Billy Goats Gruff.* Leicestershire, England: Ladybird Books.

Stevens, J. (1985). *The House That Jack Built.* New York: Holiday House.

————— (1987). *The Three Billy Goats Gruff.* New York: Harcourt Brace Jovanovich.

Stewig, J. W. (1991). *Stone Soup.* New York: Holiday House.

Turkle, B. (1976). *Deep in the Forest.* New York: E.P. Dutton.

Tyron, L. (1991). *Albert's Alphabet.* New York: Atheneum.

Underhill, L. (1987). *This Is the House That Jack Built.* New York: Henry Holt.

VanRynbach, I. (1988). *The Soup Stone.* New York: Greenwillow Books.

Watts, B. (1968). *Little Red Riding Hood.* London: Oxford University Press.

Westcott, N.B. (1991). The *House that Jack Built.* Boston, Mass.: Little, Brown.

Williams, L. (1969). *The Little Red Hen / La Pequeña Gallina Roja.* New York: Prentice Hall.

Ylla (1954). *Two Little Bears.* New York: Harper & Row.

Young, E. (1989). *Lon Po Po: A Red-Riding Hood Story from China.* New York: Philomel.

Zeddies, L., et al. *(1972). Joyfully Sing, Book One.* St. Louis: Concordia Music Education Series.

Zemach, M. (1983). *The Little Red Hen.* New York: Farrar, Straus & Giroux.

————— (1986). *The Three Wishes.* New York: Farrar, Straus & Giroux.

————— (1988). *The Three Little Pigs.* New York: Farrar, Straus & Giroux.

Zimmermann, H.W. (1989). *Henny Penny.* Toronto: Scholastic Canada.

Favorite Tales Blackline Masters

This Is the Way We Build Our House (verse)

The House That Jack Built picture cards

I Like Cake (verse)

The Cake That Mack Ate picture cards

Henny Penny picture cards

Accordion Book instructions

Little Red Hen sequence pictures

The Farmer and the Beet feltboard figures

Three Billy Goats Gruff stick puppet figures

Bear writing shape

Pig writing shape

Three Bears headband figures

Magic Pot story grid

This Is the Way We Build Our House

This is the way we build our
house, build our house,
build our house,
This is the way we build our
house
Early in the morning.

This is the way we dig a
hole . . .
This is the way we pour the
cement . . .
This is the way we saw the
wood . . .
This is the way we
hammer the boards . . .
This is the way we
shingle the roof . . .
This is the way we paint the
house . . .

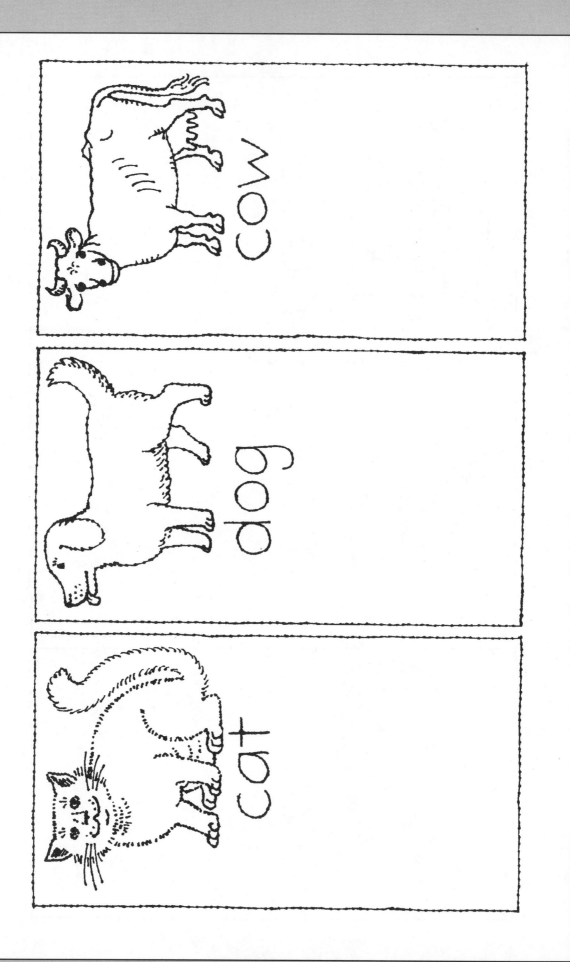

cow

dog

cat

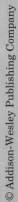

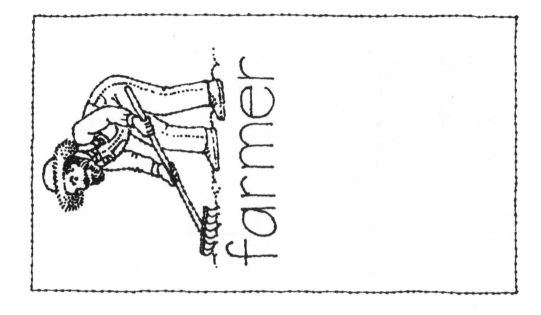

farmer

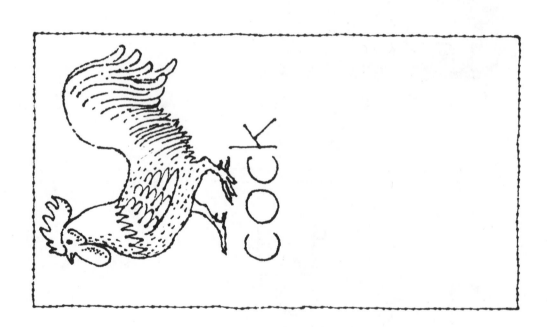

cock

I Like Cake

I like to eat cake.
   Soft sponge cake,
   Dark chocolate cake,
   Orange carrot cake,
And cake with red-colored
   sprinkles on top!

I like to eat cake.
   Very spicy cake,
   Tasty white cake,
   Fancy fruit cake,
And cake with sticky pink
   icing on top!

I like to eat cake.
   Big cakes,
   Little cakes,
   But, best of all . . .
I like birthday cake with
   bright candles on top!

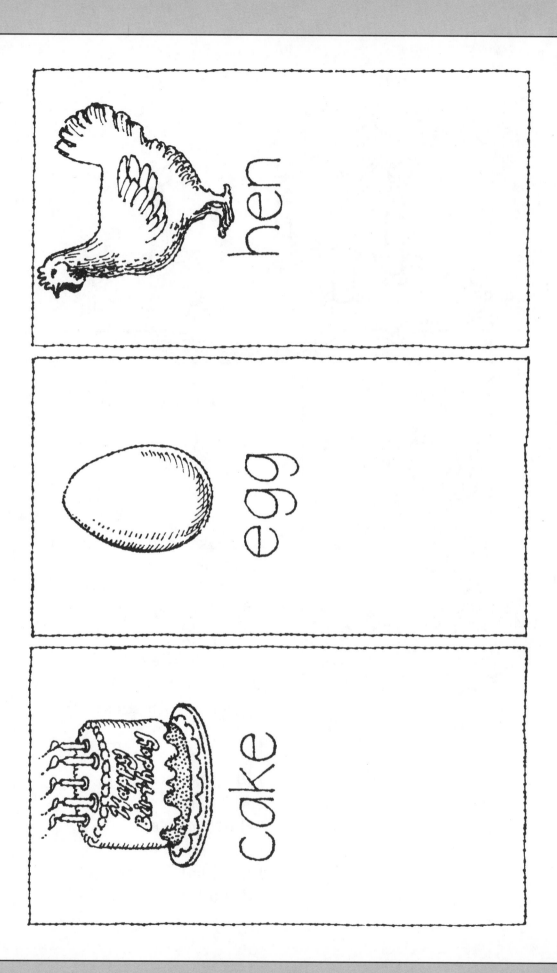

hen

egg

cake

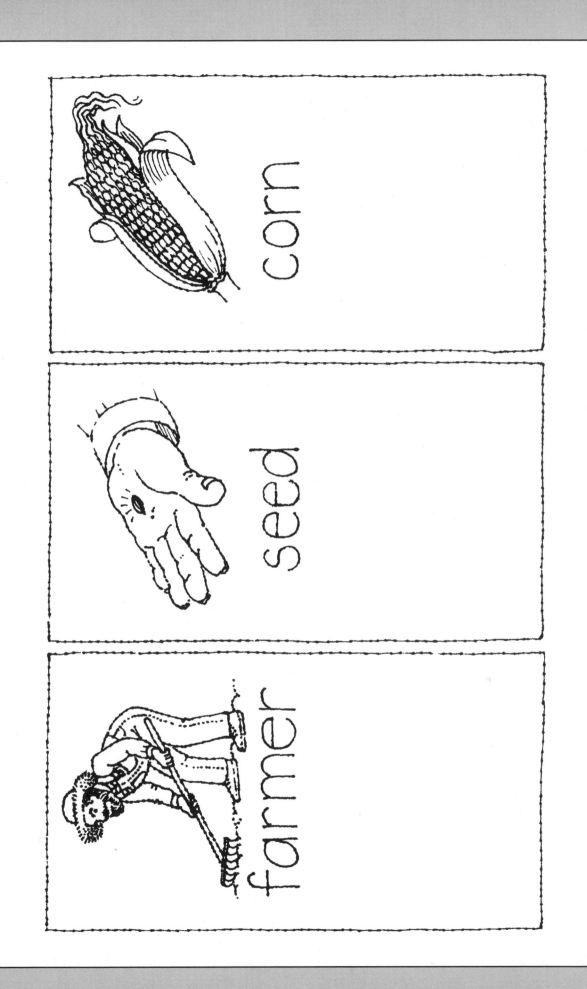

Ducky Lucky

Cocky Locky

Henny Penny

Foxy Loxy

Turkey Lurkey

Goosey Loosey

Accordion Cutout Shape Books

Directions:

1. Fold a long strip of paper into equal sections.

2. Refold the paper like accordion pleats.

3. Draw a simple shape on the top sheet.

4. Cut out the design, being careful not to cut through the side edge.

5. Illustrate and write the story on the sections.

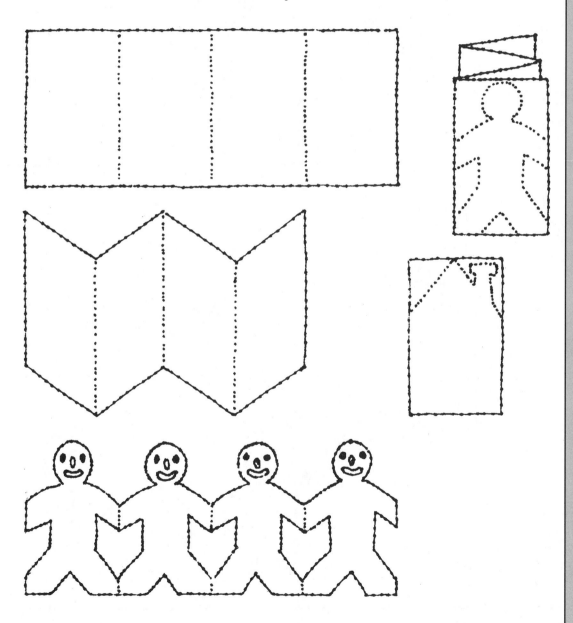

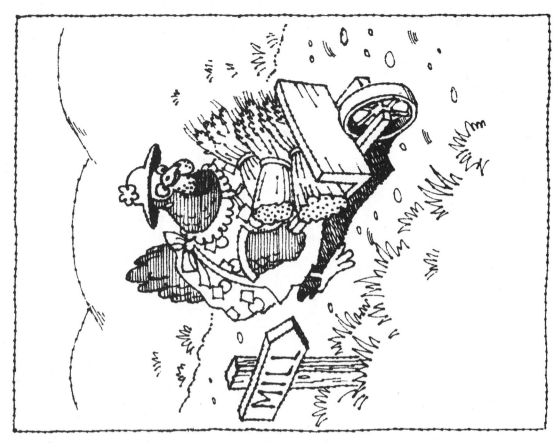

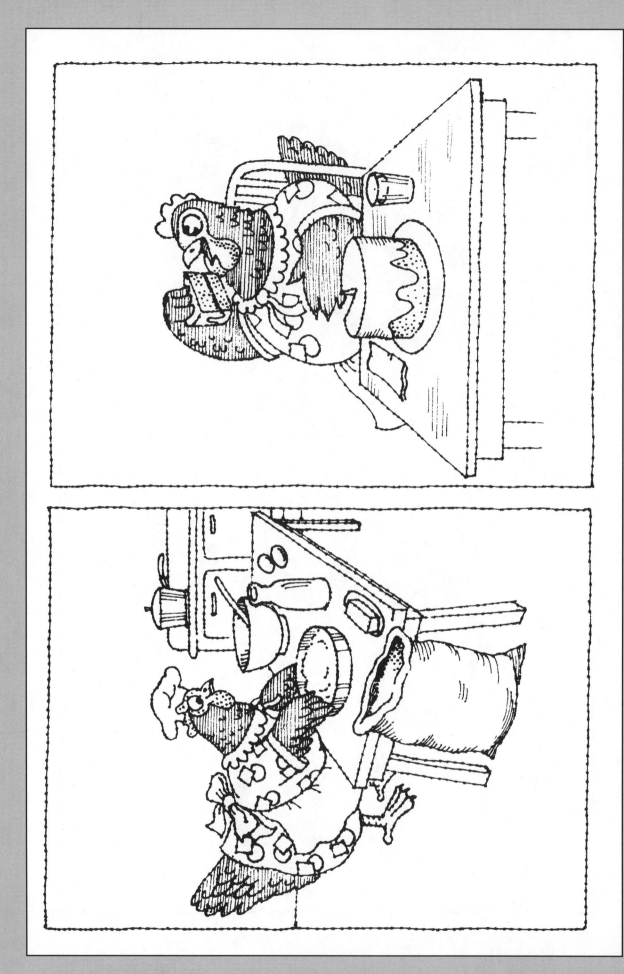

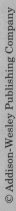

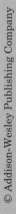

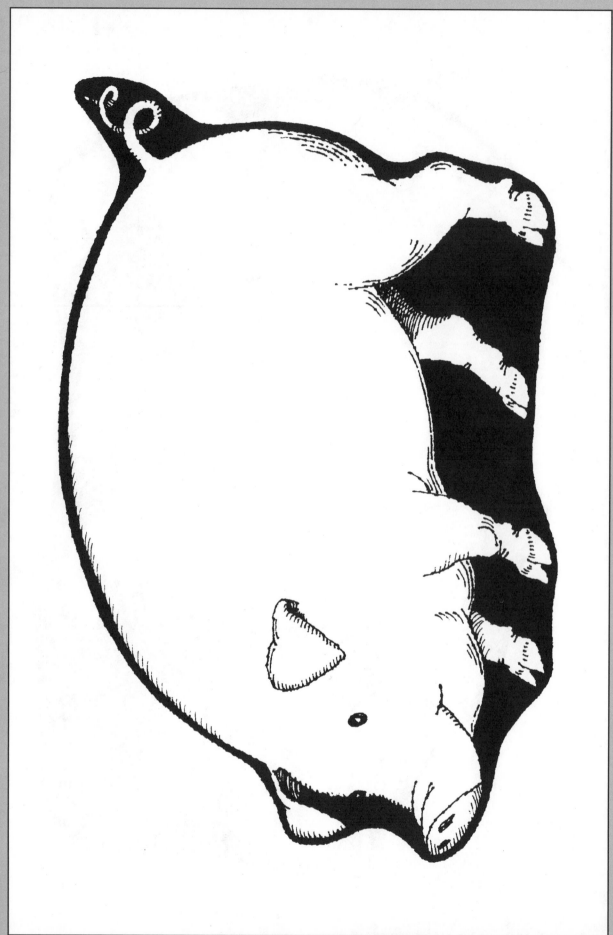

Favorite Tales / Day 11 / Pig

Favorite Tales / Day 10 / Goldilocks and the Three Bears

My Magic Pot

Friendships

Introduction to Friendships

As children enter the early primary years, they are moving beyond their egocentric stage of development to a period of continuing growth and awareness of their knowledge and understanding of themselves and others in their world. It is usually at this age that young children begin to develop best-friend relationships with one or two peers. Therefore, it is a good time to promote the growth of social behavior and responsibility (cooperation, sharing, treatment of peers). These are very important social competencies that must be developed, because the ability to form friendships is the basis of all human relationships. These skills foster a feeling of group belonging and provide opportunities to move from self toward others. The capacity to form friendships develops appropriate behavior patterns that are necessary in becoming members of the larger early primary class group.

During the early primary years, children begin to interact with different people in a variety of social contexts and develop an understanding of other children's points of view. In order to facilitate this continuing socialization, it is important to provide experiences that help children

- Develop friendships
- Participate in groups
- Be sensitive to the feelings of others
- Appreciate cultural identity and heritage
- Respect the classroom environment
- Share with others
- Develop a sense of cooperation and community
- Develop a better understanding of appropriate social behaviors
- Learn and practice social skills
- Compare themselves with others to help them develop a valid sense of identity.

Since five- and six-year-olds are just beginning to develop social responsibility and relationships with their peers, the unit on Friendships is especially relevant. The unit is meant to facilitate the transition from home to school as children move into their classroom community. Therefore, the thrust of this unit is on the development of peer interaction and social/cooperative skills, laying the foundation for the many social competencies required for success later in life.

The first week of the unit focuses on friends and friendships and why it is important to have friends. These concepts are developed in the unit through discussion, brainstorming activities, and carefully selected literature. In addition, the unit includes a variety of original poems, chants, and original songs adapted to the music of old favorites, because appropriate materials on this topic are very limited for younger children.

Since friendships may have undesirable effects (jealousy, antisocial behavior, and rejection of others) as well as desirable effects, the concept of friendship is expanded to include problems encountered between friends (arguments, friends moving away, etc.) during the second week of the unit. Opportunities for discussion are provided in order to help children clarify their developing concepts of what it is to be a friend (social responsibility). The focus during this second week is on peer friendships.

For the final week of the unit, the authors' concept of friendship is expanded to include significant others in the child's world (animals, parents, grandparents, siblings, other relatives, and community helpers). A special focus will also be placed on school buddies at this time. Community helpers are included because very young children need to understand that help is available in emergencies.

Although good literature will continue to be the main focus during the shared language period, special emphasis will also be placed on discussion, language experience, and independent writing. Both large- and small-group activities are provided. Since the books in this unit vary in difficulty, the code described in Section Two will be used again to identify easy ◇ and more difficult ◆◆ material. Whenever possible, more than one book has been recommended to help teachers select developmentally appropriate material.

Friendships Web

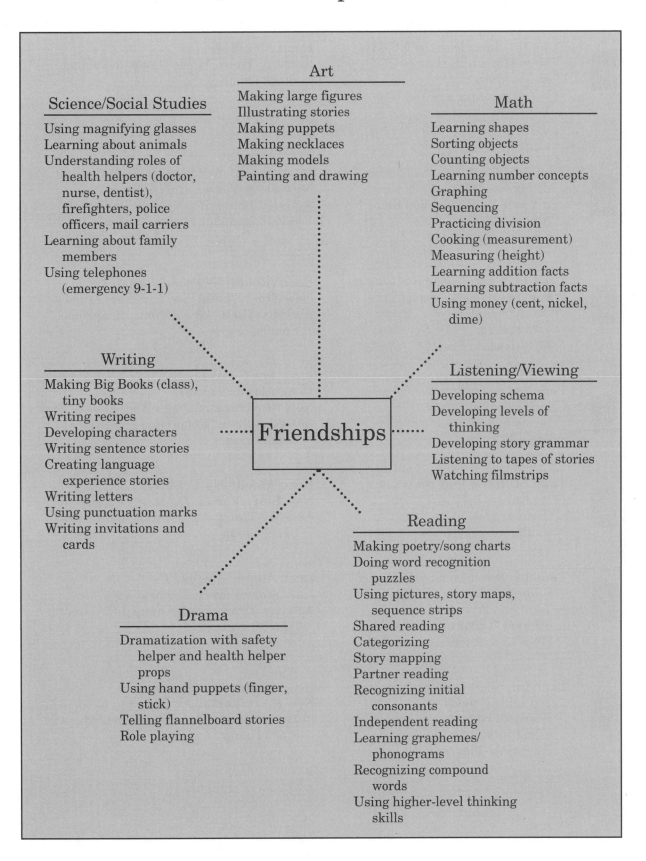

Art
Making large figures
Illustrating stories
Making puppets
Making necklaces
Making models
Painting and drawing

Science/Social Studies
Using magnifying glasses
Learning about animals
Understanding roles of
health helpers (doctor,
nurse, dentist),
firefighters, police
officers, mail carriers
Learning about family
members
Using telephones
(emergency 9-1-1)

Math
Learning shapes
Sorting objects
Counting objects
Learning number concepts
Graphing
Sequencing
Practicing division
Cooking (measurement)
Measuring (height)
Learning addition facts
Learning subtraction facts
Using money (cent, nickel,
dime)

Writing
Making Big Books (class),
tiny books
Writing recipes
Developing characters
Writing sentence stories
Creating language
experience stories
Writing letters
Using punctuation marks
Writing invitations and
cards

Friendships

Listening/Viewing
Developing schema
Developing levels of
thinking
Developing story grammar
Listening to tapes of stories
Watching filmstrips

Reading
Making poetry/song charts
Doing word recognition
puzzles
Using pictures, story maps,
sequence strips
Shared reading
Categorizing
Story mapping
Partner reading
Recognizing initial
consonants
Independent reading
Learning graphemes/
phonograms
Recognizing compound
words
Using higher-level thinking
skills

Drama
Dramatization with safety
helper and health helper
props
Using hand puppets (finger,
stick)
Telling flannelboard stories
Role playing

Outline for Friendships

1

Tune In: Select from the following:
    Mary Had a Little Lamb
    Jack and Jill
    If You're Happy and You Know It
    Two Little Dicky Birds
    Here We Go Round the Mulberry Bush

Read Aloud: *Jessica*
Activity Time: Whole Group, Individual/
    Small Group

DAY
2

Tune In: Select from the following:
    Be My Friend
    If You're Happy and You Know It
    Alphabet Song
    (Children's choice)

Read Aloud: *Will I Have a Friend?*
New Story/Verse: *Making Friends*
Activity Time: Whole Group, Individual/
    Small Group

DAY
3

Tune In: Select from the following:
    You Are My Best Friend
    Be My Friend
    Jack and Jill
    My Friends in School

Read Aloud: *My Friend John*
New Story/Verse: *See You Later, Alligator*
Activity Time: Whole Group, Individual/
    Small Group

DAY
4

Tune In: Select from the following:
    My Friends in School
    Be My Friend
    Great Friends

Read Aloud: *Together*
New Story/Verse: *That's What Friends Are For*
Activity Time: Whole Group, Individual/
    Small Group

DAY
5

Tune In: Select from the following:
    My Friends in School
    Great Friends
    (Children's choice)

Read Aloud: *We All Share*
New Story/Verse: *The Doorbell Rang*
Activity Time: Whole Group, Individual/
    Small Group

DAY
6

Tune In: Select from the following:
    Favorite Cakes
    Ten Little Friends
    (Children's choice)
    (Teacher's choice)

Read Aloud: *Alex and Roy*
New Story/Verse: *Best Friends*
Activity Time: Whole Group, Individual/
    Small Group

DAY
7

Tune In: Select from the following:
    Ten Little Friends
    Favorite Cookies
    (Children's choice)
    Over in the Playground

Read Aloud: *Let's Be Enemies*
New Story/Verse: *Angelina and Alice*
Activity Time: Whole Group, Individual/
    Small Group

DAY 8

Tune In: Select from the following:
Over in the Playground
Ten Little Friends
The More We Get Together
(Children's choice)

Read Aloud: *A Weekend with Wendell*
New Story/Verse: *Ira Sleeps Over*
Activity Time: Whole Group, Individual/
Small Group

DAY 9

Tune In: Select from the following:
The More We Get Together
Over in the Playground
Write, Write, Write a Letter
(Children's choice)

Read Aloud: *Chester's Way*
New Story/Verse: *We Are Best Friends*
Activity Time: Whole Group, Individual/
Small Group

DAY 10

Tune In: Select from the following:
Be My Friend
Write, Write, Write a Letter
You Are My Best Friend
(Children's choice)

Read Aloud: *Arnie and the New Kid*
New Story/Verse: *See You Tomorrow, Charles*
Activity Time: Whole Group, Individual/
Small Group

DAY 11

Tune In: Select from the following:
My Friends in School
Over in the Playground
The More We Get Together
(Children's choice)

Read Aloud: *Jamaica Tag-Along*
New Story/Verse: *Do Like Kyla* or *Hemi's Pet*
Activity Time: Whole Group, Individual/
Small Group

DAY 12

Tune In: Select from the following:
Write, Write, Write a Letter
This Old Man
Pet Friends

Read Aloud: Select from the following:
Amy Said
Shoes from Grandpa
New Story/Verse: *A Chair for My Mother*
Activity Time: Whole Group, Individual/
Small Group

DAY 13

Tune In: Select from the following:
Friends
Be My Friend
(Children's choice)
Five Good Police Officers

Read Aloud: *Something Special for Me*
New Story/Verse: *The Fire Station*
Activity Time: Whole Group, Individual/
Small Group

DAY 14

Tune In: Select from the following:
Write, Write, Write a Letter
Five Good Police Officers
Firefighters
(Children's choice)

Read Aloud: *My Dentist*
New Story/Verse: *My Doctor*
Activity Time: Whole Group, Individual/
Small Group

DAY 15

Culmination: Friendship Day
Tune In: Whole-group chanting and
singing favorite verses and songs
that will be presented to parents
and friends

Activity Time: Whole Group
Puppet show
Presentations to parents of favorite songs
and verses
Display of students' projects
Party time

Introduction

DAY 1

Tune In

Select from the following for unison chanting or singing.

Mary Had a Little Lamb

Jack and Jill

If You're Happy and You Know It

Two Little Dicky Birds

Here We Go Round the Mulberry Bush

Read Aloud

Read *Jessica* by K. Henkes.

Jessica shows the transition from the home environment to the classroom environment where friendships are easily formed through play. The main character in the story is an only child, a situation that has become more common in recent years. The illustrations depict children from diverse cultures, though the main character's ethnic origin is not clearly identified. The story focuses on the need for children to develop real friends rather than make-believe friends.

Prior to reading the story, clarify the concept of an imaginary friend. Ask whether children think a best friend can be imaginary and encourage them to give reasons for their answers.

Read the entire story, making sure that the children see the accompanying pictures. Point out that in many of the pictures, Ruthie, the main character, makes comments to Jessica and about Jessica, her imaginary friend. Make a tape of the story during the reading for use in the listening center.

After reading the story, discuss the following topics.

- Compare Ruthie's home friend, Jessica, to her new friend. (Literal/Comprehension—Compare/Contrast)

- Prepare a chart with the words of the last page of the story and the question, "Why was her new kindergarten friend even better?"

Brainstorm answers to this question. Use the illustrations and children's own ideas to generate more ideas. (Literal and Inferential Comprehension—Details)

● ● ● ● ● ● ● ● ● ● ● ● ● ● ● ● ● ●

Ruthie Simms didn't have a dog.

She didn't have a cat,

or a brother,

or a sister,

But Jessica was even better.

● ● ● ● ● ● ● ● ● ● ● ● ● ● ● ● ● ●

Why was her new kindergarten friend even better?

Possible reasons:

> They could go places together.
>
> They could share their dolls.
>
> They could sing songs together.
>
> They could play catch.
>
> They could dance together.
>
> They could read to each other.

After recording the responses, point out that Jessica and Ruthie have become best friends. Then brainstorm the things the children like to do with their best friends. Use the children's names in recording responses, for example:

> Anthony likes to play catch with his best friend.
>
> Maria likes to sing with her best friend.

Try to get responses from all the children in the class.

Activity Time

Whole Group

Brainstorm/categorize vocabulary related to friends.
> Read *That's What a Friend Is* by P. K. Hallinan.
> Write the word *friends* on the chalkboard in large capital letters.
> Have children brainstorm activity words that relate to friends.
> Have the group categorize the words that go together, such as words that describe friends, things you do with a friend, and so on.
> Teach the following song, using an overhead transparency or chart.

• •

Be My Friend

(tune: London Bridge is Falling Down)

_____, _____, be our friend,

Be our friend, be our friend,

_____, _____, be our friend

So we can _____ together.

Girls and boys, I'll be your friend,

Be your friend, be your friend,

Girls and boys, I'll be your friend

So we can play together.

• •

Use children's names and activities friends can do together in the appropriate blanks. The entire group may sing verse one, the child named in verse one may sing verse two, the child named in verse two may sing verse three, and so on.

Individual/Small Group

• • • • • • • • • •

Art Center
Children paint pictures of their favorite activity to do with their best friends. Help them write captions. Display the pictures for all to enjoy.

• • • • • • • • • •

Writing/Publishing Center
Provide small blank books with "What I Like to Do with My Best Friend" written on the covers.

Encourage children to write captions for each picture in their books.

• • • • • • • • • •

Listening/Viewing Center
Put the tape of _Jessica_ and a copy of the book in the center.

• • • • • • • • • •

Reading/Library Center
Add the following books:

> _The Friend_ by J. Burningham ◇
>
> _That's What a Friend Is_ by P. K. Hallinan
>
> _Hold My Hand_ by C. Zolotow

Related Reading

The Perfect Friend by J. Gantos and N. Rubel

Old Friends, New Friends by M. Thurman

 Reminder: See pages 304–305 for several figures of children that can be used to develop material for this unit.

Making Friends

Tune In

Select from the following for unison chanting or singing.

Be My Friend (tune: London Bridge Is Falling Down)

If You're Happy and You Know It

Alphabet Song

(Children's choice)

Read Aloud

Read *Will I Have A Friend?* by M. Cohen.

Recall the story about Jessica and remind the children that in that story Jessica found a new friend. In *Will I Have A Friend?* they will meet a character named Jim who is also going to school for the very first time. On the way to school, he asks his father a special question. Show the children the cover of the book and explain that the title is the special question Jim asked. Ask the children if they can figure out the question and the title.

Then ask the children how many of them found a new friend on their first day of school. Have some of the children recount their experiences or tell how they met their new friends. Before beginning the story, ask the following questions, recording responses on the chalkboard.

■ Do you think that Jim will meet a new friend?

■ If you were in Jim's place, what might you do to make a new friend?

Read the entire story, making certain that the children get a good look at the accompanying pictures. Tape the reading for use in the listening center. After reading the story, go back and check the children's responses to the questions. Discuss how Jim finally found a friend.

New Story/Verse

Making Friends by F. Rogers was specifically chosen to expand the children's concept of friends. The following key concepts are stressed.

- A friend may be a boy or a girl.
- A friend may be older or younger.
- A friend may be from your neighborhood or school.
- You may have more than one friend.
- Friends may or may not like to do the same things.
- Friends may want to do the same things in different ways.
- Friends sometimes get angry at each other.

Remind the children that Jim had trouble making a friend quickly and ask them why. Point out to the children that it is sometimes difficult to make friends.

Tell the children that in the book you are going to read to them, they will find out more information about making friends. Show the children a picture of the author, Mr. Rogers, on the back cover. Ask if they recognize him from television.

Read the book, stopping at appropriate parts for discussion. The real-life illustrations provide excellent opportunities to expand the concept of what friendships are about. Many of the concepts introduced by Mr. Rogers will be expanded later on in the unit.

Activity Time

Whole Group

Teach the following song, using an overhead transparency or chart.

• •

You Are My Best Friend

(tune: You Are My Sunshine)

You are my best friend,

My really best friend.

You make me happy

Every day.

You share your great snacks.

You share your best toys.

So please don't take my best friend away!

• •

Have children sit in a circle. Randomly distribute two sets of cards numbered from 1 to _____ (half of your class size). Have the children match their numbers to form pairs. Together, have them decide on a favorite activity good friends like to do. Then have the pairs take turns acting out their favorite activity, letting the others try to guess what the activity is.

Ask, "How do you make a friend?" Discuss responses and use them to develop a chart.

Have pairs of children dictate stories about friends. Staple the stories together and place them the reading/library center for everyone to read.

Individual/Small Group

Writing/Publishing Center

Using heart-shaped writing paper with story starters, have children complete open story frames. Story starters that could be used are given below.

A friend would _____.

Once upon a time, there were two friends _____.

My friend is always _____.

My friend is happy because _____.

My friend likes _____.

Children continue writing in their small books, *What I Like to Do with My Best Friend.*

Begin a class diary. Invite children to add a page to the class diary. Their writing should focus on acts of friendship that happen each day.

 Reading/Library Center

Add the following books:

Class Big Book *How Do You Make A Friend?*

Do You Want to Be My Friend? by E. Carle ◇

Will I Have a Friend? by M. Cohen

Three Friends by R. Krauss

One Nose, Two Hands by J. Graeme and M. Henderson

Making Friends by F. Rogers

Making Friends by E. Schick. This is a wordless book.

 Art Center

Have children make stick puppets of themselves using construction paper and ice cream sticks. These can be used in the drama center.

Have the pairs that worked together in the whole-group activity make a cooperative picture of their favorite friend activity and write a story to go with it.

 Listening/Viewing Center

Put the tape of *Will I Have a Friend?* and a copy of the book in the center.

Related Reading

Friends by H. Heine

Hug Me by P. Stren

See You Later, Alligator

Tune In

Select from the following for unison chanting or singing.

You Are My Best Friend

Be My Friend

Jack and Jill

Then introduce the children to the song, "My Friends in School" using a chart or overhead transparency. Point to the words as you sing the song several times to reinforce the key vocabulary words.

● ●

My Friends in School

(tune: The Wheels on the Bus)

My friends in school share their toys,

Share their toys,

Share their toys,

My friends in school share their toys,

All through the day.

My friends in the park push my swing,

Push my swing,

Push my swing,

My friends in the park push my swing,

All through the day.

My friends on the beach play in the sand,

Play in the sand,

Play in the sand,

My friends on the beach play in the sand,

All through the day.

● ●

Read Aloud

Read *My Friend John* by C. Zolotow.

Recall the story about making friends and remind children of some of the things they learned about good friends. Record the children's responses on chart paper before introducing the new story. Show the children the cover and ask them to read the title of the book. Read the story in its entirety, showing the pictures. You may wish to tape the reading for use in the listening center. After reading the story, ask, "Why do you think the little boy and John were good friends?"

New Story/Verse

Before reading the new story, *See You Later, Alligator* by N. M. Charles and Y. Cathcart, make sure that the children understand the following concepts:

- The tropics are very hot places.
- Different kinds of plants and animals live in the tropics.

These concepts can be developed by showing the children the front and back cover of the Big Book. If the children have difficulty identifying the key concepts illustrated, explain that the setting of the story is a very hot tropical place where alligators and crocodiles live.

Read the title of the story and write it on the board.

Begin reading the first two pages of the story, showing the pictures to the children. Ask them what they think Allie Alligator and Corky Crocodile like to do together. The children's responses throughout the discussion could be recorded as follows:

See You Later, Alligator

Our Guesses	What Happened

To expand further on the key concepts and help children make predictions, use the book's delightful pictures to discuss the setting and characters in the story.

Continue reading to page 9. Check children's predictions and write what else happened on the chart.

- What do you think Corky will do because his friend Allie has new shoes? (Inferential Comprehension—Predicting Outcomes)

Continue reading to page 13. Check children's predictions.

- What do you think Allie will do now? (Inferential Comprehension—Predicting Outcomes)

Continue reading to page 15. Check children's predictions.

- What do you think Corky will do now? (Inferential Comprehension—Predicting Outcomes)

Continue reading to page 17. Check children's predictions.

- What do you think Allie will do now? (Inferential Comprehension—Predicting Outcomes)

Continue reading to page 19. Check children's predictions.

- What do you think Corky will do now? (Inferential Comprehension—Predicting outcomes)

Continue reading to page 21. Check children's predictions.

- How do you think the story will end? (Inferential Comprehension—Cause and Effect)

Read to the end of the story. Check children's predictions.

- Discuss what happened in the story (two friends jealously began competing and trying to outdo each other). Through discussion, develop the concept that best friends do not act in this manner.

Activity Time

Whole Group

Have a display of books and pictures of crocodiles, alligators, and tropical regions. Show the children some pictures of the animals in their natural environment.

Point out to the children that both crocodiles and alligators are lizard-like animals belonging to the reptile family and that they live in tropical places. Also tell children that crocodiles can grow to be about 18 feet long, and alligators grow to be about 16 feet long. Then point out to the children that alligators live in the southern United States (Florida).

Upon completing the discussion, inform the children that the books you are showing will be in the science center if they want to find out more about crocodiles and alligators.

Show sentence strips on which these sentences have been written:

Corky: "See you later, Alligator."

Allie: "In a while, Crocodile."

Ask the children if they can remember what Corky and Allie said to each other when they went away. Explain that these remarks are written on the sentence strips. Point out to the children the meaning of quotation marks. Help them read the sentence strips.

Let pairs of children take turns reading the sentence strips. Finally, have the whole class read the sentence strips in unison.

Reread the story, inviting the children to chant any of the parts of the story they are able to read. Point to each word as both you and the children chant the story.

Chant the story with the children a second time.

Individual/Small Group

Reading/Library Center
Add the following book:

> *See You Later, Alligator* by N. M. Charles and Y. Cathcart (Big Book version)

Listening/Viewing Center
Place tapes of the following two books in the center.

> *See You Later, Alligator* by N. M. Charles and Y. Cathcart.

> *My Friend John* by C. Zolotow.

Science Center
Include books and pictures about alligators, crocodiles, and the tropics. Suggested books:

> *The Crocodile* by B. Shapiro

> *Crocodiles and Alligators* by F. Watts

Provide small blank books so that children can make books about any topic related to the display. Possible titles include "My Book of Reptiles," "All About Alligators," and "All About Crocodiles."

• • • • • • • • • •

Writing/Publishing Center

Provide children with green paper shaped like an alligator on which they can write other adventures about Allie and Corky.

Remind children to add to the class diary.

• • • • • • • • • •

Art Center

Cut two large strips of mural paper, 18 feet long for Corky and 16 feet long for Allie. Have small groups of children make large pictures of Corky and Allie and paint them. Display the mural in the Science Center, along with the books the children have written.

Have the children make models of alligators and crocodiles out of modeling clay or another material.

• • • • • • • • • •

Drama Center

Place stick puppets of Allie and Corky in the center so that children can make up short adventures about the characters. (See page 307.)

Related Reading

Rockaby Crocodile by J. Ariego and A. Dewey. This is a Filipino tale.

Frog and Toad Are Friends by A. Lobel. This book introduces the children to two more animals that are best friends. It also introduces children to a series written in simple vocabulary.

That's What Friends Are For

DAY 4

Tune In

Select from the following for unison chanting or singing.

My Friends in School (tune: The Wheels on the Bus)

Be My Friend (tune: London Bridge Is Falling Down)

Introduce the children to the poem, "Great Friends," using a chart or overhead transparency. First, read the poem to the children, pointing to each word as it is read. Then chant the verse several times, with the children joining in whenever they can. You might want to make individual copies that the children can take home or read with their friends during activity time.

● ● ● ● ● ● ● ● ● ● ● ● ● ● ●

Great Friends

I think my friends
Are really great!

They may be big,
They may be small,
They can be any
Size at all.

They like to share
All kinds of toys,
That can be played
By little girls or boys.

They like to laugh,
They like to fight,
They like to visit
And stay the night.

I think my friends

Are really great!

• • • • • • • • • • • • • • •

Read Aloud

Read *Together* by E. G. Lyon

Together emphasizes how two friends working together can do almost anything. It also offers numerous chanting opportunities. Read the entire book, showing the picture as each line is read. After reading the book, recall with the children some of the things the girls did together. Ask the children to suggest other things that can be done together.

New Story/Verse

If friends work together and cooperate, they can accomplish something worthwhile, as children will see when they read *That's What Friends Are For.* It takes place in a hot, tropical country and deals with animals who are friends, making it a good choice to follow *See You Later, Alligator.*

Show the children the cover of *That's What Friends Are For,* by F. P. Heide and S. W. Van Clief, and ask one of them to read the title. Tell them that three animals are pictured on the cover and ask if they can find them (elephant, monkey, bird).

Read the first page of the story. Ask the children the following questions:

■ Who is the main character in the story? (Literal Comprehension—Details)

■ What is Theodore's problem? (Literal Comprehension—Main Idea)

■ What do you think Theodore will do? (Inferential Comprehension—Predicting Outcomes)

Read the next page of the story to find out if the children's predictions were correct.

■ Check the previous predictions.

■ Discuss the meaning of the word *advice*. Be sure the children understand that people can give bad advice as well as good advice.

■ Using an Advice Chart to record information, ask the children the name of Theodore's friend (bird). After printing the word *bird* on the chart, ask the children what advice it gave (Literal Comprehension—Details). Record the advice on the chart, then ask the children whether the bird's advice was good or bad.

Advice Given to Theodore by His Friends

Friend	Advice Given	Kind of Advice
bird	"I would fly."	bad
daddy longlegs	"I would use my seven other legs to walk."	bad
monkey	"I would swing by my tail."	bad
crab	"I would grow another leg."	bad
lion	"I would roar for help."	bad
opossum	"Bring Theodore's cousin to him."	good

Continue reading the story in episodes, stopping to record each new animal and the advice it gives as it is introduced, following the procedure used for the bird.

After completing the Advice Chart, discuss with the children why the opossum's advice was the best.

Finally, using an overhead transparency or pocket chart, read the short verse that ends the story. Remind the children that this verse gives them some good advice on how to treat friends.

● ●

To give advice is very nice,

But friends can do much more.

Friends should always help a friend.

That's what friends are for!

● ●

Activity Time

Whole Group

Ask the children the title of the story they just heard (*That's What Friends Are For*).

■ Ask the children to recall where the story took place (setting).

■ Recall who was in the story (characters). As each character is recalled, show the children the animal's picture with its name written underneath. Number each card:

Theodore

1. bird   2. daddylonglegs   3. monkey

4. crab   5. lion   6. opossum

Have children repeat the names with you as you display the pictures.

Have the children recall what happened to Theodore at the beginning of the story. Point out that he had a problem because he couldn't walk and he wanted to visit his cousin.

Using the numbered character cards, have the children recall in sequence the advice each friend gave.

Once the sequence has been reviewed, have children retell the story using the character cards and advice chart.

Individual/Small Group

Reading/Library Center

Add the following books:

That's What Friends Are For by F. P. Heide and S. W. Van Clief

Frog and Toad by A. Lobel. You may also want to add other books from the Frog and Toad Series.

Together by G. E. Lyon

Writing/Publishing Center

Remind the children to add a page to *Our Class Diary* if they have helped a friend or have been helped by a friend either at school or at home (refer to Day Two).

Provide children with elephant-shaped paper on which they can write about Theodore and his friends.

Drama Center

Let the children volunteer to take the parts of the characters from *That's What Friends Are For*. The children can hold the picture cards or face masks in front of them to remind the audience which character they are portraying.

Provide feltboard figures from *That's What Friends Are For*. Have the children use the figures to retell the story.

Art Center

Have the children paint their favorite part of *That's What Friends Are For*. Captions could be added if desired.

Related Reading

Hello, Amigos! by T. Brown

Rainy Day Friends by R. Fahlman, J. Graeme, and M. Henderson

The Doorbell Rang

DAY 5

Tune In

Select from the following for unison chanting or singing.

My Friends in School

Great Friends

(Children's choice)

Read Aloud

Read *We All Share* by D. Corey.

Recall that in the book *Making Friends,* Mister Rogers talked about friends sharing with each other. Brainstorm with the children what things they share with their friends. Tell the children that the book you are going to read today is about how good friends share. Read the story in its entirety, showing the pictures. After completing the story, discuss the kinds of sharing described in the story.

New Story/Verse

Before reading *The Doorbell Rang,* by P. Hutchins, tell the children that they are going to hear another story about good friends sharing. Show the cover of the book and read the title of the story. Have the children look carefully at the picture on the cover. This picture depicts people of many cultures. Begin reading the first three pages of the story, ending with "the doorbell rang." Ask the following questions:

- Who is in the story? (Literal Comprehension—Details)
- Where does the story take place? (Literal Comprehension—Details)
- How many cookies did Ma make? (Inferential Comprehension—Supporting Details)
- Who do you think might be at the door? (Inferential Comprehension—Predicting Outcomes)

Continue reading the next four pages, ending with "the doorbell rang."

- Who else is in the story? (Literal Comprehension—Details)

- What happened when the two friends came over? (Literal Comprehension—Cause and Effect. Introduce the word and concept of *less* in number.)

- Who do you think might be at the door? (Inferential Comprehension—Predicting outcomes)

Continue reading the story, asking "Who do you think might be at the door?" each time the doorbell rings. Stop when each child has just one cookie left.

Have the children predict what will happen next. Then read to the end of the story to enjoy the surprise ending.

You may wish to treat the class to a tray of cookies so that they, too, will enjoy a special surprise.

 Be sure to obtain permission before allowing children to eat foods brought into the classroom in case of food allergies or other restrictions.

Activity Time

Whole Group

Have children brainstorm the names of their favorite cookies. Record their ideas on an overhead transparency or on the chalkboard).

When the list is complete, have children vote for their favorite kind of cookie. Tally the votes. Graph the results.

Tell children that you have a new verse for them. Then, using an overhead transparency or chart, teach the new verse, "Favorite Cookies."

● ●

Favorite Cookies

We like cookies—

Chocolate chip cookies,

Lemon drop cookies,

Peanut butter cookies,

And cookies with cherries on top.

We like cookies—

Oatmeal cookies,

Ginger cookies,

Fancy cookies,

And cookies with nuts on top.

We like cookies—

Jamaican crunchies,

Italian cookies,

Curry cookies,

But, best of all,

We like _____!

(Fill in the name of the cookie children
voted for in the Favorite Cookie poll.)

• •

Review the sound /el/.

Teach the letter and sound of /d/ to first graders.

Individual/Small Group

• • • • • • • • • •

Writing/Publishing Center

Provide the children with small blank books. On the covers, print "My
Little Book of *D* Things." Children should be encouraged to write words
along with the pictures.

Prepare a class book with the title "We All Share." Have children add
pages using the sentence starter "We share _____." The completed
book can then be placed in the reading/library center.

• • • • • • • • • •

Math Center

Have children divide feltboard cookies into equal groups using group pictures (two friends, three friends, and so on).

Ask children to sort collections of cookie pictures into groups. The cookies
could vary in size, color, and type, depending on students' ability. For
some classes, two elements would be sufficient for classifying.

• • • • • • • • • •

Reading/Library Center

Add the following books:

We All Share by D. Corey

Rainy Day Friends by R. Fahlman, J. Graeme, and M. Henderson

The Adventures of Charlotte and Henry by B. Graham ◆◆

The Doorbell Rang by P. Hutchins ◆◆

A Friend Like You by R. Paré

• • • • • • • • • •

Art Center

Have children paint pictures of how they share with their friends.

Related Reading

This is another book in the friend series by Lobel introduced earlier in the unit. Read aloud either the first or second story.

Frog and Toad Together by A. Lobel.

 Reminder: You will need a recipe and the ingredients to make the children's favorite cookies on Day Six.

Best Friends

DAY 6

Tune In

Select from the following for unison chanting or singing.

Favorite Cookies

(Children's choice)

(Teacher's choice)

Then introduce and teach the verse, "Ten Little Friends," using a chart or overhead transparency.

● ●

Ten Little Friends

One little, two little, three little friends,
Four little, five little, six little friends,
Seven little, eight little, nine little friends,
Ten little friends together.

Ten little, nine little, eight little friends,
Seven little, six little, five little friends,
Four little, three little, two little friends,
One little friend all alone.

● ●

This verse lends itself to dramatization, which provides the children with a concrete experience in adding one to a group until they get to ten and then subtracting one from a group until there is only one left. This verse can be used to reinforce the concept of subtraction for first graders.

Read Aloud

Read *Alex and Roy* by M. Dickinson.

Alex and Roy introduces problems that may arise in establishing and keeping good friends.

- The cover illustrates the idea that people might not like everyone they meet.
- It shows how a friendship is developed between two children from different cultures.
- It introduces the concept of anger in relationships.

Show the children the cover and read the title of the book. Ask them if they think Alex and Roy are good friends. Why? Then read the story in its entirety. After completing the story, ask the children if they think Alex and Roy are good friends now and why.

New Story/Verse

Recall with the children the names of the two storybook friends they read about in *Will I Have A Friend?* (Jim and Paul). Show the class the book as a reminder. Recall some of the activities Jim and Paul did together as you show the children pictures from the book.

Show the children the cover of *Best Friends,* which was also written by Miriam Cohen and illustrated by Lillian Hoban. Tell the class that this is another story about Jim and Paul, who became friends on the first day of school. This second story about Jim and Paul takes place much later in the school year, and Jim is beginning to think that Paul is his best friend. Note that in this story, the friendship is nearly broken up because of a misunderstanding.

Read the first eight pages, stopping at "Come on, Paul. Let's build blocks." Ask the children the following questions.

- How does Jim feel about his friend, Paul, whom he thought might be his best friend? (Inferential Comprehension—Predicting Outcomes)
- Why do you think Jim feels this way? (Literal Comprehension—Sequence of Events)
- What do you think Jim will do now? (Inferential Comprehension—Predicting Outcomes)

Continue reading the next five pages, stopping at "'Who's your best friend, Jim?' she asked."

Check the children's earlier predictions.

- How do you think Jim will answer the question, "Who's your best friend, Jim?" (Inferential Comprehension—Sequence)

Continue reading the next five pages, stopping at "Everybody is your best friend except me!"

Check the children's early inference of sequence responses.

■ Why do you think Jim and Paul are having problems with their friendship? (Inferential Comprehension—Main Idea)

To answer this question, review the incidents that have happened thus far in the story.

■ How would you feel if you were Jim? (Appreciation—Identification with Characters)

■ If you were Jim, how would you respond to Paul's outburst: "So! Everybody is your best friend except me!" (Inferential Comprehension—Predicting Outcomes)

Continue reading the next six pages, stopping at "The baby chicks will die."

Check the children's earlier predictions.

■ What do you think will happen now? (Inferential Comprehension— Predicting Outcomes. This provides children with the opportunity to solve a problem that could happen to them.)

Read to the end of the story.

Check the children's predictions. Show the children the cover of the book showing Jim and Paul as best friends.

■ How do you feel about the story ending? (Appreciative Comprehension—Emotional Response to Content)

Activity Time

Whole Group

Introduce the use of the period.

Explain that sentences usually end with a punctuation mark and that writers use several kinds of punctuation marks. Then tell students that most of the sentences they see in books use a period. Select sentences from the story as examples to write on sentence strips.

Jim was waiting outside of school.

Paul was his best friend.

Paul was late for school.

Use echo reading to help children with the sentences. Point out that the period (punctuation mark) tells them that this is the end of the sentence, so they should stop before reading the next sentence. You may also reinforce that sentences begin with a capital letter.

Introduce the use of the exclamation mark. ◆◆

Explain that sometimes writers use a punctuation mark besides a period. Select from the story sentences ending in exclamation points as examples to write on sentence strips.

Use echo reading to help children with the sentences. Model the appropriate tone of voice to show excitement as each sentence is being read.

Ask what kind of a mark children see at the end of the sentences. Have several children take turns writing exclamation marks on the chalkboard. Explain that this punctuation is called an exclamation mark, and explain why this mark may be used instead of a period.

Practice reading the sentences several times, helping the children use the right tone of voice for the sentences.

Introduce the use of quotation marks. ◆◆ Make sentence strips that include dialogue if necessary. Ask children if they notice anything special about the sentences. Elicit that some of the sentence strips include words that Paul or Jim speak.

Point out the quotation marks. You may want to highlight them in red. Ask two of the children to take the roles of Paul and Jim in order to further internalize that quotation marks signal the beginning and end of spoken words.

As preparation for cooking during activity time, write the children's favorite cookie recipe on a chart. Go over the steps. Place the chart in the cooking area for easy reference.

Individual/Small Group

• • • • • • • • •

Cooking Center

You may wish to invite several parents to help make cookies with small groups.

Be sure to obtain permission before allowing children to eat foods prepared in the classroom in case of food allergies or other restrictions.

• • • • • • • • •

Reading/Library Center

Prepare a number of sentence strips, using actual sentences from *Best Friends*. Include the sentences used in the whole-group activity. Make certain that the punctuation marks have been deleted from the sentences. Put the sentence strips into a bundle. Provide the children with two cans or boxes labeled with a large (•) or (!).

Have children work in pairs, reading the sentences to each other and placing them in the appropriate can or box.

Add the following books:

My Outrageous Friend Charlie by M. Alexander ◆◆

Best Friends by M. Cohen

Alex and Roy by M. Dickinson

Mike and Tony: Best Friends by H. Ziefert

Writing/Publishing Center

Provide children with paper cut in the shape of a chef's hat. On the hat have children write their "Recipe for a Best Friend."

Art Center

Children may paint a picture of what they like to do with their best friend or their favorite part of *Best Friends*. Captions could be written under the pictures.

Drama Center

Provide children with stick puppets of Jim and Paul. Encourage children to make up dialogue as they retell or invent stories about Jim and Paul.

Related Reading

Read aloud the third story, "Cookies," in Lobel's *Frog and Toad Together.*

Angelina and Alice

Tune In

Select from the following for unison chanting or singing.

Ten Little Friends

Favorite Cookies

(Children's choice)

Then introduce and teach the following action song, "Over in the Playground," using a chart or overhead transparency.

• •

Over in the Playground

(tune: Over in the Meadow)

Over in the playground, in the sand, in the sun,

Played little Johnny Cassidy and little Susie Chung.

"Let's build," said friend Johnny;

"We'll build," said Sue Chung,

So they built all day,

In the sand, in the sun.

(Repeat, substituting *skip, walk, run.*)

• •

Read Aloud

Read *Let's Be Enemies* by J. M. Udry.

Let's Be Enemies repeats the concept that at times good friends get angry with each other. Show the children the cover and discuss the picture. Introduce the word *enemies*. Make certain that the children have some understanding that being enemies is the opposite of being best friends.

Prior to reading the story, point out that the two main characters, John and James, were best friends at one time. Write the names on the chalkboard. Review the letter *J*. Then explain that John is telling the story about their friendship.

Read the story in its entirety. After reading the story, discuss why John decided to make James his enemy rather than his friend. Clarify that James always wants to be the boss.

New Story/Verse

Tell the children that in today's story, *Angelina and Alice* by K. Holabird, they will meet two close friends who are mice. (If you have it, read the poem "Mice," by Rose Fyleman.) Show the children the title of the story, and tell them the name of the two characters. Ask the children what they notice about the two names.

Read the first six pages, stopping at "on the playground."
Ask the children the following questions:

■ Where did the story take place? (Literal Comprehension—Details)

■ What were some of the things Angelina and Alice liked to do together? (Literal Comprehension—Details)

■ What could Alice do that Angelina could not do? (Literal Comprehension—Comparison)

■ Why was Angelina always so unhappy when she fell? (Inferential Comprehension—Character Traits)

■ Why was Angelina especially embarrassed when it happened on the playground? (Inferential Comprehension—Cause and Effect. You may wish to record responses on a chart.)

Continue reading the next six pages, stopping at "A big tear rolled down her nose." Check the children's responses to why Angelina was especially embarrassed.

■ What do you think will happen to Angelina? (Inferential Comprehension—Predicting Outcomes)

Continue reading to the end of story. Check the children's predictions.

■ Why was the festival such a great success? (Literal Comprehension — Details)

■ Why was Angelina and Alice's act so successful? (Literal Comprehension—Main Idea)

Stress that the two key reasons for their success were good teamwork and the fact that they became best friends again.

After the discussion, complete a Sequential Events Model Chart similar to the one on page 259.

Sequential Events Model Chart

Characters: Angelina and Alice

Setting: Mousie School

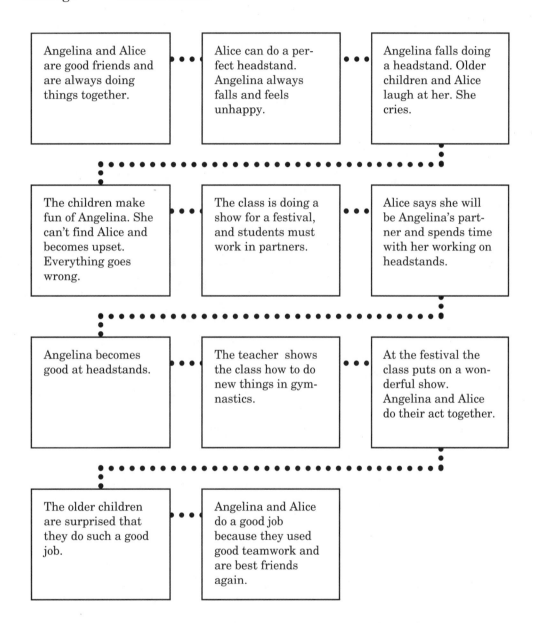

Activity Time

Whole Group

Using a chart or large sheets of newsprint that can be made into a Big Book later, have children create a Language Experience story (see page 33)—their version of the story *Angelina and Alice*. If a Big Book format is used, the children could illustrate the book in the Art Center. If a chart format is used, the children's pictures could be displayed with the chart.

Using a feltboard, overhead transparency, or chart, teach the verse "Ten Good Friends."

• •

Ten Good Friends

Ten good friends marching in a line,

Alex fell down, and then there were nine.

Nine good friends ate a snack on a plate,

Maria left for home, and then there were eight.

Eight good friends wanted to find Devon,

One went to get him, and then there were seven.

Seven good friends were playing some tricks,

Carlo went to tell the teacher, and then there were six.

Six good friends went looking for a hive,

One got lost, and then there were five.

Five good friends knocked at the school door,

One went in, and then there were four.

Four good friends decided to climb the tree,

One slipped down, and then there were three.

Three good friends looked for something new to do,

Leah fell asleep, and then there were two.

Two good friends were having lots of fun,

One was called away, and then there was one.

One good friend playing all alone

Decided just to go on home.

• •

Individual/Small Group

Art Center

Have children draw pictures for the Big Book or chart introduced during whole-group time.

Have children make mice out of modeling clay or another material.

Have children make finger puppets of Angelina and Alice.

Science Center

Place a few books about mice in the center so that children can find out more about them. Provide small blank books for children to write their information. If possible, have a real mouse in the center for one or two days.

Reading/Library Center

Add the following books:

Angelina and Alice by K. Holabird

Frog and Toad Together by A. Lobel ◆◆

The Lonely, Only Mouse by W. Smith

Let's Be Enemies by J. M. Udry

Writing/Publishing Center

Have children write stories about Angelina and Alice.

Math Center

Provide pictures of children of different heights. Children place pictures in order from tallest to shortest and from shortest to tallest.

Make pictures of mice on which numerals have been printed. Cut out a large number of cheese pieces on which number facts (addition and subtraction) have been written. Have the children match the cheese pieces with the appropriate mouse.

Discuss letter writing later in the day with first graders. Ask who has sent or received a letter. Friends often write to each other. For example, if one goes on a vacation, he or she might send a friend a card or letter; if one moves away, he or she might write; if someone is ill, friends often send that person a card or letter; invitations to birthday parties are often written.

Related Reading

The following books offer excellent examples of the importance of writing to best friends. If possible, read one of the books to the children after discussing letter writing.

A Letter to Amy by E. J. Keats Peter writes a special letter to Amy, inviting her to his birthday party. On his way to mail the letter, they meet. In order for the letter to be a surprise, Peter ignores Amy. This creates a misunderstanding that is resolved when Amy comes to the party.

A Letter for Maria by E. Lindsay. Bear decides to write a letter to his friend Maria, who is in the hospital. On the way to the mailbox his letter gets soaked, and he must deliver the letter himself.

 Reminder: Make a "Special Friends Mailbox" for the writing center as a surprise for the class next day.

Ira Sleeps Over

Tune In

Select from the following for unison chanting or singing.

Over in the Playground

Ten Little Friends

The More We Get Together

(Children's choice)

Read Aloud

Read *A Weekend with Wendell* by K. Henkes.

Often children spend the night at each other's houses. At times, this can create a problem, as in *A Weekend with Wendell*. Before reading the story, ask the children, "Who has spent a night at another child's house?" Ask what they liked best about the sleepover. Record their responses on a chart. Ask if any problems arose. Record responses.

Show the children the cover of the book, and tell them the title of the story. Point to the picture and have them find Wendell. Ask the following questions:

■ How do you think Wendell feels about going away for the weekend?

■ What do you think Wendell has packed in his suitcase?

■ How do you think the little girl feels about Wendell's weekend visit?

Read the story in its entirety, taping it for the listening center. After completing the story, ask the children the following questions:

■ What kind of a visitor was Wendell?

■ Why do you think Wendell and Sophie became good friends?

■ How do you think Wendell felt when he got Sophie's note?

New Story/Verse

Tell the children that you have another story about a boy who sleeps over at his good friend's home. Write the title, "Ira Sleeps Over," on the chalkboard, and read it to the children. Tell the children that this is the first time that Ira has been asked to sleep over, and he is very happy.

Begin reading the story, stopping at page 11, the first episode. Ask the following questions:

- Who are the characters in the story? (Literal Comprehension—Details)

- What is Ira's problem? (Literal Comprehension—Cause and Effect)

- What do you think Ira will do? (Inferential Comprehension—Sequence. Since there are only two possible answers, the class could vote.)

Continue reading, stopping at page 19, the second episode. Ask the following questions.

- Now what do you think Ira will do? Have you changed your mind? Why or why not? (Inferential Comprehension—Predicting Outcomes)

- How do you think Reggie feels about teddy bears? (Inferential Comprehension—Character Traits)

Continue reading, stopping at page 36, the third episode. Ask the children the following questions:

- How do you think Ira feels? (Literal Comprehension—Character Traits)

- How do you think Reggie feels? (Inferential Comprehension—Character Traits)

- What do you think Reggie will get? (Inferential Comprehension—Cause and Effect)

Continue reading, stopping at page 39, the fourth episode. Ask the following question:

- What do you think Ira has to get? (Inferential Comprehension—Sequence)

Read to the end of the story and discuss the questions.

Activity Time

Whole Group

This book provides a special opportunity to focus on writing thank-you letters. Tell the children that they are going to write a letter pretending to be Ira.

- Brainstorm things children would want to include in a letter if they were Ira. Record responses on a chart.

- Discuss with the children how letters begin. Write the greeting, "Dear Reggie," at the top left side of the chart.

- Then, using the Language Experience Approach (see page 33), have the children dictate the body of the letter as you write it on the chart.

- Discuss how letters end. Put the children's suggestions on a chart. Write a closing for Ira's letter.

Display the letter in the writing center to provide a model for later letter writing.

Invite the school mail carrier to the class to talk to the children about mailing letters. The mail carrier should stress the following points:

- Letters can be delivered to all parts of the world.

- Envelopes must have the correct address of the person getting the letter, and should have a return address.

- All letters must have the correct stamps.

Encourage the children to ask questions about letters and the post office.

Teach the letter and sound of /w/ to first graders.

Individual/Small Group

Writing/Publishing Center

Call attention to the Special Friends Mailbox in the center and invite the children to write thank-you letters to class friends. Have a variety of papers available for writing. Invite children to make envelopes for their letters. One-inch sticky squares can be provided for children to make stamps.

Provide children with copies of page 308 for writing.

If I was going to visit my best
friend I would take . . .

Reading/Library Center

Add the following books:

A Letter to Amy by E. J. Keats

A Letter for Maria by E. Lindsay

Ira Sleeps Over by B. Waber

Using small blank books, have the children create *W* books. Children should be encouraged to write words along with the pictures.

Add the children's version of the book *Angelina and Alice* made the previous day.

Listening/Viewing Center

Place the tape made during Read Aloud time and the book, *A Weekend with Wendell,* in the center.

Art Center

Have children illustrate their favorite part of either *Ira Sleeps Over* or *A Weekend with Wendell.* Captions can be added by the children themselves or dictated by the children to the teacher.

Related Reading

May I Bring a Friend? by B. S. de Regniers

A Letter for Tiger by Janosch

We Are Best Friends

Tune In

Select from the following for unison chanting or singing.

The More We Get Together

Over in the Playground

(Children's choice)

Teach the song "Write, Write, Write a Letter" using a chart or overhead transparency.

• •

Write, Write, Write a Letter

(tune: Row, Row, Row Your Boat)

Write, write, write a letter

To a friend or two.

Cheerfully, cheerfully, cheerfully, cheerfully

Tell them all about you.

• •

Read Aloud

Read *Chester's Way* by K. Henkes.

Chester's Way is the story of two very good friends whose friendship nearly breaks up when someone moves into the neighborhood. The story is a delightful description of how to make new friends. Before reading the story, ask the children the following questions.

■ Can anyone remember moving or going into a new neighborhood or school?

■ How did you feel about it?

■ What did you do to make friends?

Tell children that today they are going to learn about Lily and what happens when she moves into Chester and Wilson's neighborhood. Read the story in its entirety. Then discuss why Lily became a good friend.

New Story/Verse

Before reading *We Are Best Friends* by Aliki, tell the children that sometimes friends move away and often we must make new friends. Ask the children the following questions:

- Have you ever had a friend who moved away?

- How did you feel when that friend moved away?

- What did you do when that friend moved away?

Possibly the children will respond that they would either write a letter or telephone the old friend. Children may also respond that they would make new friends. This frame of reference is important in developing the story line in the book.

Read the first 12 pages of the story, stopping at "Not boring like this place." Ask the children the following questions:

- Who is in the story? (Literal Comprehension—Details)

- How do you think Peter felt about moving away? Why? (Inferential Comprehension—Character Traits)

- How do you think Robert felt about Peter moving away? Why? (Inferential Comprehension—Character Traits)

- How would you feel if you were Peter? How would you feel if you were Robert? (Appreciative Comprehension—Identification with Characters)

- How does Robert feel about Will? Why? (Inferential Comprehension—Character Traits)

- What do you think might happen next in the story? (Inferential Comprehension—Sequence)

Read the next four pages, stopping at "He has freckles." Check the children's predictions. Ask the children the following questions.

- What did we find out about Robert and Peter? (Literal Comprehension—Details)

- What do you think might happen next? (Inferential Comprehension—Sequence)

Check the children's predictions of what might happen. Ask the children the following question.

- What did we find out about best friends? (Inferential Comprehension—Main Idea)

Activity Time

Whole Group

Recall with the children that Peter and Robert wrote a number of friendly letters to each other. Make a copy of Robert's last letter to Peter, using both lowercase and capital letters. Then read the letter in unison with the children, pointing to each word as it is said. Once the children are familiar with the content, compare Robert's letter to the Language Experience thank-you letter written on Day Eight. Children's discoveries could be put on a chart. Point out that both letters are informal, but a friendly letter like the one written by Robert tells us more about the writer. Remind the children that paper and envelopes are in the writing center for anyone who wants to write a letter to a good friend.

Using an overhead transparency or chart, teach the children the following song during your music time later in the day.

• •

You Are Our Mail Carrier

(tune: You Are My Sunshine)

You are our mail carrier,

Our friendly mail carrier.

You bring us good news

Every day.

You bring us postcards,

You bring us letters,

Please don't forget

Our mail today.

• •

Teach the letter and sound of /r/ to first graders.

Individual/Small Group

• • • • • • • • •

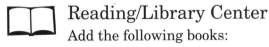 Reading/Library Center

Add the following books:

We Are Best Friends by Aliki

Harry's Smile by K. Caple ◆◆

May I Bring A Friend? by B. S. de Regniers ◆◆

Chester's Way by K. Henkes

My Friend William Moved Away by M. W. Hichman

A Letter for Tiger by Janosch

Moving Gives Me a Stomach Ache by H. McKend

Maggie Doesn't Want to Move by O'Donell ◆◆

Mitchell is Moving by N. W. Sharmat ◆◆

Moving Day by T. Tobias

Anna's Secret Friend by Y. Tsutsui ◆◆

Writing/Publishing Center

Encourage children to write letters to friends in their class or other classes, friends in the neighborhood, and other friends near and far.

Art Center

Provide children with small squares of sticky paper to design new kinds of stamps. Encourage children to put the cost on the stamp.

On large paper have children design special "friendship" stamps, using paint or crayons.

Provide children with folded paper to design friendship cards that can be sent to friends. Encourage children to write notes to their friends.

Math Center

Set up a post office where children can buy teacher-made one-cent stamps, five-cent stamps, and ten-cent stamps to put on their cards and letters. Play money can be used by the children and the postal workers. Children can take turns running the post office.

The concept of time can be reinforced by posting the times the post office will be open.

Listening/Viewing Center

Set up a telephone center where children can make imaginary phone calls to their friends. One or two phones should be provided along with a telephone directory. You may wish to develop a classroom directory with the names, addresses, and phone numbers of the children.

Related Reading

Ira Says Goodbye by B. Waber. This is a sequel to *Ira Sleeps Over,* which was used in the New Story/Verse section on Day Eight.

Reminder: Tell the children to bring in used stamps from home. Remind them to ask their parents for permission.

See You Tomorrow, Charles

DAY 10

Tune In

Select from the following for unison chanting or singing.

Be My Friend

Write, Write, Write a Letter

You Are My Best Friend

(Children's choice)

Read Aloud

Read *Arnie and the New Kid* by N. Carlson.

Ask the children if any of them have had to move and go to a new school where they knew no one. If some children respond affirmatively, ask them how it felt. If no one has entered class midyear, ask children if they can remember what it was like to come into this classroom in the fall. Record some of the responses. Show the cover of *Arnie and the New Kid* to the class and tell them the title. Ask them which character they think is Arnie and which character is the new kid in the class. If they are unable to figure out who the new kid is, tell them that Philip is the new kid. Ask students whether they notice anything special about Philip. Encourage the children to talk about their experiences. Before reading the story, tell the children that they are going to find out what happens to Philip when he comes to Arnie's school. Read the story in its entirety. After reading the story, show the children the cover to remind them how Philip felt coming to a new school. Then show them the last picture and ask them why they think Philip is so happy.

New Story/Verse

See You Tomorrow, Charles, by M. Cohen, is a story about how a blind child is finally accepted by his peers. Show children the cover of the book, and tell them the title. Ask which of the children they think Charles is.

Tell the children that Charles is blind. It is important that they understand the concept of blindness.

- Ask the children if they know what it means to be blind.

- Tell children that some blind people see light, but others do not.

- Emphasize that blind people are able to do most things that sighted people can do.

Before reading the story, brainstorm the things children think Charles will be able to do in Grade One. Record responses.
Read the first nine pages, stopping at " 'Why?' George asked."
Check the children's responses on the chart.

- Can you tell what Sammy thinks would make Charles sad? (Appreciative Comprehension—Identification with Characters. Discuss children's ideas.)

Read the next 14 pages, stopping at "It would not open!"
Ask the children the following questions:

- How would you feel if you were in a dark basement? (Inferential Comprehension—Character Traits)

- How do you think they will get out of the basement? (Inferential Comprehension—Predicting Outcomes)

Read to the end of the story.
Check the children's predictions.

- Why did the teacher tell the children they were lucky to have Charles in the class? (Inferential Comprehension—Supporting Details)

Activity Time

Whole Group

Either of the following activities can aid children in gaining a better understanding of children with special needs.

- Invite a special-education consultant or resource person in to talk to the class and demonstrate Braille and sign language. Encourage children to ask questions. Provide children with opportunities to learn some sign language.

- Invite the school nurse or an optometrist to speak to the children and respond to their questions.

Teach the consonant digraph /ch/ to first graders.
Brainstorm with the children how they might help someone who is in a wheelchair or someone who is blind.
Write a group letter inviting family friends to a special friendship day.

Individual/Small Group

Reading/Library Center

Add the following books:

The Boy Who Couldn't Hear by F. Bloom

Arnie and the New Kid by N. Carlson

See You Tomorrow, Charles by M. Cohen

I Can Hear by P. Curry

Provide the children with small blank books. On the covers print "My Little Book of *Ch* Things." ◆◆ Have children write captions to go with their pictures.

Art Center

Have children make pictures showing how they would help a handicapped person. Captions could be added.

Drama Center

Provide children with stick puppets of Arnie and Philip. Children could dramatize conversations between the two friends.

Listening/Viewing Center

Tapes of the following books could be provided along with the books.

Elihu the Elephant by G. Brennan

Grandma's Wheelchair by L. Henriod

Emil the Eagle by J. LaFleur

Select suitable filmstrips from your district resource center to expand the concepts developed earlier.

Science Center

Provide the children with some magnifying glasses and have them explore how they can be used to make print bigger. Some good resources could be pages from the telephone directory or *TV Guide*. Also place a magnifying glass where you have set up your toy telephone and telephone center.

Have an eye chart for children. Talk about some of the reasons why people go for eye tests or wear glasses. Recall magnifying glass exploration.

Have a display of Braille material for children to explore and experience how blind people read. You might want to invite a blind person to visit and demonstrate/explain how she or he reads books.

Also, place the following books in the center.

Sight by J. M. Parramón and J. J. Puig

My Sister's Silent World by C. Parraur

Seeing by H. Pluckrose

Set up a display showing pictures of a person with a seeing eye dog, people with disabilities at work and at play, and so on.

Obtain additional materials from hearing aid companies and hearing associations. They frequently provide ear charts and pamphlets at no charge. The Optometric Association, a local optometrist, or the local association for the blind may provide free resource materials.

Related Reading

Our Brother Has Down's Syndrome by S. Cairo

I Have a Sister, My Sister Is Deaf by J. W. Peterson

My Friend Leslie by H. Rosenberg

Reminder: Remember to make a copy of the large invitation so that it can be duplicated and given out to the children the following day. Also remember to bring in colored straws and balls of wool for making friendship necklaces.

Do Like Kyla or Hemi's Pet

Tune In

Select from the following for unison chanting or singing.

My Friends in School (tune: Wheels on the Bus)

Over in the Playground

The More We Get Together

(Children's choice)

Read Aloud

Read *Jamaica Tag-Along* by J. Havill.

Jamaica Tag-Along presents a typical relationship between an older brother, his little sister, and a younger friend. In this story, a big brother decides to go out to play with his friends. His little sister wants to go with him, but he refuses to take her along. She follows him anyway. Then when she decides to play by herself, a much smaller boy wants to play, too. She reacts in the same way to him as her brother did to her. Any child with an older brother or sister can easily relate to the events in the story.

Before reading the story, ask the children the following questions.

- How many of you have an older brother or sister? (Responses could be recorded on a graph.)

- What do you like about having an older brother or sister? (Record responses on a chart.)

- Is there anything you don't like about having an older brother or sister? (Record responses on a chart.)

Then refer to the charts and discuss the events of the story in relation to children's responses and their own experiences.

New Story/Verse

Select either *Hemi's Pet* by de Hamel or *Do Like Kyla* by A. Johnson for today's new story. Both books deal with siblings.

Hemi's Pet by de Hamel portrays love between an older brother and his sister. As with *Jamaica Tag-Along,* children can easily relate to this type of a brother-sister relationship.

Before reading *Hemi's Pet,* write the title on the chalkboard and read it to the group. Ask the children the following questions:

- What is a pet? (Record the children's responses on a chart.)

- What kind of a pet do you think Hemi might have? (Record the children's responses on a chart.)

Read the first six pages, stopping at "Then Hemi began to smile and smile." Ask the children the following questions:

- What did we learn about Hemi? (Literal Comprehension—Details)

- What kind of a brother do you think he was to his little sister? (Inferential Comprehension—Character Traits)

- Check Hemi's definition of a pet and the responses that were recorded. (Evaluative Comprehension—Judgments of Adequacy and Validity)

- How do you think Hemi answered Rata when she asked, "Am I your pet?" (Inferential Comprehension—Predicting Outcomes)

Read the next four pages, stopping at, "I'm looking after her today." Ask the children the following questions:

- Why do you think Hemi dresses his sister up in such a special way? (Inferential Comprehension—Predicting Outcomes)

Read the next 11 pages, stopping after the sentence, "So they let him enter Rata as a pet sister." Ask the children the following questions:

- Were your predictions right?

- How would you feel if you were Hemi? How would you feel if you were Rata? (Appreciative Comprehension—Identification with Characters)

- How do you think the story will end? (Inferential Comprehension—Predicting Outcomes)

Read to the end of the story. After completing the story, compare how the children predicted the story would end with how the story ended.

Do Like Kyla by A. Johnson portrays love between an older sister and younger sister. Written from the younger sister's point of view, it is a good follow-up to *Jamaica Tag-Along. Do Like Kyla* is also an excellent book to share orally through pictures and the many familiar words. First graders will enjoy reading the book independently.

Before reading the story, put the title on the board and read it to the children. Ask the following questions:

- Which of the children do you think is Kyla? Why? (Inferential Comprehension—Details)
- Why do you think these two girls might be good friends? (Inferential Comprehension—Details)

Read the first page of the story, stopping at "standing on the bed." Ask the children the following questions:

- Were your predictions correct?
- What other things do you think the little sister might do like Kyla on this winter day? (Inferential Comprehension—Predicting Outcomes. List predictions on the chalkboard or chart paper.)

Continue reading the entire story, stopping at appropriate places to share the beautiful illustrations that depict the warm, loving relationship between the two sisters.

Activity Time

Whole Group

In New Story/Verse the children were introduced to the concept that siblings can be friends and share good experiences. In addition, they were introduced to pets as friends. Both concepts will be extended in the book *I Really Want a Dog* by S. Breslow and S. Blakemore. Before reading the book, the following activities are suggested:

- Invite children to tell the kinds of pets they have. Record their responses on a chart, listing each type of pet along with the names of the children who have that kind of pet.
- Ask the children who do not have pets what kind of pet they would like if they could have one.

Tell the children that they will hear a story about a little boy who wanted a dog for a pet. Read *I Really Want a Dog* in its entirety. After reading the book, brainstorm with the children what they would do if they had a dog. Record their responses. Once the activity has been completed, responses can be chanted in unison with the children, developing vocabulary (reading, writing, listening, speaking). Tell the children that they can make a page called "If I had a pet . . ." for the class Big Book during activity time. This activity is a good one to do with older buddies.

Review the letter and sound of /p/.

Tell children that there will be a special Friendship Day on the last day of this unit. Tell them that the friendship necklace will be given to someone who is a special friend to them. Show the class a sample necklace and the materials to be placed in the art center:

- Pieces of colored wool (30 inches long)

- Box of wide straws in various colors
- Scissors
- Stack of 3-inch squares cut from red construction paper
- Heart templates
- Sparkles
- Marking pens and crayons

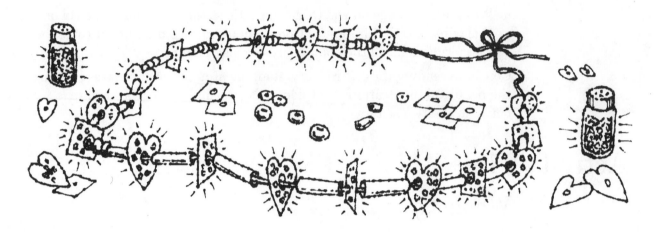

Demonstrate how to make the necklaces.

Individual/Small Group

Reading/Library Center

Add the following books:

Bobo's Dream by M. Alexander. This book without words is also available as a Big Book.

I Really Want a Dog by S. Breslow and S. Blakemore

Hemi's Pet by de Hamel

I Love My Baby Sister (Most of the Time) by E. Edelman ◆◆

We're Very Good Friends, My Brother and I by P. K. Hallinan

We're Very Good Friends, My Sister and I by P. K. Hallinan

Jamaica Tag-Along by J. Havill

Sara Loves Her Big Brother by R. Hooker

Do Like Kyla by A. Johnson

A Boy, a Dog, and a Frog by M. Mayer. This book without words is available as a Big Book.

My Brother Oscar Thinks He Knows It All by L. W. Tyler

Art Center

Provide large sheets of paper that have been folded in half. One half is for a picture and the other half is for a story, "If I Had a Pet . . ." Stories can be written at the writing center.

Children can put together friendship necklaces with materials provided (see Whole-Group Activity).

Writing/Publishing Center

Provide small blank books with "My Little Book of *P* Things." written on the covers.

Provide small blank books on which a variety of titles have been written, such as "My Sister," "My Brother," "My Sister and Brother," and "Our Baby."

Housekeeping/Dramatic Play Center

Encourage adult or parent role playing by providing dramatic-play props (briefcases, hats, wigs, eyeglass frames, purses).

Provide puppets of family figures for dramatization.

Science Center

Add any books that you can find about pets.

Related Reading

One of the following books without words may be read and discussed later in the day. The focus of both books is a brother and sister enjoying each other's company. One focuses on a real adventure, the other on an imaginary adventure. Both books have great potential for developing oral language.

The Gift by J. Prater. In this book a brother and sister create an imaginary adventure using an empty box.

Rain by P. Spier. This book depicts a real adventure that a brother and sister have in the rain.

If these books are not available, *Big Sister and Little Sister* by C. Zolotow or *Anna in Charge* by Y. Tsutsui may be read. The children were introduced to Anna on Day Ten.

Reminder: Make sure the children take home their invitations inviting family friends to the special Friendship Day.

A Chair for My Mother

Tune In

Select from the following for unison chanting or singing.

Write, Write, Write a Letter

This Old Man

Teach the song "Pet Friends," using a chart or overhead transparency.

● ●

Pet Friends

(tune: Mary Had a Little Lamb)

Peter had a little dog, little dog, little dog,

Peter had a little dog

Whose bark was always heard.

And everywhere that Peter went, Peter went, Peter went,

Everywhere that Peter went

The dog was sure to go.

Alice had a little rabbit, little rabbit, little rabbit,

Alice had a little rabbit

Whose ears were soft and pink.

And everywhere that Alice went . . .

The rabbit was sure to go.

André had a little cat, little cat, little cat,

André had a little cat

Whose fur was soft as silk.

And everywhere that André went . . .

The cat was sure to go.

Gloria had a little bird, little bird, little bird,

Gloria had a little bird,

Whose song was sweet and soft.

And everywhere where that Gloria went . . .

The bird was sure to go.

Xavier had a little fish, little fish, little fish,

Xavier had a little fish,

Whose tail was gold and brown.

And everywhere that Xavier went . . .

The fish was sure to go.

Substitute children's names and pets or favorite animals
to create new verses.

Read Aloud

Read either *Amy Said* by M. Waddell or *Shoes from Grandpa* by M. Fox.

Amy Said introduces the concept that an older relative can also be a good friend. In this book, a young, mischievous boy tells us about his visit at Gran's house with his older sister, Amy. The two children get into all kinds of mischief until their ever-patient Gran finally says "That's enough! NO MORE!'

Before reading the story, ask the children if they have ever stayed over at their grandmother's. Tell them that today's story is about a brother and sister who visit their grandmother. Read the story in its entirety, and then discuss it with the children.

Shoes from Grandpa by M. Fox is also about an older relative who is a friend. Grandpa starts a humorous series of events when he gives Jessie a new pair of shoes for her birthday. The story, told in rhyme, is a variation of *The House That Jack Built* and has a funny ending.

New Story/Verse

A Chair for My Mother by V. B. Williams includes the following features:

- single-parent family
- working mother
- inner-city setting
- neighbors helping in time of need
- introduction of firefighters
- close relationship between three generations
- emphasis on sharing and helping others

- emphasis on the extended family (grandparents, uncle, aunt)
- roles of a wide array of family members

Before reading the story, it is important to develop the concept of helping. Good friends help their friends when they are in need. Promote class discussion with the following questions.

- Have you ever had an older friend help you? How?
- Have you ever helped an older friend? How?

Record responses on a chart. Introduce the concept of natural disasters and the need for the community to work together.

Tell the children that in the story they will hear something sad that happens to a little girl and her family. Write the title *A Chair for My Mother* on the board. Ask the children if anyone can read the title.

Begin reading the first four pages, stopping at ". . . into the jar."

- What characters have we met in the story? (Literal Comprehension — Details)
- What have we learned about the characters? (Literal and Inferential Comprehension—Character Traits)
- Why do you think they are putting all their coins into a jar? (Inferential Comprehension—Predicting Outcomes)
- How long do you think it will take to fill the jar? (Inferential Comprehension—Predicting Outcomes)

Read the next four pages, stopping at ". . . time ago."

- Were your predictions correct?
- What other characters did you meet in the story? (Literal Comprehension—Details)
- Why did Mother need to buy a new chair? (Literal Comprehension—Cause and Effect)

Tell the children that we are now going to hear the little girl's story about the big fire in their other house. Read the next six pages, stopping at "But the rooms were very empty."

- What other characters did you meet in the story? (Literal Comprehension—Details)
- How did her uncle and aunt help them? (Literal Comprehension—Details)
- What do you think will happen next in the story? (Inferential Comprehension—Predicting Outcomes)

Continue reading the next four pages, stopping at ". . . put it in."

Check the children's predictions. Discuss the ways in which the neighbors and family members helped the family.

Check the children's earlier predictions about how long it would take to fill the jar with coins.

- What do you think that the family will do now that the jar is filled to the top? (Inferential Comprehension—Predicting Outcomes)

Read to the end of the story. Check the children's predictions.

Activity Time

Whole Group

Read *Coco Can't Wait!* by T. Gomi, which is a translation of the Japanese story *Hyaku Aitaina*. It tells about Coco's desire to visit her grandmother and her grandmother's desire to visit her granddaughter. Problems arise because they both decide to leave their houses at the same time and keep missing each other along the way. Much of the story is told through pictures, providing many opportunities for language development. The children will enjoy this humorous tale with its happy ending. In addition, its limited vocabulary and simple text make it an easy-reading book.

Invite a grandparent in to speak with the class about what his or her schooldays were like, what he or she likes about being a grandparent, what his or her grandparents were like, and so on. Have children work cooperatively to write a thank-you note to the visitor.

Using the Language Experience Approach (see page 31), brainstorm ways in which children help neighbors and family friends. Chart their responses under appropriate headings.

Ask the children if any of them have received letters or cards from an older family member or friend. Record their responses in a list.

Before reading the book, *Dear Daddy* by P. Dupasquier, explain to the children that this book is a collection of letters written by a little girl to her father whose job takes him far away. The letters were written over a long time. Show the children the cover, which shows the envelope addressed to Sophie's dad. Read the envelope and discuss the airmail sticker and name and address of Sophie's father.

Show the sets of pictures on the first two-page spread of the book. Discuss the pictures with the children. Make certain they understand that the top picture shows something about what the father is doing while the bottom picture shows something that Sophie is doing. Since the book contains parts of many letters over a period of time, you might want to to say the words, "Dear Daddy," at the beginning of each two-page spread.

Upon completion of the story, remind the children that they may use the letter paper in the writing center to write letters to a relative or friend who lives far away.

Individual/Small Group

 ### Reading/Library Center

Set up a display of pictures of family members from magazines, showing as many different ethnic groups as possible.

Add the following books:

The Two of Them by Aliki

Aunt Nina, Goodnight, by F. Brandenberg

Dear Daddy by P. Dupasquier

Coco Can't Wait! by T. Gomi ◇

Grandpa's Face by E. Greenfield ◆◆

We're Very Good Friends series by P. K. Hallinan

The Gift by J. Prater

Rain by P. Spier

Anna in Charge by Y. Tsutsui

Amy Said by M. Waddell

A Chair for My Mother by V. B. Williams

Big Sister and Little Sister by C. Zolotow

 ### Writing/Publishing Center

Provide children with small blank books on which a variety of titles have been written: "My Favorite Aunt," "My Grandparents," "My Favorite Uncle," "My Good Neighbor," "If I Were an Aunt or Uncle."

Provide paper for children to write letters to family or friends that live far away. Encourage the children to address envelopes.

Math Center

Provide boxes of play money for counting by ones and twos.

Provide two-piece puzzles, matching the cost of the stamp to the correct amount of money to be paid for the stamp. With younger children you might want to picture only pennies.

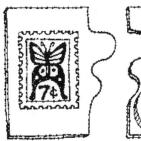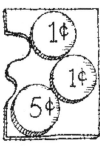

Bring in a small jar of coins. Have children guess the number of coins in the jar and write their guesses on a sign-in record sheet.

• • • • • • • • • •

 ## Art Center

Provide children with paper and colored markers and crayons to make thank-you cards for someone older who has done something nice. Encourage the children to write a thank-you message.

Provide children with blank books on which "My Family Album" has been written. Encourage them to draw pictures and to write something to go with each picture.

Have children continue making friendship necklaces.

• • • • • • • • • •

 ## Listening /Viewing Center

Select suitable filmstrips from your district resource center to expand concepts developed earlier.

Related Reading

The following read-aloud books may be read for enjoyment.

Chester and Uncle Willoughby by P. K. Edwards

Amber's Other Grandparents by P. Bonnici

Aunt Nina and Her Nephews and Nieces by F. Brandenberg

Grandpa's Face by E. Greenfield

I Love You Forever by R. Munsch

I Know a Lady by C. Zolotow

Reminder: Take time to plan Friendship Day with the children. Have them decide their favorite friendship verses and songs to present on the special day and the kind of snacks and drinks they would like to prepare for their guests.

The children should be encouraged to pick out some of their best work from their writing folders to be displayed. The children could also put on puppet plays with some of the puppets used throughout the unit. Props might be used to dramatize some of the verses. Discuss with the children whom they might invite to the Friendship Day celebration, with or without their parents.

The Fire Station

Tune In

Select from the following for unison chanting or singing.

Friends

Be My Friend

(Children's choice)

Then teach the children the following number verse using an overhead transparency or chart. Once the children become familiar with the verse, have them chant it several times. This verse could also be dramatized.

• •

Five Good Police Officers

Five good police officers standing by the store,

One became a traffic officer and then there were four.

Four good police officers watching over me,

One took home a lost boy, and then there were three.

Three good police officers, all dressed in blue,

One saved a puppy, then then there were two.

Two good police officers—how fast they run!

One helped a lady, and then there was one.

One good police officer saw some smoke that day,

She called the firefighters, who went right away.

• •

Read Aloud

Read *Something Special for Me* by V. B. Williams.

Something Special for Me continues the story of Rosa, who was introduced to the children on Day Twelve of this unit. In an episode of that book, the children were introduced to firefighers, whose roles will be discussed. The first part of the book reviews some of the story events, especially focusing on the money jar that was used to save money for the chair. The book clearly establishes the warm friendship that was developed between Rosa and her mother.

Show the children the cover of *Something Special for Me* and ask them if they can recall the name of the little girl in the picture (Rosa). Remind them that they have already heard a story about her in *A Chair for My Mother.* Have the children recall some of the events in that story. Then read the new story in its entirety and discuss the ending.

New Story/Verse

Recall with the children that friends can be old as well as young. Also remind them that other adults as well as family members can be friends. Have the children recall people who were good friends to Rosa and her family. Record the children's responses (neighbors, firefighters, Josephine). Point out to the children that firefighters are very special friends because they help keep us safe. Ask the children if they can name any other special adult friends that help keep them safe. Record their responses (crossing guards, police officers). If the children name persons such as nurses, doctors, explain that they are health helpers rather then safety helpers.

Show the class the cover of *The Fire Station* by R. Munsch. Ask the children to tell you about what is happening in the picture.

- Do you think that the little girl and boy are good friends? Why or why not?

Read the first six pages, stopping after "Let's go into the enormous fire truck." Ask the children the following questions:

- What are the names of the two children? (Literal Comprehension— Details)

- How old do you think they are? (Inferential Comprehension—Details)

- What do we find out about Sheila? (Inferential Comprehension— Character Traits)

- What do we find out about Michael? (Inferential Comprehension— Character Traits)

- What do you think is going to happen next in the story? (Inferential Comprehension—Predicting Outcomes. Record the children's predictions.)

Read the next eight pages, stopping at ". . . drove them away." Ask the children the following questions:

- Were some of your predictions correct? (Check the children's earlier predictions.)

- How do you think Sheila and Michael felt? (Inferential Comprehension—Character Traits)

- How would you feel if you were Sheila? How would you feel if you were Michael? How would you feel if you were the Fire Chief? (Appreciative Comprehension—Identification with Characters)

- How do you feel about Sheila and Michael's adventure? (Appreciative Comprehension—Identification with Content)

- What do you think will happen to Michael when he gets home? (Inferential Comprehension—Predicting Outcomes. Record the children's responses.)

- What do you think will happen to Sheila when she gets home? (Inferential Comprehension—Predicting Outcomes. Record the children's responses.)

Read the next four pages, stopping at "...got clean." Ask the children the following questions:

- Were some of your predictions correct? (Check the children's predictions.)

- Do you want to add any more predictions to what will happen to Sheila?

Continue reading to the end of the book. Ask the children the following questions:

- Were some of your predictions correct?

- Do you think this story could really have happened? Why or why not? (Evaluative Comprehension—Judgments of Reality or Fantasy)

Activity Time

Whole Group

Referring to the display of pictures, books, and other materials about police officers and firefighters, have a discussion with the children about how police officers and firefighters keep us safe. Make frequent reference to the pictures and other materials to clarify concepts developed. Then write two group stories: "Our Friends the Firefighers" and "Our Friends the Police Officers." Use the Language Experience Approach (see page 33). After writing the stories, have the children read them in unison several times.

Ask the children if any of them can tell you their telephone number. After several children have responded, write the number 9-1-1 on the board. Ask the children if they recognize this special telephone number. Discuss the importance of knowing this number and giving accurate information over the telephone. Ask the children when this number should be used. Record their responses. Emphasize the meaning of *emergency*. Then ask the children what types of information they would have to give to the other person on the telephone. Record the responses, making certain that the children realize that they must be able to tell exactly why help is needed, tell their name and their parents' first and last names, tell their correct address, and tell their correct telephone number.

Stress with the children the importance of being a good listener. Then bring in two telephones. One will be used by the teacher who will act as the emergency dispatcher, and the other will be used by individual children who will be asking for emergency help. Then have the children role play various emergency situations such as the following: They see smoke and flames coming from their neighbor's house; their garage is on fire; or they find a lost child on their front stairs.

Teachers might want to invite a police officer, a firefighter, or a school crossing guard to speak to the class and answer their questions. Any of these visitors would present an excellent opportunity to discuss seeking a police officer's aid when in trouble, not talking to or going with strangers, and practicing fire safety in the home.

Teach the children the following poem, using a chart or overhead transparency.

• •

Firefighters

Ten little firefighters, sleeping in a row;

Ding, dong, goes the bell, down the pole they go.

Jumping on the engine, oh, oh, oh,

Putting out the fire shhhhhhhhhhhhhhhhhhhhhhhhhh.

And home again they go

Back to sleep again,

All in a row.

Anonymous

• •

Individual/Small Group

• • • • • • • • •

Reading/Library Center

Set up a display of books, pictures, and other materials about police officers and firefighters.

Add the following books:

When There Is a Fire Go Outside by D. Chlad. This book gives many good tips on fire safety, as well as making children aware that a fire plan is important for safety.

Fire! Fire! by G. Gibbons

Fire Fighters by R. Maass. This book shows photographs of firefighters and what they do.

The Fire Station by R. Munsch

Fire Fighters and Fire Engines by L. Peter

All Aboard Fire Trucks by T. Slater

Check your school library and your local library for the latest books about police officers and firefighters, since new books are being published all the time.

Block Center

Add appropriate props to promote dramatic play of emergency situations. Blocks can be used to construct buildings. Suggested props:

Firefighters

- hoses (old garden hose, vacuum cleaner hose)
- helmets
- small fire trucks
- small ladders
- black boots

Police Officers

- whistles
- hats
- traffic signs
- badges
- pad of traffic tickets
- pencils

Math Center

Add the following book:

Fire Engine Shapes by B. McMillan. This is a concept book of shapes found around the fire station. The pictures are colorful.

Writing/Publishing Center

Provide children with small blank books on which the following titles have been printed: "If I Were a Firefighter," "If I Were a Police Officer," and "Emergency! Call 9-1-1!"

Listening/Viewing Center

Select suitable filmstrips from your district resource center to expand the concepts developed in this section.

Housekeeping/Dramatic Play Center

Place one of two phones in the housekeeping center, and the other at a desk called the Emergency Center. Real working phones can often be obtained from your local telephone office. Post a sign on which the emergency number, 9-1-1, has been written. This will provide the opportunity for children to dramatize emergency situations using the information discussed earlier.

Art Center

Have the children continue making friendship necklaces.

Invite children to paint pictures of firefighters and police officers in action. Encourage them to write a few sentences about their paintings. Display the pictures in the classroom.

DAY

My Doctor

Tune In

Select from the following for unison chanting or singing.

Write, Write, Write a Letter

Five Good Police Officers

Firefighters

(Children's choice)

On Day Thirteen, children expanded their knowledge about adult friends who help keep them safe (firefighters and police officers). Today the focus moves to adult friends who help keep them healthy and strong. The dentist, doctor, and nurse are the health helpers with whom most children have had some contact.

Read Aloud

Read *My Dentist* by H. Rockwell.

Before reading *My Dentist,* show the children the cover of the book. Put the title on the chalkboard and ask the children if they can guess which friend they will meet in the story. Ask the following questions:

- How many of you have been to the dentist? (Responses could be recorded on a graph.)

- What is the name of your dentist?

- Is your dentist a woman or man?

- Why do you go the dentist? (Brainstorm and record responses.)

- What things might you find in a dentist's office? (Record responses on a chart.)

Read the book in its entirety. The illustrations show clearly what equipment is found in the dentist's office. If the children have never gone to a dentist, this book will explain what happens during a visit to the dentist. The detailed pictures should help to take away any fear and apprehension that children often feel about unfamiliar places and people.

After reading the book, discuss the list children compiled of equipment that might be found in a dentist's office. Find out what other things need to be added to the list.

Contact the American Dental Association, Order Section CAT77, 211 E. Chicago Avenue, Chicago, IL 60611, for free materials.

New Story/Verse

Remind children that there are adult friends who help keep them healthy. Ask the children to name as many as they can. The children are likely to mention the nurse and family doctor and maybe the eye doctor. Ask the children the following questions:

- How many of you have visited the doctor? (Responses could be graphed.)

- What happened when you visited the doctor? (Record responses.)

- Was your doctor a woman or a man? (Responses could be graphed.)

Today's new story, *My Doctor,* is also written by H. Rockwell. This book presents clear illustrations on the equipment used by most doctors when children are getting their checkup. If the children have never gone to a doctor, this book will help remove any fears they may have about a visit to the doctor.

Show the children the cover. Write the title on the chalkboard and have the children read the title. Before reading the book, show the children the title page. Discuss the people in the picture. The picture shows the reception room, both Mom and Dad bringing children to visit the doctor, the receptionist answering the phone, and the pediatrician.

Read the first page of the book. Ask the children the following questions.

- Why do you think the little boy is in the doctor's office? (Inferential comprehension—Predicting Outcomes. List predictions on the chalkboard.)

- Why is the doctor washing her hands? (Inferential Comprehension— Details. The children should be be made aware that washing hands helps prevent the spread of germs.)

Continue reading the entire story, stopping at particular words that may require further clarification. If possible, have available samples of doctor's equipment so that children can see and touch them. Some of the items can be readily obtained from the school nurse. A toy doctor's kit may also be used. Terms that may need clarification include *stethoscope, tongue depressor, special type of flashlight, plastic mallet, thermometer,* and *gauze pads.*

Check children's predictions that were made before reading the story.

Activity Time

Whole Group

Refer to the display of pictures, books, and other materials about doctors and discuss how doctors help people. This activity helps develop an understanding of key words that were introduced earlier. It also helps to increase the children's listening and speaking vocabularies. After the discussion, write a story, *Our Friend the Doctor,* using the Language Experience Approach (see page 33). Have the children read the story in unison several times.

Teach the children the following poem, using a chart or overhead transparency.

● ●

Call 9-1-1

If you need a doctor to come quick, quick, quick,

Call 9-1-1 and say, "Someone is very sick, sick, sick!"

Give your name, your phone number, your address and street.

Then the doctor will come quickly to your street.

If you need firefighters to put out a fire one day,

Call 9-1-1 and say, "Put out the fire right away!"

Give your name, your phone number, your address and street.

Then firefighters will come quickly to your street.

If you need police officers to save someone one day,

Call 9-1-1, and say, "Someone needs help right away!"

Give your name, your phone number, your address and street.

Then police officers will come quickly to your street.

● ●

Since this unit introduces a number of compound words such as *mailman, firefighter, policeman, policewoman, mailbag,* this is an excellent time to review compound words.

Additional practice should be provided for children to role play calling 9-1-1 in emergency situations. Refer to the four-point chart developed on Day Thirteen with information that the children must be able to tell the emergency dispatcher. Again, stress that children must be good listeners and remain calm. Suggested emergency situations include: someone has fainted and won't wake up; there is a fire in the field behind your house; something has fallen on your father while he was working in the garage, and the object is too heavy for you to move; and the babysitter has fallen down the stairs and can't move one leg.

Invite the school nurse to come to talk to the children about health helpers. Ask the nurse to talk about his or her own job. The children should be made aware that nurses can be either men or women.

Individual/ Small Group

Reading/Library Center

Set up a display of books, pictures, and other materials about dentists, nurses, and doctors.

Add the following books:

Visiting the Dentist by Althea

When I See My Dentist by S. Kuklin

When I See My Doctor by S. Kuklin

A Trip to the Doctor by M. Linn

A Trip to the Dentist by M. Linn

My Doctor by H. Rockwell

My Dentist by H. Rockwell

Nicky Goes to the Doctor by R. Scarry

What Happens When I Go to the Doctor by H. Slater

What Happens When I Go to the Dentist by H. Slater

Check your school library and your local library for the latest books about doctors, nurses, and dentists, since new books are being published all the time.

Provide children with the following puzzles and matching activities. Use different cuts for each puzzle to make activities self-correcting.

- Match the names of helpers with pictures. Helpers include firefighter, mailcarrier, dentist, doctor, nurse, police officer, and eye doctor.

- Match the name of the adult helper with the name of something the person uses on the job. ◆◆

Writing/Publishing Center

Provide the children with small blank books on which the following titles have been printed: "My Friend the Nurse," "My Friend the Doctor," and "My Friend the Dentist."

Provide children with sentence starters such as the following:

- If I were a doctor I would _____.

- If I were a dentist I would _____.

- If I were a nurse I would _____.
- If I were a toothbrush I would _____.
- If I worked at the hospital _____.
- When I was sick _____.

Math Center

Provide the children with measuring tapes or yardsticks so that they can work cooperatively measuring each other. The information can be recorded on a class measurement sheet and posted in the center. Have someone measure you, too. If possible, measure the principal or other staff members.

Housekeeping/Dramatic Play Center

Set up a doctor's office near the housekeeping center with a receptionist and a waiting room. Magazines and books should be made available for reading in the waiting room. The children can bring dolls from the housekeeping center to see the doctor. The following props should be provided:

- nurse's cap
- doctor's coat and mask
- stethoscope
- kit or bag
- prescription pad and pencil
- baby scale and ordinary scale
- tape, cotton, bandages
- unbreakable plastic "medicine" bottles
- eye chart
- tape measure or height chart

Listening/Viewing Center

Select suitable filmstrips from your local resource center to expand the concepts developed earlier.

Block Center

Add appropriate objects such as a doctor's car, ambulance, and so on to help promote dramatic play.

Art Center

Have children paint pictures of themselves visiting either the doctor or the dentist. Children should be encouraged to write a few sentences about their visit. Display the pictures in the classroom.

Drama Center

Add appropriate puppets to the center (doctors, police officers, firefighters, nurses).

Related Reading

Going to the Doctor by F. Rogers.

Reminder: Remind the children to tell their parents that tomorrow is the special Friendship Day Celebration.

Friendship Day (Culmination)

Tune In

All the children's favorite verses and songs will be chanted or sung to parents and friends.

The songs and verses are on charts that have been put together to form one large book.

Activity Time

For the celebration children will chant their favorite friendship verses, sing their favorite friendship songs, and present their puppet shows in small cooperative groups. The children will show their special guests the materials and projects they have worked on during the unit.

Party Time

As the parents and special friends are being seated, have children place their friendship necklaces around the neck of one of the guests. As they do this children can sing the song "The More We Get Together The Happier We'll Be." Then snacks and drinks the children have chosen can be served. Before the special guests leave, the children will present them with the specially prepared thank-you cards.

 Be sure to obtain permission before allowing children to eat foods prepared in the classroom in case of food allergies or other restrictions.

One treat could be Friendship Soup.

Recipe: Friendship Soup

- vegetables, a variety (have children bring them to share with their friends)
- stock cubes (beef or chicken)
- alphabet noodles/rice
- water

References

Alexander, M. (1970). *Bobo's Dream.* New York: Dial Press.

Alexander, M. (1989). *My Outrageous Friend Charlie.* New York: Dial Books.

Aliki (1982). *We Are Best Friends.* New York: Mulberry Books.

————— (1987). *The Two of Them.* New York: Mulberry Books.

Althea (1990). *Visiting the Dentist.* New York: McClanahan.

Ariego, J., and A. Dewey (1988). *Rockaby Crocodile.* New York: Greenwillow Books.

Arthur, C. (1979). *My Sister's Silent World.* Chicago, Ill.: Children's Press.

Bloom, F. (1977). *The Boy Who Couldn't Hear.* London: The Bodley Head.

Bonnici, P. (1985). *Amber's Other Grandparents.* London: The Bodley Head.

Brandenberg, F. (1983). *Aunt Nina and Her Nephews and Nieces.* New York: Greenwillow Books.

————— (1989). *Aunt Nina, Goodnight.* New York: Greenwillow Books.

Brennan, G. (1984). *Elihu the Elephant.* Milwaukee, Wis.: Ideal.

Breslow, S., and S. Blakemore (1990). *I Really Want A Dog.* New York: Dutton Children's Books.

Brown, T. (1986). *Hello, Amigos!* New York: Henry Holt.

Burningham, J. (1975). *The Friend.* New York: Thomas Y. Crowell.

Cairo, S. (1985). *Our Brother Has Down's Syndrome.* Toronto: Annick Press Ltd.

Caple, K. (1987). *Harry's Smile.* Boston, Mass.: Houghton Mifflin.

Carle, E. (1971). *Do you Want to Be My Friend?* New York: Thomas Crowell.

Carlson, N. (1990). *Arnie and the New Kid.* New York: Viking Penguin.

Charles, N.M. and Y. Cathcart (1991). *See You Later, Alligator.* Richmond Hill, Ontario, Canada: Scholastic Canada.

Chevalier, C. (1982). *Grandma's Wheelchair.* Chicago, Ill.: Albert Whitman.

Chlad, D. (1982). *When There Is a Fire Go Outside.* Chicago, Ill.: Children's Press.

Cohen, M. (1967). *Will I Have A Friend?* New York: Macmillan.

————— (1971). *Best Friends.* New York: Macmillan.

————— (1983). *See You Tomorrow, Charles.* New York: Greenwillow Books.

Corey, D. (1980). *We All Share.* Chicago, Ill.: Albert Whitman.

Curry, P. (1984). *I Can Hear.* Los Angeles, Calif.: Price Stern Sloan.

de Hamel. (1986). *Hemi's Pet.* Auckland, N.Z.: Reed Methuen.

de Regniers, B. S. (1980). *May I Bring A Friend?* New York: Atheneum.

Dickinson, M. (1981). *Alex and Roy.* London: Scholastic.

Dupasquier, P. (1986). *Dear Daddy.* New York: Puffin Books.

Edelman, E. (1985). *I Love My Baby Sister (Most of the Time).* New York: Puffin Books.

Edwards, P. K. (1987). *Chester and Uncle Willoughby.* Boston, Mass.: Little, Brown.

Fahlman, R., J. Graeme, and M. Henderson. (1990). *Rainy Day Friends.* Don Mills, Ontario: Addison-Wesley.

Fox, M. (1990). *Shoes from Grandpa.* New York: Orchard Books.

Gantos, J. and N. Rubel (1979). *The Perfect Friend.* Boston, Mass.: Houghton Mifflin.

Gibbons, G. (1987). *Fire! Fire!* Mt. Rainer, Md.: Gryphon House.

Gomi, T. (1984). *Coco Can't Wait.* New York: William Morrow.

Graeme, J. and M. Henderson (1990). *One Nose, Two*

Hands. Don Mills, Ontario: Addison-Wesley.

Graham, B. (1987). *The Adventures of Charlotte and Henry.* New York: Viking Penguin.

Greenfield, E. (1988). *Grandpa's Face.* New York: Philomel Books.

Hallinan, P. K. (1973). *We're Very Good Friends, My Brother and I.* Nashville, Tenn.: Ideals Children's Books.

———— (1977). *That's What a Friend Is.* Nashville, Tenn.: Ideals Children's Books.

———— (1989a). *We're Very Good Friends, My Aunt and I.* Nashville, Tenn.: Ideals Children's Books.

———— (1989b). *We're Very Good Friends, My Father and I.* Nashville, Tenn.: Ideals Children's Books.

———— (1989c). *We're Very Good Friends, My Grandma and I.* Nashville, Tenn.: Ideals Children's Books.

———— (1989d). *We're Very Good Friends, My Grandpa and I.* Nashville, Tenn.: Ideals Children's Books.

———— (1989e). *We're Very Good Friends, My Mother and I.* Nashville, Tenn.: Ideals Children's Books.

———— (1989f). *We're Very Good Friends, My Sister and I.* Nashville, Tenn.: Ideals Children's Books.

———— (1989g). *We're Very Good Friends, My Uncle and I.* Nashville, Tenn.: Ideals Children's Books.

Havill, J. (1989). *Jamaica Tag-Along.* New York: Scholastic.

Heide, F. P., and S. W. Van Clief. (1971). *That's What Friends Are For.* New York: Scholastic.

Heine, H. (1986). *Friends.* New York: Aladdin Books.

Henkes, K. (1986). *A Weekend with Wendell.* New York: Greenwillow Books.

———— (1988). *Chester's Way.* New York: Puffin Books.

———— (1986). *Jessica.* New York: Puffin Books.

Henriod, L. (1982). *Grandma's Wheelchair.* Chicago, Ill.: Albert Whitman.

Holabird, K. (1987). *Angelina and Alice.* New York: Clarkson, N. Potter.

Hooker, R. (1987). *Sara Loves Her Big Brother.* Niles, Ill.: Whitman.

Hichman, M. W. (1979). *My Friend William Moved Away.* Nashville, Tenn.: Abingdon.

Hutchins, P. (1989). *The Doorbell Rang.* New York: Scholastic.

Janosch. (1984). *A Letter for Tiger.* London: Scholastic Book Services.

Johnson, A. (1990). *Do Like Kyla.* New York: Orchard Books.

Keats, E. J. (1968). *A Letter to Amy.* New York: Harper & Row.

Krauss, R. (1975). *Three Friends.* New York: Scholastic.

Kuklin, S. (1988a). *When I See My Dentist.* Mt. Ranier, Md.: Gryphon House.

———— (1988b). *When I See My Doctor.* Mt. Ranier, Md.: Gryphon House.

LaFleur, T. (1984). *Emil the Eagle.* Milwaukee, Wis.: Ideals Children' Books.

Lindsay, E. (1988). *A Letter for Maria.* London: Scholastic.

Linn, M. (1988). *A Trip to the Dentist.* New York: Harper & Row.

———— (1988). *A Trip to the Doctor.* New York: Harper & Row.

Lobel, A. (1970). *Frog and Toad Are Friends.* New York: Harper & Row.

———— (1970). *Frog and Toad Together.* New York: Scholastic.

———— (1971). *Frog and Toad.* New York: Harper & Row.

Lyon, G. E. (1989). *Together.* New York: Orchard Books.

Maass, R. (1989). *Fire Fighters.* New York: Scholastic.

Mayer, M. (1967). *A Boy, a Dog, and a Frog.* New York: Dial Books.

McKend, H. (1988). *Moving Gives Me a Stomach Ache.* Windsor, Ontario: Black Moss Press.

McMillan, B. (1958). *Fire Engine Shapes.* New York: Lothrop, Lee & Shepard.

Munsch, R. (1986). *Love You Forever: For Their Child Forever.* Scarborough, Ontario: Firefly Books.

——— (1986). *The Fire Station*. Toronto: Annick Press.

O'Donell (1987). *Maggie Doesn't Want to Move*. New York: Four Winds Press.

Parramón, J. M., and J. J. Puig (1985). *Sight*. New York: Barron.

Paré, R. (1984). *A Friend Like You*. Toronto: Annick Press.

Parraur, C. (1979). *My Sister's Silent World*. Chicago, Ill.: Children's Press.

Peter, L. (1987). *Fire Fighters and Fire Engines*. Los Angeles, Calif.: Price Stern Sloan.

Peterson, J. W. (1977). *I Have a Sister, My Sister Is Deaf*. New York: Harper & Row.

Prater, J. (1987). *The Gift*. New York: Picture Puffins.

Pluckrose, H. (1986). *Seeing*. Danbury, Ct.: Watts.

Rockwell, H. (1973). *My Doctor*. New York: Macmillan.

——— (1975). *My Dentist*. New York: Greenwillow Books.

Rogers, F. (1986). *Going to the Doctor*. New York: G. P. Putnam's Sons.

——— (1987). *Making Friends*. New York: G. P. Putnam's Sons.

Rosenberg, M. (1983). *My Friend Leslie*. New York: William Morrow.

Prater, J. (1987). *The Gift*. New York: Puffin Books.

Schick, E. (1969). *Making Friends*. New York: Macmillan.

Scarry, R. (1972). *Nicky Goes to the Doctor*. New York: Western Publishing.

Shapiro, B. (1983). *The Crocodile*. Richmond Hill, Ontario: Scholastic-TAB Publications.

Sharmat, M. W. (1978). *Mitchell Is Moving*. New York: Scholastic.

Slater, H. (1991a). *What Happens When I Go to the Dentist*. Frome, Somerset: Teeney Books.

——— (1991b). *What Happens When I Go to the Doctor*. Frome, Somerset: Teeney Books.

Slater, T. (1991). *All Aboard Fire Trucks*. New York: Platt and Munk.

Smith, W. (1989). *The Lonely, Only Mouse*. London: Penguin Books

Spier, P. (1982). *Peter Spier's Rain*. New York: Doubleday.

Stren, P. (1977). *Hug Me*. New York: Harper & Row.

Thurman, M. *Old Friends, New Friends*. Toronto: New Canadian Publications.

Tobias, T. (1976). *Moving Day*. New York: Alfred A. Knopf.

Tsutsui, Y. (1987). *Anna's Secret Friend*. New York: Viking Penguin.

——— (1988). *Anna in Charge*. New York: Viking Penguin.

Tyler, L. W. (1989). *My Brother Oscar Thinks He Knows It All*. New York: Puffin Books.

Udry, J. M. (1961). *Let's Be Enemies*. New York: Harper & Row.

Waddell, M. (1989). *Amy Said*. Boston, Mass.: Little, Brown.

Waber, B. (1972). *Ira Sleeps Over*. New York: Scholastic.

——— (1988). *Ira Says Goodbye*. Boston, Mass.: Houghton Mifflin.

Watts, F. (1989). *Crocodiles and Alligators*. New York: Franklin Watts.

Williams, V. B. (1982). *A Chair for My Mother*. New York: Scholastic.

——— (1983). *Something Special for Me*. New York: Harper & Row.

Ziefert, H. (1982). *Me Too! Me Too!* New York: Harper & Row.

——— (1982). *Mike and Tony: Best Friends*. New York: Harper & Row.

Zolotow, C. (1966). *Big Sister and Little Sister*. New York: Harper & Row.

——— (1968). *My Friend John*. New York: Harper & Row.

——— (1969). *The Hating Book*. New York: Harper & Row.

——— (1972). *Hold My Hand*. New York: Harper & Row.

——— (1984). *I Know a Lady*. New York: Greenwillow Books.

Friendships Blackline Masters

Friends in school figures

My Friends in school (song)

Allie and Corky stick puppet figures

Suitcase writing shape

Call 9-1-1 (verse)

People stick puppet figures

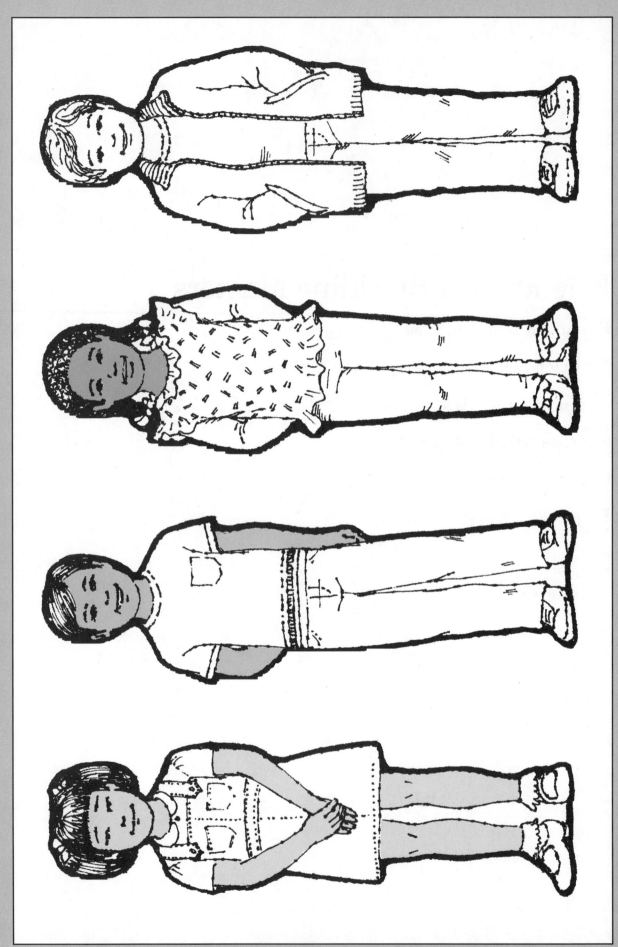

Friendships / Day 1 / Friends in School

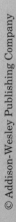

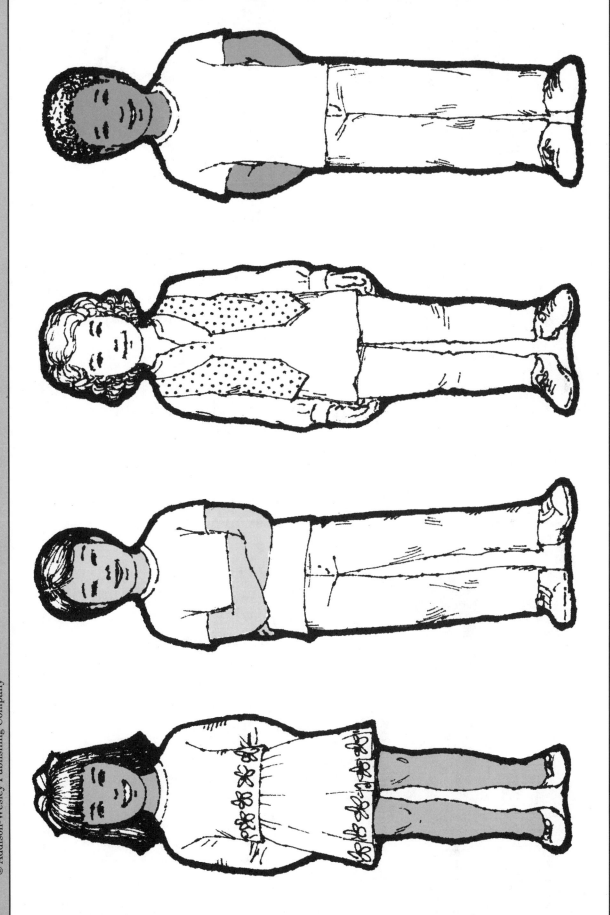

My Friends in School

(tune: The Wheels
on the Bus)

My friends in school share
    their toys,
Share their toys,
Share their toys,
My friends in school share
    their toys,
All through the day.

My friends in the park push
    my swing,
Push my swing,
Push my swing,
My friends in the park push
    my swing,
All through the day.

My friends on the beach play
    in the sand,
Play in the sand,
Play in the sand,
My friends on the beach play
    in the sand,
All through the day.

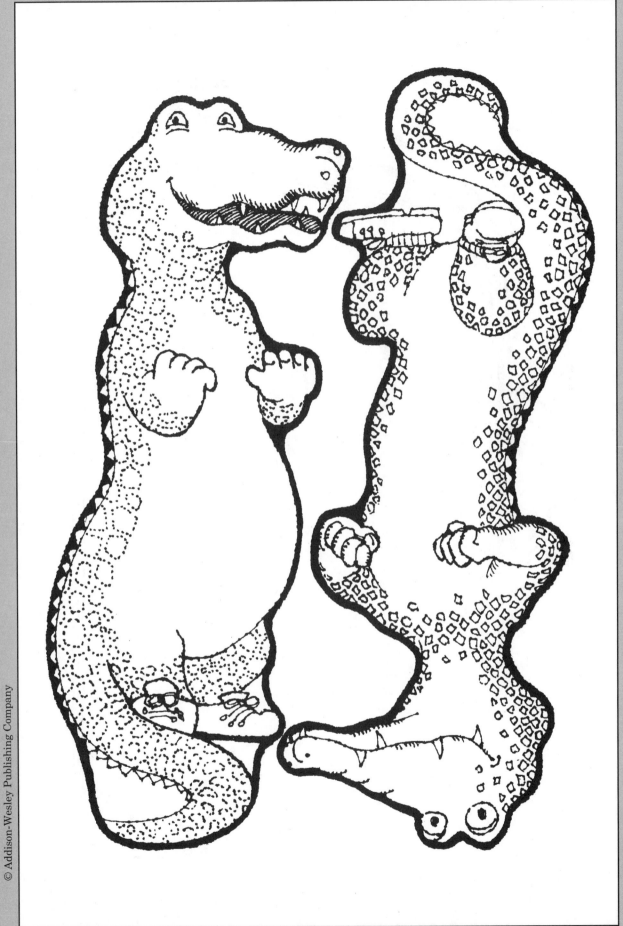

Friendships / Day 3 / Allie and Corky   307

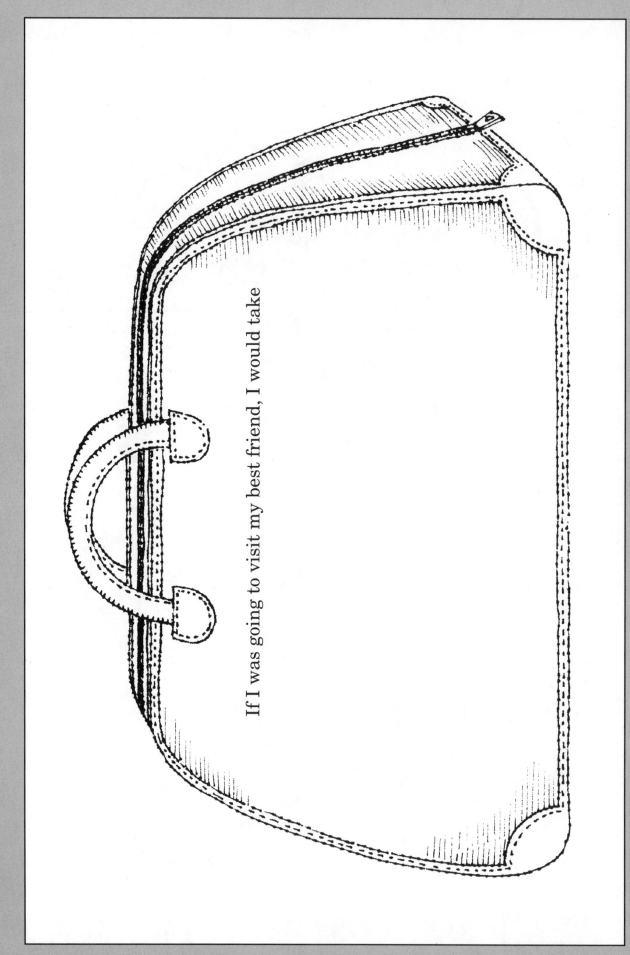

If I was going to visit my best friend, I would take

Call 9-1-1

If you need a doctor to come
  quick, quick, quick,
Call 9-1-1 and say, "Someone
  is very sick, sick, sick!"
Give your name, your phone
  number, your address and
  street.
Then the doctor will come
  quickly to your street.

If you need firefighters to
  put out a fire one day,
Call 9-1-1 and say, "Put out
  the fire right away!"
Give your name, your phone
  number, your address and
  street.
Then firefighters will come
  quickly to your street.

If you need police officers to
  save someone one day,
Call 9-1-1, and say,
  "Someone needs help right
  away!"
Give your name, your phone
  number, your address and
  street.
Then police officers will come
  quickly to your street.

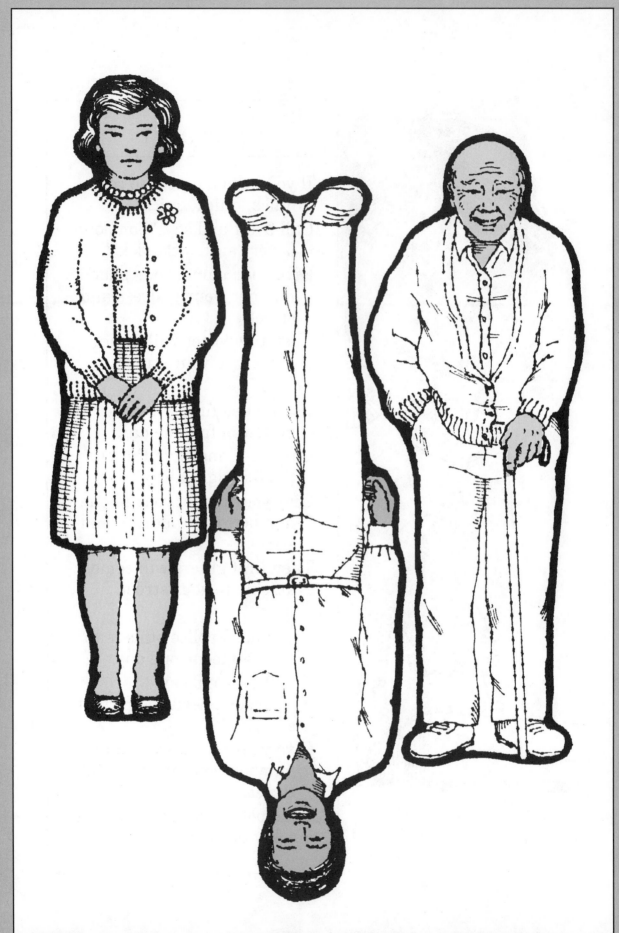

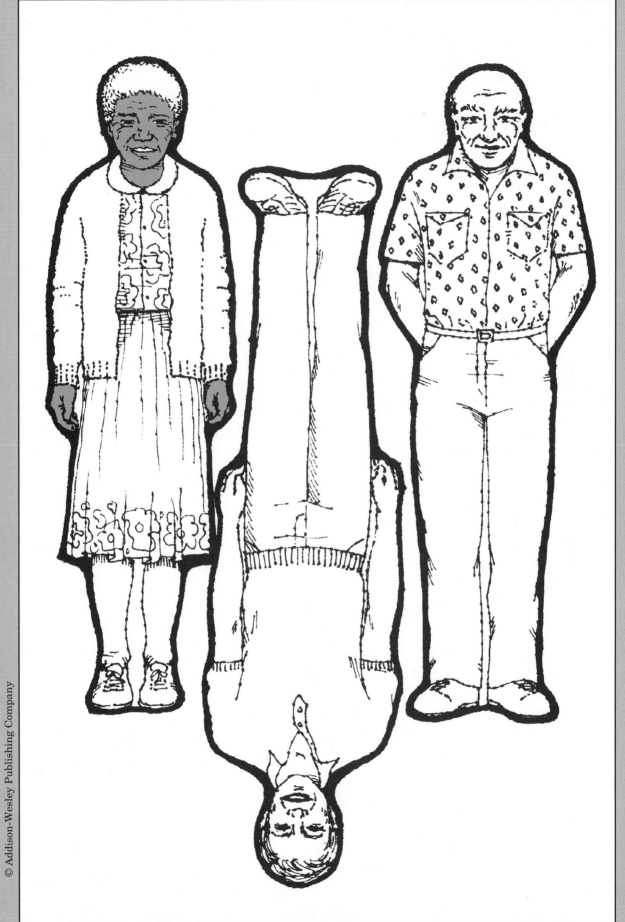

SECTION

4

Appendix

Assessment During the Early Primary Years

Assessment Instruments

Assessment During the Early Primary Years

Assessment is a continuous process that should take place daily through a systematic observation and recording of children's behavior in the classroom. It utilizes many informal techniques such as checklists, rating scales, samples of children's natural writing, and tapes of children's storytelling and reading. These assessment instruments should reflect the objectives of your program and should be developmentally and culturally appropriate for the children you are assessing. Taken all together, the techniques provide teachers with valuable information about their children, which can then be evaluated by teachers and children alike. This analysis provides direction for teaching and learning.

The information obtained from these informal assessments should be kept in a teacher portfolio as well as in the children's own personal portfolios. All samples in the portfolios should include the child's name and date of assessment. Sample materials gathered over time and placed in the portfolio are an excellent way for teachers to evaluate developmental growth in their children. The samples can also be used during parent conferences to show developmental growth over time.

It is suggested that assessment be carried out in the following areas.

I. Cognitive Domain

A. Writing

Dated samples of writing should be collected throughout the year. This includes information sheets, information from brainstorming, letter writing, creative writing, and so on. By comparing a child's writing samples at different times of the year, the teacher is able to evaluate the young child's development from drawing pictures or making squiggles to making letters to inventing spellings to writing actual words.

B. Listening

Observe children in conversation as they work in whole-group situations and smaller cooperative groups. It is also important to note how children process information in presentations, speaking, dramatization, writing, and drawing.

C. Speaking

Listen to how the child responds to questions asked by you or other children in the class. Also note how individual children respond as a member of a group.

- Can the child pronounce words clearly?

- Can the child participate in oral interactions?
- Can the child understand the language of others when spoken to?
- Can the child speak in complete sentences?
- Can the child identify similar sounds?
- Can the child differentiate similar sounds?
- Can the child be understood by others?
- Can the child use a wide range of words appropriately?

D. Reading

A wide range of informal assessment procedures are recommended to assess the child's growth in emergent reading. Observe your children for evidence of the following:

- Shows an interest in print.
- Uses left-to-right direction as well as top-to-bottom direction.
- Attempts to read print around the classroom and in books.
- Can recognize some of the letters of the alphabet.
- Knows a number of words by sight.
- Attempts to read and reread familiar songs, stories, and verses.
- Uses reading-like behavior.
- Attempts to read Big Books, following the print.
- Monitors and attempts to self-correct reading.
- Is able to retell a story after it is read.
- Begins to use graphophonic cues as an aid to word recognition.
- Makes appropriate predictions when reading new material.
- Is developing concepts of story grammar (setting, characters, problems, episodes, and solutions).

In order to assist teachers in assessing reading growth, a number of assessment instruments are included in this section of the book.

Although many of them are specific to a particular story or verse or strategy, they can be adapted to meet your assessment needs. The assessment instrument sheets are not designed to be handed to the student. They simply provide a frame for discussion and record keeping.

II. Affective Domain

Children who have a positive outlook toward literacy become better readers and writers than the children who do not have a positive attitude. Therefore, it is important for teachers to discover how children feel about activities related to reading and writing and about themselves as learners. The answer to these two questions can readily be discovered through classroom observations and conferences. The child who eagerly seeks out print and books found within the classroom is sure to have a positive attitude toward reading and toward himself or herself as a reader. The same can be said about the child who eagerly attempts to write words, sentences, and stories. The earlier this positive attitude toward literacy is nurtured and formed, the greater is the chance that it will continue into adult life. This positive attitude is very important, because the focus of any literacy program is to produce lifelong readers and writers.

Strategies at a Glance

In order to effectively conduct ongoing assessment, it is important to know what strategies are presented throughout the units. The following strategies chart presents the specific strategies in each of the four units (Volumes One and Two) by first outlining the major emphases, then giving the outline of punctuation, word, and comprehension strategies to be developed each day.

Strategies Chart

Volume One, Unit One, Part One: Old Favorites: Nursery Rhymes

Major Emphasis: Development of basic sight vocabulary; direction words; story grammar (setting, characters, problem, events, solution); four levels of comprehension (literal, inferential, evaluative, appreciative); listening skills; relationship between reading and writing; and initial letter names.

Story/Verse	Word Strategies and Punctuation	Comprehension Strategies
Introduction	Mother Goose album (key vocabulary)	Comparing/contrasting chart
Humpty Dumpty	Mother Goose album Rhyming words Phonogram /al/ Key word box Growing nursery rhyme Dictionary	Story grammar Literal, inferential, evaluative comprehension Character chart
Two Little Dicky Birds	Nursery rhyme Dictionary Mother Goose album Letter *P*	Character chart Following sequence Graphing Sequencing Comparing (big/small)
Twinkle, Twinkle Little Star		Following sequence Categorization (day/night) Sequencing
Little Miss Muffet	Key word box Letter *M* Mother Goose album	Character chart Beginning/middle/end Categorization (big/little) Evaluative comprehension
Little Bo-Peep	Letter *L* Consonant digraph /sh/ Phonogram /ēp/ Key word box	Story grammar Literal, inferential, evaluative comprehension Character chart Developing sentence sense
Mary Had a Little Lamb	Mother Goose album	Story grammar Character chart Graphing responses
Little Boy Blue	Letter *B* Phonogram /ēp/ Compound words Letter of invitation Mother Goose album	Literal, inferential, evaluative comprehension Character chart Story grammar Following sequence

Jack and Jill	Letter *J* Phonogram /il/ Mother Goose album	Literal, inferential, evaluative comprehension Beginning/middle/end Categorization (up/down) Story sequence Character chart
Pussy-cat, Pussy-cat	Phonogram /at/ Mother Goose album	Literal, inferential comprehension Character chart Webbing
One, Two, Buckle My Shoe		Following directions Sequencing events

Volume One, Unit One, Part Two: Old Favorites: Favorite Tales

Major Emphasis: Further development of sight vocabulary; fluency in reading; story grammar; four levels of comprehension; beginning, middle, and end; and initial letter names.

Story/Verse	Word Strategies and Punctuation	Comprehension Strategies
Introduction	Letter *P*	
The House That Jack Built	Phonogram /ak/ Rhyming words Alphabet cards (key vocabulary)	Sequencing events
The Cake That Mack Ate	Letter *M* Rhyming words Alphabet cards (key vocabulary)	Sequencing events Comparison/contrast

Teeny Tiny Woman	Letter *T*
	Phonogram /el/
	Personal alphabet books
	    (key vocabulary)
		Episodes
		Sequence
		Literal, inferential
		    comprehension
		Comparison/contrast (tiny/big)

Henny Penny	Phonogram /an/
	Personal alphabet books
	    (key vocabulary)
		Story grammar
		Sequencing events
		Literal, inferential
		    comprehension

The Gingerbread Man	Letter *H* Personal alphabet books (key vocabulary)	Story grammar Following sequence

The Little Red Hen	Personal alphabet books (key vocabulary)	Story grammar Literal, inferential comprehension Circle story map Compare/contrast chart Advanced organizers
The Farmer and the Beet	Letter *F* Personal alphabet books (key vocabulary)	Story grammar Advanced organizers
The Three Billy Goats Gruff	Personal alphabet books (key vocabulary)	Story grammar Episodes Story sequence
Goldilocks and the Three Bears	Personal alphabet books (key vocabulary)	Literal, inferential comprehension Sequencing events Following directions Categorization
The Three Little Pigs	Personal alphabet books (key vocabulary)	Story grammar Literal, inferential comprehension Story map frame
Little Red Riding Hood	Personal alphabet books (key vocabulary)	Story grammar Advanced organizers Literal, inferential comprehension Sequential events model
Stone Soup	Letter *S* Personal alphabet books (key vocabulary)	Story grammar Compare/contrast chart
Strega Nona	Letter *M* Personal alphabet books (key vocabulary) Beginning/middle/end	Story grammar Literal, inferential comprehension

Volume One, Unit Two: Friendships

Major Emphasis: Development of concepts related to the unit theme; awareness of the dimensions of friends; reading in episodes; story grammar; literal, inferential, evaluative comprehension; use of punctuation marks; letter writing; story writing; letter names, phonograms, and blends.

Story/Verse	Word Strategies and Punctuation	Comprehension Strategies
Jessica		Literal, inferential comprehension Story web
Making Friends	Class diary	Brainstorming in cooperative groups
See You Later, Alligator	Use of quotation marks Class diary	Literal, inferential, evaluative comprehension Compare/contrast chart
That's What Friends Are For	Class diary	Episodes Story grammar Literal, inferential, evaluative comprehension Sequence of events
The Doorbell Rang	Letter *D* Phonogram /el/	Story grammar Literal, inferential comprehension Story web
Best Friends	Review use of period Quotation marks Exclamation marks	Literal, inferential, evaluative, appreciative comprehension Following directions Sentence sorting
Angelina and Alice	Letter writing	Episodes Literal, inferential, evaluative comprehension Sequential events model
Ira Sleeps Over	Letter *W* Thank-you letter	Episodes Story grammar Literal, inferential comprehension
We Are Best Friends	Friendly letter Letter *R*	Story grammar Literal, evaluative, appreciative comprehension
See You Tomorrow, Charles	Consonant digraph /ch/	Story grammar Literal, inferential, evaluative, appreciative comprehension

Do Like Kyla *Hemi's Pet*	Review letter *P*	Episodes Story grammar Inferential, evaluative, appreciative comprehension
A Chair for My Mother	Family album Letter writing	Episodes Story grammar Literal, inferential, evaluative comprehension
The Fire Station		Episodes Story grammar Literal, inferential, evaluative comprehension

My Doctor	Review compound
	  words
		Literal, inferential
		  comprehension
		Vocabulary match-up puzzles

Volume Two, Unit Three: Food from the Farm

Major Emphasis: Development of concepts related to the unit topics: simple notetaking (making lists); elementary research strategies; four levels of comprehension; sequential charting of information; and structure of language.

Story/Verse	Word Strategies and Punctuation	Comprehension Strategies

My First Visit to the Farm		Introduction of K-W-L Strategy
		  chart
		Comparison/contrast chart
		Literal, inferential, evaluative
		  comprehension

My Big Farm Book	Farm Dictionary
	  (whole class/individual)
	My Little Farm Book
		K-W-L Strategy chart
		Season cycle chart of farm
		  chores

Farmer Joe Goes to the City	Farm Dictionary Past tense: *-ed* My Little Farm Book	Story grammar Literal, inferential, appreciative comprehension
The Little Wooden Farmer	Farm Dictionary My Little Farm Book	Literal, inferential, appreciative comprehension
Field Trip		Simple notetaking/lists

The Very Busy Spider	Review of punctuation
	  (period/question mark)
	Farm Dictionary
		Sequential events chart
		K-W-L Strategy chart
		Matching character and
		  dialogue

Where's Henrietta's Hen?	Farm Dictionary
	Positional words
	Thank-you letters
	My Little Farm Book
		Animal Products from the
		    Farm chart
		Organizing information in
		    chart format: simple
		    list/notes
		Sequence of events
		Literal, inferential,
		    appreciative comprehension

A Visit to the Dairy Farm	Farm Dictionary
	Letter *C*
	My Little Farm Book
		Animal Products from the
		    Farm chart
		K-W-L Strategy chart
		Following directions
		Literal, inferential, evaluative
		    comprehension

The Goat in the Rug	Invitation letter
	Farm Dictionary
		Animal Products from the
		    Farm chart
		K-W-L Strategy chart
		Sequencing
		Animal Products chart
		Literal, inferential, evaluative
		    comprehension

Pigs	Farm Dictionary
	My Little Farm Book
		Animal Products from the
		    Farm chart
		Literal, inferential, evaluative,
		    appreciative comprehension

A Seed Is a Promise	Farm Dictionary	K-W-L Strategy chart categorization
Oranges	Farm Dictionary My Little Farm Book	Sequencing events Plant Products from the Farm chart
Growing Vegetable Soup	Farm Dictionary Farm Counting Book Word picture puzzles My Little Farm Book	Sequencing events Plant Products from the Farm chart
Bread, Bread, Bread	Farm Dictionary Plural *-s* My Little Farm Book Alphabetization	Sequencing events Plant Products from the Farm chart

Volume Two, Unit Four: Dragons from East and West

Major Emphasis: Development of consolidating schema for narrative mode; episodes; story grammar; four levels of comprehension; character development; sight vocabulary; variety of story maps; relationships among listening, reading, and writing; and the structure of language.

Story/Verse	Word Strategies and Punctuation	Comprehension Strategies
The Knight and the Dragon	Review letters *C* and *D* Little Book of Dragons Big Book of Dragons	Episodes Story grammar Literal, inferential comprehension
Chin Chiang and the Dragon's Dance	Little Book of Dragons Big Book of Dragons Key vocabulary list	Episodes Story grammar Literal, inferential, appreciative comprehension
The Paper Bag Princess	Little Book of Dragons Big Book of Dragons Little Dragon dictionary Key vocabulary list	Episodes Story grammar Literal, inferential, evaluative, appreciative comprehension Sequence strips Vocabulary/concept puzzles
Jane and the Dragon	Little Book of Dragons Little Dragon dictionary Big Book of Dragons Key vocabulary list	Episodes Story grammar Literal, inferential, evaluative, appreciative comprehension
The Dragon's Cold	Little Book of Dragons Letter writing Contractions	Episodes Story grammar Literal, inferential comprehension Mapping story events
Harriet and William and the Terrible Creature	Little Book of Dragons Big Book of Dragons Little Dragon Dictionary Key vocabulary list	Story grammar Literal, inferential comprehension Compare/contrast chart Circle story map
World Famous Muriel and the Scary Dragon	Little Book of Dragons Big Book of Dragons Dragon Number Book	Story grammar Literal, inferential, appreciative comprehension
The Tough Princess		Story grammar Literal, inferential comprehension Diagraming story events Venn diagram Compare/contrast chart

Drango Dragon	Little Book of Dragons Letter writing Big Book of Dragons Key vocabulary list	Story grammar Literal, inferential, evaluative, appreciative comprehension
Beware the Dragons!	Little Book of Dragons	Story Grammar Literal, inferential, evaluative, appreciative comprehension Mapping story events Matching sentence parts
The Popcorn Dragon	Little Book of Dragons Compound words	Story grammar Literal, inferential, evaluative, appreciative comprehension Circle story map Matching sentence parts
Dragon for Breakfast	Little Book of Dragons Compound words Plural *-s*	Story grammar Literal, inferential, evaluative, appreciative comprehension Matching sentence parts
How Droofus the Dragon Lost His Head	Little Book of Dragons Compound words Key vocabulary list	Story grammar Literal, inferential, evaluative, appreciative comprehension Story map Comparison chart Matching sentence parts; Character question cards
The Fourth Question	Little Book of Dragons Thank-you cards	Story grammar Literal, inferential, appreciative comprehension Following directions

Assessment Instruments

My Child as a Reader and Writer

Nursery Rhyme Interview

Story Conference

Comprehension Checklist

Sample of Story Comprehension *(Paper Bag Princess)*

Nursery Rhyme Assessment (Name That Character)

Favorite Tales Survey

Identifying Feelings

Sample Oral Cloze Technique ("Humpty Dumpty")

Sample Sentence Verification *(Pigs)*

My Child as a Reader and Writer
(An Observation Guide for Parents)

Name _____

Teacher _____   Date _____

Indicate your observation of your child's reading and writing by responding to the following questions. Please comment on your observation.

	Yes/No	Comments
I Reading		
A. Does my child enjoy getting a book for a present?		
B. Does my child have books of her or his own? How many?		
C. Does my child have a special place to keep her or his books?		
D. Does my child look at books or pictures on her or his own?		
E. Does my child like me to read to her or him? (brings books from the library to share; likes regular bedtime stories)		
F. Does my child read stories or verses to me? (shares verses or stories read at school; reads or attempts to read her or his library book)		

G. Does my child try to read in everyday situations? (street signs, store signs, cereal boxes, newspapers, magazines, TV advertisements)		
H. Does my child try to talk about or retell the stories or verses heard at school?		
I. Does my child try to retell the story that I read at home?		
J. Does my child try to read new words? (uses letter sounds and meaning clues to read street and store signs)		
K. Does my child try to read along with me on favorite parts of the story or sentences that are said over and over again?		

	Yes/No	Comments
II Writing		
A. Can my child write her or his name?		
B. Does my child like to write letters?		
C. Does my child have a collection of paper, pencils, and crayons?		
D. Does my child like to receive notes from me and others?		
E. Does my child ask me or others to write words or notes to people?		

F. Does my child have a chalkboard or magnetic board? Does my child have chalk or magnetic letters?		
G. Do I encourage my child to invent his or her own spellings?		
H. Do I encourage my child to make labels for photo albums, household items, and so on?		
I. Do I encourage my child to make words or write stories for picture books?		

Nursery Rhyme Interview

Name _____

Date _____

A. What is your favorite nursery rhyme?

_____

B. Say the nursery rhyme.

Fluent

Good Memory

Some Difficulty

C. Who are the characters in your nursery rhyme?

_____   _____

D. Tell me what happens in the nursery rhyme.

Recall   1. _____

3. _____

2. _____

3. _____

4. _____

major events noted _____ missed _____ in order _____

E. Show series of sequence cards (2-4)

Put in order _____

Trouble with   beginning _____

middle _____

end _____

Story Conference

Name _____

Story Title _____ Date _____

A. Who do you think is the most important character?

_____

Why? _____

B. Where does the story happen? _____

C. Tell me the story in your own words.

Beginning	Middle	End

(Write down responses; check sequence against book.)

Trouble with   beginning _____

middle _____

end _____

D. What was the problem in the story?

_____

How was the problem solved?

_____

E. Did you like the story?

Why or why not? _____

_____

© Addison-Wesley Publishing Company

Comprehension Checklist

Date _____

Student
Names

	A. Participated in echo reading	B. Identified one major character	C. Explained why character is major	D. Identified setting	E. Recalled events correctly — Beginning — Middle — End	F. Identified major problem	G. Identified major solution

Paper Bag Princess Recall

After children have heard *The Paper Bag Princess,* have individuals tell you everything that they remember about the story. Check items recalled in the beginning, middle, and end.

Name _____

Date _____

Events

Beginning:

_____ Elizabeth, a princess, wants to marry Ronald.

_____ A dragon burns castle.

_____ The dragon carries off Ronald.

_____ Elizabeth, wearing a paper bag, follows the dragon.

Middle:

_____ Elizabeth finds the dragon's cave and knocks on the door.

_____ The dragon slams the door.

_____ Elizabeth knocks again.

_____ Elizabeth asks if the dragon can burn forests.

_____ The dragon burns the forests.

_____ Elizabeth asks if the dragon can fly around world.

_____ The dragon flies around world.

_____ The dragon falls asleep.

End:

_____ Elizabeth goes into the dragon's cave.

_____ Elizabeth finds Ronald.

_____ Ronald tells Elizabeth she is a mess.

_____ Elizabeth tells Ronald he is a bum.

_____ Elizabeth leaves Ronald and they don't get married.

Name That Character

This assessment instrument could be administered either to individual children or to small groups of children during a conference in order to measure recall of main characters from rhymes introduced during the Nursery Rhyme section of Old Favorites.

Name _____

Date _____

Read the questions and note the number of correct responses.

1. Who was frightened by the spider?

_____

2. Who fell asleep under the haystack?

_____

3. Who lost her sheep?

_____

4. Who fell off the wall?

_____

5. Who had a lamb that went to school?

_____

6. Who had so many children she did not know what to do with them?

_____

7. Who went up the hill to get some water?

_____

8. Who rode through the air on a very fine gander?

_____

Favorite Tales Survey

Give the child the oral clue. Have the child identify the story related to the clue.

Name _____

Date _____

Clue	Story Title
Papa bear, Mama bear, Baby bear	
a troll under a bridge	
a red cape	
a straw house	
three bowls of porridge	
a fish that grants wishes	
a hen who has to plant wheat all alone	
a huffing, puffing wolf	
a sick grandmother	
a hen who wants to tell the king that the sky is falling	

Identifying Feelings

Before reading a story to the children, ask them to think about how the characters in the story felt. After reading the story, complete the questionnaire for each student separately, reading aloud the feeling words and asking how one or more characters felt at the beginning, middle, and end of the story.

Name _____

Date _____

happy   sad   worried   mad   surprised   lonely

Story _____

Characters	Beginning	Middle	End
_____			
_____			
_____			

Tell how the characters felt at the beginning, middle, and end of the story. Why do you think the character felt this way?

_____

_____

_____

_____

_____

_____

Oral Cloze Technique

Oral cloze is an excellent technique to use with emergent readers. It provides information on the child's comprehension ability as well as his or her understanding of semantic and syntactic cues.

Humpty Dumpty

Read the connected prose to the child and pause before the word to be added. Write down the word elicited from the child in the space provided.

Humpty Dumpty sat on a _____.

Humpy Dumpty had a great _____.

All the king's _____ and all the king's _____

Couldn't put Humpty Dumpty _____ again.

Sentence Verification

Name _____

Date _____

Book: *Pigs*

Read each sentence to the children. Tell them that they are to answer each sentence by saying yes or no. This assessment can be done in small groups. Give children YES cards and NO cards. Children respond to each question by showing the YES or NO card. Record the responses of the individual children.

1. In the beginning Megan thought pigs were smart.   YES   NO

2. Megan left the pigpen gate open.   YES   NO

3. The pigs were happy to get out of the pigpen.   YES   NO

4. Megan found the pigs in her mother's bedroom.   YES   NO

5. The pigs were eating her father's newspaper and drinking his coffee.   YES   NO

6. The pigs were sitting on the desks working on schoolwork.   YES   NO

7. The teacher thought the pigs were smart.   YES   NO

8. A pig drove the schoolbus back to the farm.   YES   NO

9. The pigs went right to the pigpen.   YES   NO

10. Megan will let animals out of their pens again.   YES   NO